D1293221

The Melancholy Science

*An Introduction to the Thought
of Theodor W. Adorno*

European Perspectives
A Series of the Columbia University Press

The Melancholy Science

An Introduction to the Thought
of Theodor W. Adorno

Gillian Rose

New York   Columbia University Press   1978

Published in 1978 in Great Britain by The Macmillan Press Ltd
and in the United States of America by Columbia University Press

Library of Congress Cataloging in Publication Data

Rose, Gillian.
　　The melancholy science.

　　(European perspectives)
　　Bibliography:　p.
　　Includes index.
　　1.　Adorno, Theodor W., 1903–1969.　2.　Frankfurt
school of sociology.　3.　Communism and society.
I.　Title.
HM22.G3A37　　1978　　　　301.092′4　　　　78–1555
ISBN 0–231–04584–0

Printed in Hong Kong

Contents

Acknowledgements

Many people have inspired, helped and criticised this work at various stages. I wish to thank especially Sir Isaiah Berlin, Julius Carlebach, Leszek Kolakowski, Steven Lukes and Sabine MacCormack.

I wish to thank the following people who read and commented on all or part of the manuscript in its final stages: Zev Barbu, Tom Bottomore, Frank Glover-Smith, E. F. N. Jephcott.

In addition I wish to thank Ulrike Meinhof, who checked all my translations and retranslations from the German, and Rogers Ragavan who gave me unstinting assistance in secretarial and practical matters. I am also grateful to the Librarian of St Antony's College, Oxford, for her patience in supplying books over the past few years, and to St Antony's College for their support. I wish to thank the Social Science Research Council, the University of Sussex and the Deutsche Akademische Austauschdienst for financial help during the course of the research, which was partly conducted at the Free University, West Berlin, and at the University of Constance, West Germany.

My special thanks are given to Stefan Collini, Herminio Martins, John Raffan and Jacqueline Rose.

Preface

'The melancholy science' which this book expounds is not a pessimistic science. By introducing *Minima Moralia* as an offering from his 'melancholy science' – an inversion of Nietzsche's 'joyful science' – Adorno undermines and inverts the sanguine and total claims of philosophy and sociology, and rejects any dichotomy such as optimistic/pessimistic for it implies an inherently fixed and static view.

Adorno's work draws on traditions inherited from Marxian and non-Marxian criticism of Hegel's philosophy, and on the pre-Marxian writings of Lukács and of Benjamin as much as on their Marxian writings. Interpretation of Adorno suffers when his aims and achievements are related solely to Marx or to a Marxian tradition which is sometimes undefined and sometimes overdefined, and, equally, when he is judged solely as a sociologist. Here, Adorno's thought is introduced and discussed in its own right, 'immanently', to use his own term. Where appropriate, Adorno's engagement with and transformation of the many intellectual traditions which inform his work is examined.

Adorno's thought depends fundamentally on the category of reification. This category has attained a strangely dominant role in much neo-Marxist and phenomenological literature and in recent sociological amalgams of these two traditions. It is used to evoke, often by mere suggestion or allusion, a very peculiar and complex epistemological setting which is rarely examined further or justified. In the Marxian tradition 'reification' is most often employed as a way of generalising Marx's theory of value with the aim of producing a critical theory of social institutions and of culture, but frequently any critical force is lost in the process of generalisation.

Adorno's work, the most ambitious and important to have emerged from the Institute for Social Research before 1969, is the most abstruse, and, in spite of its great influence, still the most misunderstood. This is partly a result of its deliberately paradoxical, polemical and fractured nature which has made it eminently quotable but egregiously misconstruable. Yet, as I try to show, Adorno's *œuvre* forms a unity even though it is composed of fragments. In the last five years all the major works and many of the minor works of Adorno, Lukács and Benjamin have been translated or are in the process of being translated into English. In spite of this increasing recognition of their importance there exists as yet little systematic study of their work.

I have not attempted to be exhaustive in my treatment of Adorno's work. In particular, his writings on music, which constitute over half of his published work, do not receive detailed attention. Although Adorno acknowledged the importance of his collaboration with Horkheimer, his debates with Lukács and with Benjamin reveal more of the inspiration which structures his thought, and I have therefore concentrated on those aspects. While I argue that Adorno's texts must be read from a methodological point of view with close attention to stylistic features, I have, nevertheless, reconstructed his ideas in standard expository format.

Chapter 1

The Crisis in Culture

The Frankfurt School, 1923–50

All the tensions within the German academic community which accompanied the changes in political, cultural and intellectual life in Germany since 1890 were reproduced in the Institute for Social Research from its inception in Frankfurt in 1923.[1] These changes were widely diagnosed as a 'crisis in culture'.[2] By this very definition the 'crisis' was deplored yet exacerbated. The Institute carried these tensions with it into exile and when it returned to Germany after the war and found itself the sole heir to a discredited tradition the inherited tensions became even more acute. These tensions are evident in the work of most of the School's members, and most clearly, self-consciously and importantly in the work of Theodor W. Adorno.

From 1890 the German academic community reacted in a variety of ways to the sudden and momentous development of capitalism in Germany, and to the new role of Germany in the world. This resulted in disillusionment with various scientific and philosophical methods, and the pedagogical and philosophical revival which followed occurred across the political spectrum, to the extent that the spectrum was represented in the universities. The different attempts to 're-engage learning' and reinvigorate German life have been indicted for their political naïvety and irresponsibility.[3] Although the Frankfurt School was deliberately set up to be outside the academic community, the aims and work of the Institute amount to a most ambitious attempt to 're-engage learning'.[4] For, on the one hand, the School tried more concretely than any university department to reunify the fragmented branches of knowledge in the social sciences without sacrificing the fruits of any of them. Neo-Marxist, it was not deterred by academic cries against 'materialism' and 'materialist' methods. On the other hand, the School faltered in its attempt to redefine Marxism intellectually and politically for its generation. By the early thirties, it had dropped its orientation towards the workers' movement, a process which was capped by the replacement of Carl Grünberg by Max Horkheimer as director of the Institute, and by the substitution of the *Zeitschrift für Sozialforschung* (Journal for Social Research) edited by Horkheimer for Grünberg's *Archiv für die Geschichte des Sozialismus und der Arbeiterbewegung* (Archive for the History of Socialism and the Workers' Movement).[5] It even dropped its interest in class analysis and increasingly turned its attention to the analysis of culture and authority. Instead of politicising academia, it academised politics.[6] This transposition became the basis for its subsequent achievements. Yet time and time again, the history of the School reveals this tension: as an institution, it reaffirmed and reinforced those aspects of German life which it criticised and aimed to change, just as it reaffirmed and reinforced those aspects of the intellectual universe which it criticised and aimed to change. Only if this is realised can the goals, achievements and failures of the School and of the work of Adorno be defined and assessed.

During the thirties, first in Germany and later in exile, the School is best examined in the same light. Under Horkheimer's directorship, it avoided the pedantry and conservatism of the universities, while engaging in sociological research which united theoretical and empirical inquiry.[7] Many of the themes which recur in the articles and books by members of the School published during this period echo themes raised throughout the German academic world,[8] such as the lamented fragmentation of knowledge, the appeal to an often diffuse notion of 'totality' as the lost perspective, the attack on positivism and the recovering of traditions. All of these emphases and the academic assumption that to 're-engage learning' would be to rescue society from the ravages of capitalism and modernity were epidemic in Germany until 1933.[9] Yet the Frankfurt School, although implicated in this more than its own rhetoric or scholarship to date suggests, deserves different treatment too. The special case of the School has always rested on its particular fusion of the Idealism, which arose in opposition to neo-Kantianism, with the revival of Marxism after the First World War.

It may be said that the members of the School were addressing themselves in their collaboration during the upheavals of the thirties to the question which Marx asked at the end of the *1844 Manuscripts*, 'How do we now stand in relation to the Hegelian *dialectic*?'.[10] They asked this question for their generation, which was the generation younger than Lukács', disappointed with the working class since 1919, but, unlike him, increasingly disillusioned with the development of communism in Russia during the twenties. Like Lukács, the School considered that to be consistent with Marx, it was necessary to take account of flourishing non-dialectical philosophies and sociologies,[11] just as Marx had scanned the philosophy and political economy which flourished in his day. On the one hand, the School was dismayed that the social sciences had developed so separately from each other and sought to combat this fragmentation. On the other hand, Horkheimer did not believe that one man alone could undertake research in all the relevant fields.[12] The members of the School tended to specialise while, at the same time, breaking down the established barriers between philosophy and sociology in their particular areas. Horkheimer was particularly concerned to take advantage of the developments in empirical research techniques which in Germany had occurred quite apart from developments in theoretical sociology and at a time when almost every German professor of sociology considered it incumbent on him to produce a theoretical sociology.[13] By combining several empirical methods in any inquiry, he believed that the evils of too restricted an empiricism could be avoided. This unity underlying the work of the members of the School is evident in the various publications of the thirties, in the *Zeitschrift* and most clearly in joint works such as *Autorität und Familie* (Authority and the Family).[14] However, from the outset, the inheritance of non-Marxist critical traditions affected the style and presentation of many of the contributors. This inheritance from non-Marxist criticisms of Hegel's system, for example, those of Schopenhauer and Nietzsche, tolerates idiosyncracy and hence makes for another kind of fragmentation. It is this inheritance from a tradition which has itself never been widely understood even within Germany which, paradoxically, has often increased the School's appeal, while at the same time, exposing it to misinterpretation. But it has prevented the work of the School from having a more cogent and continual impact on sociology.

Many of these non-Marxist influences, Hegelian and post-Hegelian, were present in Lukács' writings too, especially up to 1923.[15] The School rejected many of Lukács' assumptions and theories, particularly the idea of the working class as the subject/object of history and the notion of 'imputed' class consciousness. However, a subject/object dichotomy was retained, and ideas from the non-Marxist critical traditions developed in a way which affected the style of the work of many members of the School. Many of Lukács' central concepts were thus retained, such as 'subject', 'object', 'fetishism' and 'reification', but they attained a quite different status. The School sought to define Marxism as a mode of cognition *sui generis* on the assumption that there is no longer any privileged carrier of that cognition, any universal class.[16] The influence of Lukács on the School has been both underestimated[17] and over-estimated,[18] and nowhere have the continuities and discontinuities been adequately traced.

Similarly, the continuity of the dispute, which has become notorious since 1964 as the *Positivismusstreit* (the Positivist dispute),[19] with the polemics undertaken by the School since its earliest days, has been overlooked. This has contributed to the many failures on the part of the School's opponents to understand the terms of the later debate.[20] From the late twenties, members of the School conducted disputes with various forms of philosophical and sociological absolute systems, positivisms and relativisms.[21] It may be said that some form of dispute concerning 'positivism' is as old as Marxism itself. After 1950 the adversaries changed, but the enterprise did not. It involves demonstrating the social necessity of the position which is criticised, while rejecting, in more strident tones, its claim to absolute validity.

The discontinuity in the membership of the School, especially after the war when very few returned to Germany, has meant that the School's general theory of change in the social organisation of production, which underlies all its other work, is difficult to identify. In the post-war writing of Horkheimer and Adorno the theory of change in late capitalism is implicit but not directly presented in any one place. These ideas were originally formed in the attempt to analyse the development and success of the Nazis in Germany, and always bore the mark of this origin.[22] Friedrich Pollock's article 'State Capitalism', written in 1941,[23] offers an example of the difficulties which beset the School's analysis of capitalism and which reappear in Adorno's works in an indirect and inverted form. Pollock pictured state capitalism as a system where the state has taken over the organisation of production and replaced price and market mechanisms by its own plans. Power to command instead of the profit motive becomes the motor of this system, which has taken over from monopoly capitalism and which may proceed under a totalitarian or democratic political structure. An image of a static and stable regime emerges, although it is not clear to what extent this 'ideal-type' is intended to offer an historical analysis or a prediction.[24] Pollock relies inconsistently on Marx's method for analysing capitalism and his account lacks cogency because of this. He presupposes Marx's theory of value and commodity production and hence, however unemphatically, the distinction between use-value and exchange-value, but he does not go on to develop on this basis a notion of labour-power and of the extraction of surplus value and thus of class formation. Instead, the state appears as a force *sui generis* in Pollock's account and there is no attempt to relate the posited change in its role to the underlying processes of production. These processes are merely declared to be no longer operative. This leaves Pollock, as it will leave Adorno, without a satisfactory theory of the historical development of capitalism and without an adequate theory of the state.

Dialectic of Enlightenment, which Adorno wrote with Horkheimer in the

United States in the early 1940s, might be considered the School's response to Marx's critique of political economy.[25] In this book Horkheimer and Adorno attempt to decode the history of the philosophical subject as the domination of nature whether under the guise of myth or of enlightened reason.[26] The book is concerned with 'instrumental reason', or, as it is also called, 'technological' reason, but not with technologies for the domination of nature.[27] Instrumental reason is seen as a feature of both pre-capitalist and capitalist societies, although it only becomes a structuring principle in capitalist societies. Ideas are developed here which Adorno was investigating in his empirical work at the same time, especially the 'culture industry' and 'anti-semitism', but he did not share Horkheimer's concern with instrumental reason and the logic of domination. The concept of reification and Marx's theory of value are much more important in Adorno's analysis of society. Adorno and Horkheimer fused – each in his own way in his individual works – the Nietzschean and Weberian hyperbole which is so evident in *Dialectic of Enlightenment*.

During the years of the School's exile in America, especially in the late thirties and during the forties, the conflict in its position was particularly acute: it was more critical than ever of German society while at the same time more concerned than ever to carry on and develop those aspects of that society and its culture which it deemed worthy of defence.[28] This was a brave stance in a dilemma shared by other German *émigré* intellectuals and writers. However, it resulted in serious lacunae in the School's work, visible most clearly in the separation which occurred between their theoretical and empirical work. The membership of the School changed considerably during its years in America due to the departure of several members. Horkheimer carried on publishing the *Zeitschrift* in German until 1940.[29] Meanwhile he and Adorno were engaged in empirical work which was published in English. Throughout the forties they both continued writing and publishing their theoretical work in German and their empirical work in English. From 1941–4 especially, they did no empirical work and wrote together in German. This partly reflects the fact that the empirical work was commissioned – and Adorno, especially, needed the money – but it also reflects a deeper ambivalence. Horkheimer had always been more sympathetic to learning about and using empirical techniques than Adorno.[30] Adorno, in fact, conducted in collaboration with others more empirical work than Horkheimer during these years, yet he displayed the split in the School's position most clearly. He was most hostile to American culture and strongly identified with German culture during these years.[31] Later, in response to criticism of his work on American popular music and on authoritarianism, he referred to their theoretical underpinning in *Dialectic of Enlightenment*[32] which, however, was only available in

German. These conditions led to Adorno's worst work on jazz and popular culture.

The Frankfurt School, 1950–69

The history of the Institute in Germany after 1950 is the most important and complex but the least documented. Horkheimer, Adorno and Pollock returned to West Germany and re-established the Institute for Social Research in Frankfurt. Horkheimer became the rector of the University of Frankfurt, and in 1953 Adorno too accepted a chair at the university. Thus the activity of the Institute was no longer to be explicitly divorced from teaching. This turned out to be both an advantage and a disadvantage. It increased the intellectual and political influence of the Institute in the fifties but also contributed to its decline in the sixties. During these two decades the tension between the Institute's role as part of established academia, which it now increasingly became, and as critic of German society was at its most acute. By the mid-sixties the Institute was uncomfortable in many ways, unable to satisfy the state or its students. This has caused its achievement to be underestimated.

The story of the School after 1950 is the story of Horkheimer and Adorno and the ideas which they brought back with them from America. While many early members of the Institute had drifted away from it and remained in America after the war, Horkheimer and Adorno had in many ways drawn closer together.[33] They decided to return to West Germany, unlike Ernst Bloch and Bertolt Brecht who returned to East Germany,[34] because they were committed to redefining 'critical theory' in a way that would take account of the experience of the previous twenty years. This meant for them combating the official communism of Eastern Europe as much as fascism and the 'culture industry', which were the social phenomena associated more in their minds with Western Europe and America. The two men took up and propagated a position which defied the terms of the Cold War. They were equally critical of East and West and did not succumb to the ideological excesses characteristic of the period of German reconstruction. This isolated them and the faculties of sociology and philosophy of the University of Frankfurt. Not only did they preserve and continue a Marxist discourse, but they resisted the intellectual tide in Germany which disowned Nietzsche and even, for a period, Max Weber along with most of the tradition of theoretical sociology. By contrast, Lukács, now in Hungary, discredited both Nietzsche and Weber and German social thought in general in his book *Die Zerstörung der Vernunft* (The Destruction of Reason).[35] In most West German universities the theoretical tradition in sociology was rejected or ignored, and empirical research methods, copied from American ones, were enthusiastically embraced in order to assess, for example, the effects of the war on family structure and adolescent socialisation and to assist the rebuilding of the infrastructure of the country. This was in marked contrast to the heterogeneous mushrooming of sociological systems which had preceded the Nazi seizure of power. In Frankfurt too, research techniques developed in America were imported and others were developed. Further studies on prejudice were carried out as well as research in other branches of empirical sociology. Concern with the establishment of democracy in Germany was evident in some of these works.[36] At the same time Adorno was very hostile to the use of empirical techniques divorced from any critical concern.[37] The Frankfurt School continued their pre-war emphasis on the mixed use of such techniques within an interdisciplinary theoretical approach. Students at Frankfurt University in the fifties were taught sociology, philosophy and psycho-analysis in a way which reproduced the peculiar perspective of the School.[38] A precarious and short-lived independence was achieved, and throughout the fifties the Institute was vigorous in its publishing and the professors confident in their teaching.[39]

At the same time, the attitudes which were gradually to isolate Horkheimer and Adorno from their students were discernible. In many ways the two men never recovered from the war, and their courage and originality in redefining a role for the School in West Germany were always allied with ideas which remained more hidebound. The book *Aspects of Sociology*, published under Horkheimer's and Adorno's auspices and largely written by them, reveals some of the problems.[40] It is an introductory text in sociology written in a clear and simple style, which discusses the key sociological concepts of the time. There is no chapter on the concept of class. The method employed is to retrace the history of each concept usually from its original, substantive meaning in the Greek. According to the authors, as such concepts are made into sociological ones, they tend to become rigidified into positivistic and formal categories. The book aims to recover and release the substantive connotations of the concepts by thus criticising their static, ahistorical use in contemporary sociology. This 'restitutive' approach, while it had considerable critical power, produced essays in the tradition of cultural criticism, but no overall strategy for a unified sociology. It displayed the authors' preoccupation with fascism and the 'culture industry' and how their views on these matters had not developed any further after their return to Germany.

Horkheimer and Adorno produced much more important works after 1950 than this small, unpretentious volume, but each evolved his own idiosyncratic brand of criticism and wrote largely in essay form.[41] Yet their intellectual development was not similar. Adorno became increasingly involved in writing his *Ästhetische Theorie* (Aesthetic Theory)[42] in the sixties. The students at Frankfurt were increasingly dissatisfied with

Horkheimer's and Adorno's withdrawal from sociology and their
unwillingness to commit themselves to any political activity.[43] Although
by the late sixties Jürgen Habermas was also under fire from students for
political reticence, it is evident that Habermas' work marks a radical
break with the School on several other scores. It is not dialectical, nor
essayistic, nor is it concerned with questions of aesthetics. It also marks a
deep break with Horkheimer and Adorno's work on many epistemological issues, but a strong continuity lies in its engagement with Marx.

By the end of 1969 Horkheimer was no longer active due to ill-health,
Adorno had died, and Habermas had withdrawn from teaching after the
student occupation of that year. Horkheimer and Adorno appear to have
been the last great 'mandarins'. They created an academy precisely to
criticise traditions which the academic community abused or ignored.
Yet neither men, Adorno least of all, was a 'public' man. They were not
suited for responsibility in the sense of providing any platform. Hence
they seemed to recreate the evils of the old academic community –
indulging in intense, idiosyncratic cultural criticism deeply imbedded in
the scholarly and institutional constraints which they were committed to
transcend.[44]

Adorno

The tensions noted in the institutional character of the School are
especially evident in Adorno's writings, above all in the way he defined
his relationship to tradition. On the one hand he was opposed to all
philosophical and sociological systems, yet on the other, he wanted his
fragments to be read as if they were systematic.[45] He stressed the necessity
of understanding social phenomena from the perspective of the 'totality',
yet denied the possibility of grasping the 'totality'. On the one hand, he
was always searching for a style for philosophy and sociology which
would be the equivalent of the search for a modernist style which has
concerned twentieth-century musicians and novelists; on the other hand,
he produced cultural criticism which greatly circumscribed and criticised
any such search. He turned Marxism into a search for style, and yet
combined this with the old Hegelian and Marxist claims that he was
founding the one valid science.

Adorno was born in Frankfurt am Main in 1903, the son of a Jewish
wine merchant whose name, Wiesengrund, he bore until the war years
when he became known by his mother's maiden name, Adorno.[46] He was
interested in music and philosophy from his early teens,[47] and studied
philosophy at the University of Frankfurt, where his teachers were
representatives of the various forms of neo -Kantianism which dominated
philosophy departments in Germany at that time. In 1924 he submitted
his doctoral dissertation on Husserl to the Frankfurt Univer-

sity philosophy faculty.[48] From early 1925 to 1928, he studied music in Vienna as a pupil of Alban Berg. At the same time he wrote his *Habilitation* on Kant and Freud, submitted it for examination in Frankfurt in 1927, but withdrew it again before it was examined. This was partly due to his growing involvement with Marxism and especially to the influence of his friendships with Walter Benjamin and Max Horkheimer. After his return to Frankfurt in 1928, Adorno worked on a book on Kierkegaard which he hoped to submit as his new *Habilitation*.[49] He started teaching philosophy at the university in 1931 but was not a member of the Institute until 1938 when he went to New York. He was editor of the *Musikblätter des Anbruchs*, a music journal published in Vienna, from 1928 until late 1930.[50] In September 1933, on his thirtieth birthday, he was deprived of his *venia legendi* (right to teach) by the Nazis and moved to Berlin.[51] In the spring of 1934 he left Germany and came to London. He really wanted to return to Vienna, but his application to continue his studies at the University of Vienna was rejected by the philosophy department. By October he was ensconced in Oxford, where he remained for over three years, hoping to obtain the Oxford D.Phil., which he regarded as the nearest equivalent to the German *Habilitation*.[52] After a brief visit to New York in June 1937, he finally moved there in February 1938 without submitting for the Oxford degree. Meanwhile Horkheimer had found work for him with Paul Lazarsfeld on the Princeton Radio Research Project.[53] Although Adorno had by now published several pieces in the *Zeitschrift*, it was only after his arrival in America that he became a member of the Institute, working half for it and half for the Radio Project. In 1941, he went with Horkheimer and other members of the Institute to live in California where he collaborated with Horkheimer, Hanns Eisler, Thomas Mann and the research team of *The Authoritarian Personality* on projects in philosophy, music, literature and sociology. In late 1949 he went back to West Germany, to the University of Frankfurt, returning to America briefly in 1951 and for a year to Los Angeles, 1952–3, in both cases to organise research projects which he had undertaken to complete. He taught at the University of Frankfurt and was the director of the Institute until his death in 1969.[54]

Every year from 1920, his seventeenth, to 1969, the year of his death, Adorno published on music. These writings range from minor reviews and articles to major books. Adorno's ideas on the complex relationship between the author as composer and the author as critic are clearer in the case of music than in the case of philosophy and sociology. For where music is concerned he always considered himself to be both composer and critic.[55] He identified closely with the Vienna school of *neue Musik*, and the activity of composing within the new style and of defining the new music in articles and personal correspondence were inseparable activities for him.[56] At the same time, Adorno was one of the sternest critics of this music from both a musical and a sociological standpoint.[57] Where philosophy and sociology are concerned it is not so easy to distinguish the 'composer' from the 'critic' but it is equally important to do so, for Adorno's criticism of philosophy and sociology is deeply allied to his search for a new style for these enterprises as it is more obviously in the case of his work in music.

Adorno's collected works will comprise twenty-two volumes. He wrote in many forms and produced essays, reviews, radio broadcasts, slim volumes of short articles, monographs and long books. Half of his published work is on music. Only two volumes in the collected works are called by their editors 'sociological writings'.[58] The first of these volumes contains Adorno's criticism of sociology, the second, his empirical work. Yet, as the editors warn, the work in these two volumes is not 'merely' sociological, nor do they contain the whole of Adorno's 'sociology'.[59] The philosophical and sociological principles which structure his criticism of philosophy, sociology, music and literature are always the same. Adorno tried to develop a critique of society by producing a critique of its intellectual and artistic products.

Chapter 2

The Search for Style

Morality and Style

It is impossible to understand Adorno's ideas without understanding the ways in which he presents them, that is, his style, and without understanding the reasons for his preoccupation with style. It is, however, Adorno's theory of society which determines his style, and that theory can only be understood if one knows how to read his texts. This chapter is concerned with the relationship between Adorno's ideas and their heterogeneous presentation; the subsequent chapters are concerned with the grounding of the ideas. The glossary included at the end of the book may be consulted at this stage for a protreptic account of terms mentioned in this chapter. Adorno explicates his style most fully in the essay *Der Essay als Form* (The Essay as Form),[1] and in the book *Minima Moralia*.[2] It is in these that his engagement with Nietzsche is most evident. Much of Adorno's critique of philosophy and of sociology is drawn from his reception of Nietzsche's philosophy.

Adorno opposed the separation of philosophy from sociology since it amounted, in his opinion, to the separation of substantial issues from the development of methodology and empirical techniques. His own concern with 'method' and 'style' was of a different order. Adorno's 'methods' present seminal ideas; they are not devices imposed on material in order to organise and explain it. 'Method' (and even more 'style') means for him the relation between ideas and the composition of texts. It does not mean devising procedures for applying theories.

Adorno's works are exemplars of negative dialectic, that is, they are informed by the idea that concepts, as ordinarily used, are distorting and mask social reality. Adorno thus had to find an alternative way of using concepts, and the relation of a thought or a concept to what it is intended to cover, its object, is problematic. It follows from this that standard modes of communication are also inadequate, since they depend on the ordinary use of concepts. The question of communicating his ideas becomes the question of what the reader should experience when confronting the text, and Adorno insists that expressing the relation of the thought to its object should be prior to any concern with ease of communicating that thought. As he tersely puts it, 'Truth is objective, not plausible'.[3] He is not unconcerned with communication, but aims to find alternative modes of communication. Criticism and composition in Adorno's works are thus inseparable.

Adorno describes his programme, as presented in his book *Negative Dialectic*, as an anti-system,[4] and his texts may be equally well described as anti-texts – as he in fact describes Hegel's texts.[5] Most of Adorno's books consist of reprinted articles which were first published in journals as essays, articles, notes, monographs or reviews. Others were originally radio broadcasts, and a few were introductions to or synopses of academic conferences.[6] He gave them titles which stress their fragmentary nature, such as 'notes', 'prisms', 'models'.[7] Adorno wrote in a variety of styles, some more, some less abstruse. He is, however, notorious for his esoteric style. There is less unity in his style than this reputation suggests, and his ideas are presented in both more and less accessible ways. It is difficult to understand this reputation because Adorno discussed his method and style in everything he wrote, often at the expense of discussing the ostensible subject of the piece. In addition he wrote specific essays on titles,[8] on punctuation,[9] on his use of foreign words,[10] on different kinds of texts,[11] on form,[12] on syntax and on semantics.[13] His articles on literature are largely concerned with language and style.[14] Writers, musicians, philosophers and sociologists are discussed by Adorno as if they shared his preoccupation with style. Every critical essay on another's work emphasises the relation between thought and its presentation. This concern is equally evident in his major works which display, *prima facie*, more continuous texts.[15] Almost every page of these works includes a self-conscious reference to method and style.

Adorno uses several stylistic strategies in the attempt to present the object of his thought and to 'see beyond' the subject.[16] When he discusses 'thought' and 'mind' he uses impersonal and passive constructions. 'Thought' and 'mind' are not attributed to 'us' but are frequently personified, sometimes by dramatic metaphor.[17] Other stylistic strategies are directed at the experience of the reader. He describes these strategies as 'shock',[18] 'exaggeration',[19] 'fantasy',[20] or 'provocative formulations'.[21] An idea 'provocatively formulated' may be left and not enlarged upon, but may be restated later in the text with many different emphases. This gives an impression of confusion, but in fact amounts to a set of parallaxes, apparent displacements of an object due to changes of observation point. This is quite consistent with the idea that the object cannot be captured, and that a *set* of presentations may best approximate it. Adorno sometimes calls this a 'constellation',[22] and he also describes this way of composing texts as 'paratactic',[23] 'concentric',[24] 'as a spider's web',[25] and as a 'densely woven carpet'.[26] In letters to Rolf Tiedemann, Adorno explained the construction of his *Ästhetische Theorie* (Aesthetic Theory), and although he says that his previous books were conventional by comparison, the difference is only one of degree.[27] The *Ästhetische Theorie* was written 'concentrically, in equally weighted, paratactic parts which are ordered around a middle point which is expressed by the constellation of the parts'.[28] 'Parataxis' means placing propositions one after the other without indicating relations of co-ordination or subordination between them. In another letter he explains why he writes in this paratactic manner

> . . . from my theorem that there are no philosophical first prin-
> ciples, it follows that one cannot construct a continuous argument with
> the usual stages, but one must assemble the whole from a series of
> partial complexes . . . whose constellation not [logical] sequence
> produces the idea.[29]

Adorno explains in several places why he disregards the norms of standard philosophical argument,[30] but he does not describe the mode, half way between argument and trope, which he puts in its place – chiasmus. (Chiasmus is a grammatical figure by which the order of words in one clause is inverted in a second clause.) Adorno usually inverts the terms of the second of two antitheses in order to turn them into a chiasmus,[31] thus: ab ba. Each antithesis is usually a tautology which has importance in itself. The use of chiasmus stresses the transmutation of processes into entities which is the fundamental theme of Adorno's work. He presents this theme in this way in order to avoid turning processes into entities himself. Sometimes he uses chiasmus directly, for example, 'the subject is the object, the object is the subject'; or, 'history is nature, nature is history'. At other times it can be seen to inform the whole structure of a piece. His article on static and dynamic as sociological categories depends overall on the development of the chiasmus 'static presupposes dynamic, dynamic results in static'.[32] This chiasmus reveals a more general one which, in many versions, underlies all Adorno's thinking and which shows how he moves from criticism of intellectual and artistic products to criticism of society. Thus science misrepresents society as static and invariant; society has produced the static and invariant features which science describes,[33] or, methodology is made more important than its object (in non-dialectical sciences):(what has happened to) the object has determined methodology.

The Essay as Form

Adorno considered his essay of this title, written between 1954 and 1958,[34] to be one of the earliest statements of his programme.[35] This is a strange judgement because the piece is concerned with issues raised by Adorno since 1931,[36] but it does indicate the importance which he attached to it. The title alludes to Lukács' essay 'On the Nature and Form of the Essay' which introduced Lukács' book *Soul and Form*, published in Hungarian in 1910 and in German in 1911.[37] Adorno's essay introduces the first of his four small volumes of notes on literature. He repeats many of Lukács' points, especially the idea that the essay is a 'modest' form which makes no claim to capture the ultimate, or the actuality of life.[38] Lukács was developing Georg Simmel's distinction between life and form,[39] whereas Adorno considers the essay to be the form best suited to a philosophy which has renounced the philosophical system.[40] In both discussions there is little or no reference to society.

Adorno justifies the use of the essay in several ways. It is best suited for criticism of cultural products (*Gebilde*, 'forms') without itself relying on any notion of origin, first principles, the given or the immutable.[41] While he considers that the essays of Simmel, Lukács, Benjamin and Rudolf Kassner shared features with his essays, he is in fact prescribing how the essay should be constructed and how it should function.[42] An essay always takes a cultural product as its object, interprets such products as social and historical formations[43] and assesses their truth content from that perspective.[44] However, Adorno says much less about how the essay should examine a work than he does about how it should proceed itself. He states that the theme of the essay is the relation between culture and nature,[45] but that this theme must be presented in a way which does not reproduce a cultural form of the kind which is being examined. The essay has all the features of the 'anti-system'. It proceeds by way of parallaxes which Adorno describes here as 'experimenting': 'For whoever seeks to criticise must necessarily experiment. He must create conditions under which an object becomes visible anew . . .'[46]

Adorno enlarges his position by pitting it against three of Descartes' four rules of method in his *Discourse on Method*.[47] He thus opposes the second rule, to divide the object 'into as many parts as possible, and as seems necessary in order to resolve it in the best way',[48] as a version of the traditional theory that analysis of elements is the same as the analysis of the structure of being, or that an ordering schema of concepts corresponds to the order of reality.[49] He rejects Descartes' third rule, 'to proceed according to my thoughts, thus commencing with objects that were the most simple and easy to understand, in order to rise gradually as it were by degrees to knowledge of the most complex'.[50] Thinking for Adorno starts from the complex and is not separated into progressive stages. The fourth rule is also disputed, 'to make enumerations so complete and summations so general "that one would be sure to have left nothing out"'.[51] Adorno starts from the assumption of a split and antagonistic reality which cannot be adequately represented by any system which makes its goals unity and simplicity or clarity.[52] The essay, on the other hand, 'thinks in breaks (*in Brüchen*) because reality is brittle (*brüchig*) and finds its unity through the breaks, not by smoothing them over'.[53] It lies between art and science,[54] and, since it takes historical and cultural products as its object, results in a philosophy of culture (*Kulturphilosophie*).[55] Adorno claims that this does not diminish its value, but that the essay is the 'critical form *par excellence*'.[56] Adorno is well aware that any form which abandons the conventions of discursiveness runs the risk of being obscure or arbitrary or even a vehicle for shallow thinking, and of smudging the distinctions between these faults.[57]

Adorno's dicta concerning the relation between thought and style also apply to the use of language. Hence the distinction between the expression (*Ausdruck*) of truth and communication (*Mitteilung*) of it[58] affects the use of words as well as the overall structure of Adorno's texts.[59] One outcome of this is his refusal to define terms,[60] another is that the same term is used in many different senses. He believes that it is impossible to eliminate the 'mythical remainder' from language and that therefore this aspect of language must be enlisted in the expression of truth, and not expunged from it.[61] By 'mythical remainder', Adorno means that history is congealed in language and that to rationalise language by purifying words of acquired connotations is impossible. Therefore any attempt to do so merely results in creating another kind of myth.[62] The demand that ideas should be expressed clearly and simply amounts to a demand that 'expressive residues' should be eliminated for the sake of ease of communication, according to Adorno. This does not result in an 'objective', 'scientific' style but in a kind of distortion. Conversely, whenever he examines a work of philosophy, sociology or art, he is as much concerned with its linguistic features as with any other feature. One of his best known books, *Jargon of Authenticity*,[63] is a criticism of a particular use of language. Criticism of language (*Sprachkritik*), like criticism of cultural forms (*Kulturkritik*), is philosophy and criticism of society for Adorno.

Minima Moralia

Minima Moralia is Adorno's best-written book and the most successful stylistically. It was written between 1944 and 1947 in German when he was in America. It consists of three parts divided according to when they were written. Each part is divided into around fifty sections and each section is numbered and headed by a title. Adorno subtitled the whole book 'Reflections from Damaged Life' and each section contains a reflection or an 'essay' in the sense of a short tentative on a theme. Most sections cover only a page or less, although a few are several pages long. A section is often connected closely with the succeeding one. In the dedication, Adorno justifies the form of the book in much the same way in which he justified the essay in *Der Essay als Form*. The book was written 'from the standpoint of subjective experience'.[64] It contains reflections on personal experiences, on society, on art, on philosophy, on psychology, and on a host of related topics.

If *Minima Moralia* is written from 'the subjective standpoint', then *Negative Dialectic* is written from 'the objective standpoint'.[65] The second of these books, although fragmentary like the first, constitutes the most direct statement of Adorno's ideas, free of irony. *Minima Moralia* is much less formal in its tone and often lyrical in style and relies greatly on 'indirect methods', especially ironic inversion.[66] This indirect and more idiosyncratic way of presenting his ideas is what Adorno means by 'the subjective standpoint'. In *Minima Moralia* Adorno's use of ironic inversion is most explicit, while in other texts the inverted ways in which he presents his ideas about society are less obvious because the irony is less obvious. Adorno, like many essayists and ironists, has thus been read far too literally, and this is partly because some of his texts are stylistically much more meticulous than others.

Minima Moralia is ironic in the two standard senses of the word: 'expression of meaning by use of words normally conveying the opposite meaning', and 'apparent perversity of fate or circumstance'. Adorno takes well-known titles of works, phrases and ideas and changes one or two words so as to convey the opposite meaning. He proceeds to expound the idea involved as if he took the new meaning literally. This device is designed in fact to revert attention to the original idea and thus to reassess it. Sometimes he uses the original phrase and conveys the ironic inversion in his discussion. Sometimes he just states the inversion and does not discuss it. Furthermore, all these inversions of well-known ideas imply that society has undergone an extremely perverse fate, and has turned into the obverse of its ideals, but any literal or simple reading of this is also undercut. For, according to Adorno, in philosophy and sociology 'nothing is meant in a completely literal manner, neither statement of fact nor pure validity', and he warns that 'dialectical knowledge is taken all too literally by its opponents'.[67] If someone asks that we do not take him literally, then we should, presumably, not take the advice not to take him literally, literally. To follow the original injunction consistently means both that we must sometimes not take it literally and that sometimes we must. This would seem a chaotic principle for exegesis, but in fact Adorno usually undermines his own hyperbole and auxesis quite clearly himself.[68] In this way Adorno manages to criticise society and present his ideas without grounding them in any of the ways which he considers illegitimate.

An example of ironic inversion is 'The Health unto Death',[69] the title of a section and an inversion of Kierkegaard's title *The Sickness unto Death*,[70] and which introduces reflections on society's definition of health and normality.[71] Another example is 'This side of the pleasure principle',[72] an inversion of the title of Freud's book *Beyond the Pleasure Principle*.[73] The whole book, however, is based on three key inversions. The first is indicated by the title *Minima Moralia* which alludes to Aristotle's *Magna Moralia* and also suggests Nietzsche's *Beyond Good and Evil*.[74] The second major inversion is 'The whole is the false',[75] an inversion of Hegel's principle 'the whole is the true'.[76] The third inversion is contained in his description of the book as 'the melancholy science' (*die traurige Wissenschaft*)[77] which is an allusion to Nietzsche's book *The Joyful Science* (*die fröhliche Wissenschaft*).[78] Sometimes Adorno makes the inversion of a theme clear by setting one section up as the direct antithesis of another, usually the preceding one[79] and by also making it clear that neither are to be taken literally.[80] As in all his texts, some passages contain explicit directions for reading the book,[81] and in other places he describes his method

> . . . limitation and reservation are no way to present the dialectic. Rather, the dialectic advances by way of extremes, driving thoughts with the utmost consequence to the point where they turn back on themselves, instead of qualifying them.[82]

Adorno discusses irony too 'by way of extremes'. He defines irony as 'the difference between ideology and reality', and says that this difference 'has disappeared'.[83] Hence the classic procedure of irony which 'convicts its object by presenting it as what it purports to be . . . and without passing judgement . . .'[84] is no longer possible, because there is no point in unmasking failure to measure up to a standard when the standard is 'itself a lie'.[85] Yet Adorno does believe that some standards are not lies; he does add interpretation to irony, and he does use irony in the way in which he defines it and says that it is no longer possible to use it. For his definition of irony is the same as what he elsewhere describes as 'the immanent method': if 'Irony says: such it [ideology] claims to be, but such it [reality] is',[86] then irony works in the same way as the 'immanent' procedure which takes the 'objective idea'[87] of a work, whether philosophical, sociological, literary or musical, and 'confronts it with the norms which it itself has crystallized'.[88] Adorno explains the rationale of this 'immanent procedure'[89] in terms which are identical with his delineation of 'irony's medium' as 'the difference between ideology and reality', namely, 'It takes seriously the principle that it is not ideology in itself which is untrue but rather its pretension to correspond to reality'.[90] These procedures, however named, are 'objectivist' ones, that is, they are designed to make the object 'speak for itself'. Thus whether Adorno writes from the 'subjective standpoint' or from the objective standpoint,[91] his methods turn out to be fundamentally the same.

This discussion of Adorno's method in *Minima Moralia* is not intended to tone down the ideas or to deflect attention from what Adorno says. *Minima Moralia* is the book in which Adorno most appears to describe society. However, if one reads it literally, it appears to be self-contradictory and self-defeating, owing to the prevalence of ideas such as 'the total society', 'the end of the individual', and 'complete reification', which imply that no critical consciousness is possible. In order to see that this is not the case, it is necessary to know how to interpret these ideas, in short, to understand the workings of Adorno's dialectic.

The Tradition of Irony

Adorno's engagement with Nietzsche is evident throughout his work. He believed that he was confronted by the same paradox which beset Nietzsche, namely, how to present or ground a philosophy or point of view when the aim of that philosophy is to criticise reality or society altogether and thus the prevailing norms of philosophical or sociological discourse as well. Both writers, therefore, according to Adorno use 'indirect methods'[92] to express their criticism and to avoid grounding their philosophy in the ways which they deem undesirable. Adorno self-consciously but unobtrusively weaves many of Nietzsche's positions into his own thought, often by inverting them as a way of appropriating them. For example, Adorno's pronouncement that 'Life does not live' (*Das Leben lebt nicht*),[93] which introduces the first part of *Minima Moralia*, is an inversion of the message which runs through Nietzsche's philosophy – the commandment to 'live life'. These connections between Nietzsche and Adorno inform all of the latter's *oeuvre*, but they are most explicit in *Minima Moralia*.

Like Nietzsche, Adorno's work is inimitable and idiosyncratic and his convictions are often arrogantly stated in a way which contrasts strangely with the modest attempt to present a philosophy which is ungrounded and ungroundable. Yet both Nietzsche and Adorno undercut and contradict even their most sacred assertions and provide instructions for interpreting their strongly-voiced claims. The works of both must be read from a methodological point of view and not literally. In both cases too, their work was designed to resist popularisation, but in effect encouraged it. They tried, in very different ways, to make their style esoteric in order to defy the norms which they opposed, and they wrote in essays or in fragments to avoid the appearance and presuppositions of the traditional philosophical system. Yet fragments and aphorisms are easily detachable and equally easily misunderstood, since their significance can only be appreciated on the basis of an understanding of the whole of which they are the fragments – hence the paradoxes that such idiosyncratic and radical thinkers can be so widely and quickly assimilated but so often misunderstood. Nietzsche wrote for the most part a lapidary, brilliant German which was often deceptively clear, while Adorno's German ranges from the poetic to the obtuse. Both men, nevertheless, fired the imagination of the younger generation, and had a strong effect on the work of their respective epigoni.

Adorno shared Nietzsche's programme of a 'transvaluation of all values'.[94] 'Morality', 'values' and 'norms' do not imply a moral dimension distinct from other dimensions but characterise the construction and imposition of 'reality'. Nietzsche, according to Adorno, refused 'complicity with the world'[95] which, where Adorno is concerned, comes to mean rejecting the prevalent norms and values of society on the grounds that they have come to legitimise a society that in no way corresponds to them – they have become 'lies'.[96] Adorno shared Nietzsche's epistemological aim to demonstrate that the apparent fixity of the world or values arises from the systematic debasement of dynamic aspects of reality in our thinking and philosophy. Like Nietzsche, Adorno was a moralist, concerned to find a method by which his alternative moral perspective could be conveyed, but he faces the difficulties of justifying a moral position when he has apparently rejected all morality, of stating that position when he has rejected the prevalent norms of communication, and of adhering to any position at all without reaffirming the superior status of static as opposed to dynamic ways of thinking. Nietzsche called one of his books by the provocative title *Beyond Good and Evil*, but its theme is 'the *conscience* of method'.[97] Similarly *Minima Moralia* is preoccupied with 'the morality of thinking'[98] and with 'morality and style'.[99]

In the book *Dialectic of Enlightenment*, which Horkheimer and Adorno wrote together, they developed the idea that society, culture and language as a whole are ideological or a 'lie'. This amounted to an announcement that the prevailing ideology is impenetrable and that there is no universal class which is the carrier of privileged alternative knowledge. They also exposed ambivalences in the original ideals of the Enlightenment to show how it is that an ideology which describes society so inadequately and incorrectly has yet attained unchallenged hegemony. They trace the idea of 'enlightenment' from the Kantian notions of autonomy and organisation[100] to Nietzsche's exposure of 'enlightenment' as the unity of reason and domination.[101] The dialectic is between two aspects of the concept of reason (in Kant), one which

> as the transcendental, supraindividual self, . . . comprises the idea of a free human social life in which men organize themselves as the universal subject and overcome the conflict between pure and empirical reason in the conscious solidarity of the whole. This represents the idea of true universality: utopia. At the same time, however, reason constitutes the court of judgement of calculation, which adjusts the world for the ends of self-preservation and recognizes no function other than the preparation of the object from mere sensory material in order to make it the material of subjugation.[102]

This duality is the Enlightenment's notion of reason between freedom and subjugation, a duality heightened in the subsequent course of history, has given rise to a 'dialectic of enlightenment'.[103] The second aspect of reason has informed men's *activity*, while the first set of connotations has prevailed as the ideal which masks that activity. This interpretation of reason (*Vernunft*) owes a lot to Nietzsche and the authors credit him with this, 'Nietzsche was one of the few after Hegel who recognized the dialectic of enlightenment'.[104] They quote Nietzsche's view that '. . . princes and statesmen should be unmistakably aware that everything they do is an intentional lie . . .'.[105] It is a 'lie' or 'false' because it involves 'the reduction and malleability of men',[106] but also because Nietzsche has an instrumental theory of truth. Truth is whatever is imposed as truth and thus has no ultimate validity. Truth, for Nietzsche, is 'will to power'. Thus when he says that something is 'false' or a 'lie' he too is using 'false' as an instrument and imposition. Hyperbole is thus a form employed obliquely to counteract the prevailing imposition, and the content of any proposition presented by such means is not to be taken literally. Although Horkheimer and Adorno did not subscribe to an instrumental theory of truth they took over Nietzsche's position in a way which enabled them to point out the universality of domination.

In *Minima Moralia*, Adorno argues that in order to avoid the 'lie' or 'sheer falsehood' and to expose it for what it is, Nietzsche pretends to be an amoralist who rejects the moral distinctions of the world, sometimes by also playing the role of the immoralist, who opposes what the world approves and emphatically endorses what it disapproves. Adorno construes other writers in a similar way; 'Did not Karl Kraus, Kafka, even Proust prejudice and falsify the image of the world in order to shake off falsehood and prejudice?'.[107] He considers that he is the amoralist for his own time as Nietzsche was for his, 'As a guarantee of his undiminished resistance, he [the amoralist] is still as alone in this as in the days when he turned the mask of evil upon the normal world, to teach the norm to fear its own perversity'.[108] The position of the amoralist is a profoundly moral one, 'Anti-morality, in rejecting what is immoral in morality, . . . inherits morality's deepest concern . . .'.[109] The way in which Adorno describes Nietzsche's position is very close to his own discussion of irony and of the immanent method:

> Nietzsche belongs to that tradition of bourgeois thinkers who since the Renaissance have revolted against the untruth of society and cynically played its reality [*deren Wahrheit*] as an 'ideal' against its ideal, and by the critical power of the confrontation have helped that other truth [i.e. its ideal] which they mock most fiercely as the untruth . . .[110]

Pitting reality against ideals is a way to criticise both the ideals and the reality without assuming a different fixed reality or a dogmatic standpoint. Adorno, of course, belongs to this tradition too.

For both Nietzsche and Adorno, according to the latter, it is necessary to show how entities are constructed out of the dynamic processes of the world or of society in order to explain how the ideas and beliefs (or 'norms' or 'values') about the world which are the targets of their criticism have attained hegemony. To examine the formation of beliefs about the world or about society is equally to examine the formation of the world or of society and, *ex hypothesi*, to criticise such beliefs is to criticise society or the world. For example, the mode of production of commodities gives rise to systematically mistaken beliefs about them, such as that (exchange) value is a property of the commodity. This belief is inseparable from the formation of the commodity *qua* commodity, that is, from the production of value in exchange. The processes which underlie the formation must not be made into ontological principles since they would then display precisely those features of reality which are being exposed as apparent. In Nietzsche's case, 'will to power' constitutes the world and our mode of thought; in Adorno's case, processes of production (mode of production) constitute society and our mode of thought. Both writers stress an underlying 'reality' as process or, as they call it, *Werden* (becoming). 'Becoming' is a notoriously vague emphasis shared by many philosophers and sociologists but meaning many different things. Neither Nietzsche nor Adorno refers to it as *the principle* of reality, nor do they intend it to refer to *events* rather than entities.

Adorno thus revived Nietzsche's emphasis on *Werden* as the basis of his own denial of the possibility of grounding philosophy or sociology on a first principle, and of his criticism of the traditional subject/object dichotomy. Marx and most post-Hegelian philosophical and social thought may also be construed as refusing such grounds.[111] Adorno considered, however, that Nietzsche's version was the most successful and appropriate for his time, because he believed that only the ironist or the stylist consistently refuses to reground his thought. Adorno, like Lukács, is known for having developed a Hegelianised Marxism. However, Adorno's thought cannot be understood unless it is realised that any 'Hegelian' terminology is reintroduced on the basis of a Nietzschean inversion.[112] This is not true of Lukács' work. Adorno was concerned to show, too, that fresh attempts to ground philosophy and sociology on indubitable first principles which had occurred since Nietzsche and Lukács wrote were just as illegitimate as the classical ones. Adorno in fact considered that Lukács' Marxist writing constituted precisely such an attempt. The main targets of Adorno's criticism were the twentieth century attempts to break out of philosophical idealism which he believed had relapsed back into it, such as the philosophy of Husserl and of Heidegger, and sociological 'relativisms' which rely on classificatory principles to ground their object, for example, the 'situational' aspects of Karl Mannheim's concept of total ideology.[113]

Hence, for Adorno, Nietzsche's 'liberating act, a true turning point of Western thought . . .', that he 'refuses homage to the speculative concept, the hypostasis of the mind'[114] is still pertinent and valid for the criticism of philosophical and social thought. Adorno means that 'mind' (*Geist*) has been falsely made into the autonomous foundation of knowledge in philosophical systems. The notion of 'mind' itself is merely a construct, a formation, which has acquired the status of an eternal and immutable principle. 'Truth' (and identity) does not consist of correspondence between consciousness and reality or between concepts and their objects, it is an instrument imposed on the reality which it constructs. Adorno thus developed Nietzsche's criticism of 'identity philosophy' in his own restatement of the Marxian criticism of Hegel and philosophy and sociology. He is perhaps the only neo-Marxist to make Nietzsche's criticism of logic (identity) into social criticism.

Adorno's criticism of our usual way of thinking, which he calls 'identity thinking', is based on an instrumental notion of logic, on a 'will to identity' and, as in Nietzsche's case, this does not involve denying the laws of thought. This criticism attempts to yield insight into the way concepts are formed and imposed. Adorno quotes Nietzsche's attack on the traditional idea of logic, 'Nothing occurs in reality which strictly corresponds to logic'[115] and endorses this point, although he concedes that it is not the same as Hegel's criticism of traditional logic. Adorno is more concerned with the Nietzschean perspective that to say that two things are identical is to make them identical, than with the Hegelian emphasis that to say that two things are identical is to assume incorrectly that they are independent of each other. Many passages in *Negative Dialectic* allude to Nietzsche's strictures on logic and Adorno's position is only cogent when understood in this light. He exposes the motive behind the construction of philosophical and sociological systems as a will to control the entire world by construing it as identical to the concepts of the system

> Great philosophy was accompanied by a paranoid zeal to tolerate nothing else and to pursue everything else . . . The slightest remnant of non-identity sufficed to deny an identity conceived as total.[116]

Adorno considers that this 'desire to control' determines every individual judgement as well as the impulse to construct systems, ' . . . the will to identify works in every synthesis'.[117] Although Adorno relates this interpretation of identity to a specific historical mode of production,[118] he also bases it on a more general 'anthropological' account which is not attributable to any specifiable carrier, man or class. Adorno exclaims, somewhat rhetorically, that desire for the unity of thought has its origin in the battle for self-preservation. It arises from the impulse to devour anything which is different and which is thus considered to be inferior. Hence, 'The system is the belly turned mind, and rage is the mark of each and every idealism'.[119] Adorno attributes this insight to Nietzsche.[120] For example, 'It is our needs that interpret the world; our drives and the For and Against. Every drive is a kind of lust to rule.'[121]

Adorno calls the function of thought which constructs and controls nature (the world, society) the 'pragmatic' aspect of identifying.[122] He does not deny that this aspect of identifying is necessary for thinking, but he dramatises it by calling it 'false', because any thinking which is determined by the desire to control the world cannot qualify for the status of 'truth' in the conventional, disinterested sense of truth. He occasionally describes the 'necessary illusions' of capitalist society, an idea and phrase which come from Marx, in very Nietzschean terms, 'Illusion is the most *efficacious* [*das Allerwirklichste*] reality'.[123] Adorno uses this Nietzschean perspective to emphasise that concepts are imposed. He considers that a perspective based on a theory of interests or 'will' yields more insight into social mechanisms than, for instance, Durkheim's structural approach, because it is able to see the universal coercive mechanism of thought as a formation, whereas Durkheim could only consider the coercive function of thought as a 'given'.[124]

Adorno calls Nietzsche 'the dynamic thinker *par excellence*'.[125] Nietzsche granted full status to the dynamic aspects of reality and conceived of the apparently fixed aspects as having been formed out of the dynamic:

It is axiomatic (for a transformed aesthetics) that what has become can also be true [*dass auch das Gewordene wahr sein kann*]. This mode of cognition was developed in the late works of Nietzsche in opposition to traditional philosophy. The traditional view which was demolished by him, should be turned on its head thus: only what has become is true [*Wahrheit ist einzig als Gewordenes*].[126]

Adorno was impressed by Nietzsche's accusation that traditional philosophers 'hate' 'the very idea of becoming . . . What is, does not *become*; what becomes, *is* not . . .'.[127] In his essay *Der Essay als Form*, Adorno makes the same point 'It [the essay] escapes the dictate of attributes which have been ascribed to ideas since the definition of the Symposium, "of being eternal and neither becoming nor passing away, neither changing nor decreasing"; "a Being which is by itself, for itself, eternal and of one form". . . '.[128] Nietzsche demonstrated that many of the most cherished philosophical concepts such as 'cause' and 'effect', 'ego', 'reason', 'being', 'subject' and 'object' were 'reifications' and 'fetishes', constructions based on specific prejudices of philosophers which lead to faulty thinking.[129] Nietzsche actually used the word *Verdinglichung* and his work is certainly one of the lost sources of the concept. The role it performs in Adorno's work owes much to Nietzsche. Adorno adopted Nietzsche's way of presenting concepts so as to avoid the assumptions under attack. He thus refuses to define concepts and frequently quotes Nietzsche to explain this, 'all those concepts in which a total process is semiotically [*semiotisch*] embraced escape definition; only that is definable which has no history'.[130] For Adorno, to define a concept would be to use the kind of thinking which he is criticising. Adorno tries to make Nietzsche's point about history into one about society too. He takes over Nietzsche's idea that concepts are 'masks' and that they hide their origins and asserts that this is due to 'real domination'.[131]

Nevertheless, Nietzsche and Adorno each found a way to assert alternative values, by demonstrating that apparently eternal values have been erected in a way which hides their formation. Adorno sometimes expresses his position by dissenting vigorously from the one to which Nietzsche adhered. At the very end of his essay on form, he quotes a passage from Nietzsche, 'If we affirm one single moment, we thus affirm not only ourselves but all existence . . . and in this single moment of affirmation, all eternity was called good, redeemed, justified, and affirmed'.[132] Nietzsche's 'message' is to live each instant of life, of becoming, as if it were eternal, '. . . beyond terror and pity, *to realise in oneself* the eternal joy of becoming . . .',[133] '. . . that the will to life may assert itself eternally . . .',[134] '*Eternal* life, eternal recurrence of life . . .'.[135] Nietzsche's tirades against modern culture and prevalent values arose from his belief that they 'denied life'. Nietzsche entitled one of his books *The Joyful Science* and his 'method' (the science) is designed to convey these values. Adorno rejects not the method, nor the emphasis on instants as opposed to the eternal verities of traditional philosophy, but the affirmation of 'life'. This is why the first words of the dedication of *Minima Moralia* describe the work as 'the melancholy science', why the book is subtitled 'Reflections from Damaged Life', and why the aphorism 'Life does not live' introduces the first part of the book.

Furthermore, it is only from the Nietzschean perspective that sense can be made of Adorno's combination of a commitment to process and formation with the lack of any proleptic account of history. Adorno rejects all forms of historicism, whether empiricist or Hegelian. He is thus engaged in 'interventions' (*Eingriffe*), the title of one of his essay collections, designed to prevent the affirmation of society. He comments on Nietzsche's alternative in the concluding paragraph of the essay on form, 'For the happiness of the instant which was sacred to Nietzsche, it [the essay] knows only the name of the negative'.[136] Adorno interprets Nietzsche's teaching as *amor fati* and as consecration of a new myth (as Nietzsche intended), because such teaching continues to mask the society which underlies it.[137] Both Nietzsche and Adorno resisted assimilation of their work by the culture which they were criticising, but Nietzsche did not refuse to affirm 'life' because he could not affirm his culture. For Adorno 'life' could not be affirmed as something apart from the life of a culture or society and its possibilities. Nietzsche in this sense had no concept or theory of society. Adorno too seeks to affirm 'life' but, given the present society, to affirm life is to affirm that society and thus a 'life which does not live'. Adorno instead affirms hope for a 'life (that is, a society) which lives'. He accuses Nietzsche of bowing down before 'the powers that be'[138] and of denying the validity of the hope that existence might be better.[139] Yet Adorno is aware of Nietzsche's argument against hope; it is the argument against philosophical idealism:

> Nietzsche in the *Antichrist* voiced the strongest argument not merely against theology but against metaphysics, that hope is mistaken for truth; that the impossibility of living happily, or even living at all, without the thought of the absolute, does not vouch for the legitimacy of that thought.[140]

Nevertheless, Adorno opts for the ungroundable and unjustifiable hope at the risk of relapsing into philosophical idealism.[141] Thus Adorno is not a pessimist because, in spite of the gloomy picture which he dialectically paints of society, he is always concerned in his own work and in the assessment of the work of others, to achieve a style which will best intervene in society. Adorno never specifies any particular political goal of his 'interventions'. He says that they should not glorify the past, nor set up alternative dogmas. To avoid such absurdity, they should be constantly provocative.[142]

Thus the notion of a 'dialectic of enlightenment' is an interpretation of Nietzsche, and not of Max Weber,[143] and the emphasis on the social imposition of concepts is also based on an interpretation of Nietzsche not of Durkheim. However, Adorno's work displays the serious difficulties inherent in any attempt to make Nietzsche's ideas into sociological ones, whether within a Marxist or non-Marxist context. Adorno is aware that Nietzsche has no general concept of society nor thus of a specific kind of society, for example, capitalist society. Nietzsche's criticism of 'values' and his exposure of the 'will to power' by which concepts and ideas are imposed, do not logically depend on being located in a subject, social or non-social, nor thus in a social group or class.[144] It is precisely such presuppositions which Nietzsche was refusing. Sociologically, his perspective has often been used to stress the universality and impersonality of domination, but it cannot provide any sociological theory of the origin or workings of that 'domination', that is, any theory of power.[145] *Dialectic of Enlightenment* illustrates the difficulty of linking a general theory of the domination of nature with a theory of a specific kind of society. In Adorno's work the link is established by the theory of reification which purports to describe the mechanism of domination in a specific mode of production. This theory, too, is presented in a variety of ways, some of them apparently self-contradictory, such as 'total reification', 'total control', 'the end of the individual'. For Adorno is dramatising these ideas, presenting them *as if* they were absolutely and literally true, in order to undermine them more effectively.

Chapter 3

The Lament over Reification

Reification as a Sociological Category

The concept of reification has been overworked in sociology and thus made to bear an enormous amount of theoretical responsibility. The reasons for this need to be recovered in order to reassess the suitability of 'reification' for such a central theoretical role.

Marx reconstructed the way specific social relations between men result in a definite mode of production (or form of society) which he also described as a social form.[1] Where capitalism is concerned, Marx started his analysis from the commodity form as the most elementary and crucial social form:

> What I started out from is the simplest social form in which the labour-product is presented in contemporary society, and this is the '*commodity*'. I analyse it, and right from the beginning, in the *form in which it appears*.[2]

His theory of value established that ' . . . exchange-value is the *only form* in which the value of commodities can manifest itself or be expressed'.[3] Capitalism, as a mode of production, depends, *inter alia*, on the value-form, the commodity-form, the money-form.[4] They are some of its particular social forms.

After he had developed the theory of value and the theory of commodity fetishism in the first part of the first volume of *Capital*, Marx did not derive from these theories any detailed accounts of other capitalist social institutions (that is, of the organisation of bureaucracy, of religion, of law) or of culture.[5] Marx might have derived many more social forms specific to capitalism from his model of the value-form than he did.

The concept of reification in the later neo-Marxist tradition was devised in order to generalise Marx's theory of value as the model of capitalistic social forms, and to apply it to social institutions and to culture. Emphasis on the theory of commodity fetishism has obfuscated the importance of the structure of the theory of value on which the cogency of 'commodity fetishism' depends. 'Reification' has often been used in order to generalise the theory of value and of commodity fetishism without taking up the theory of surplus value or any theory of class formation, and without developing any theory of power and the state.

Historical

The Abuse of 'Reification'

Unlike the Marxian concept of 'alienation' and the Durkheimian concept of 'anomie',[6] 'reification' has no canonical source, and it has become prominent and debased as much by insinuation as by scrupulous examination. Frequently, most of nineteenth-century German social thought has been construed as contributing to the debate over reification: 'The concept of reification, one of the most important legacies of the German intellectual tradition to modern social thought . . .',[7] and Marx is seen as merely one of the contributors, 'Though Schiller, Hegel, Marx, Simmel, and others have worked with the idea (if not always the term) of reification . . . '.[8] This debate concerns the origin and demise of reification, the point in history at which reification irrupted into society, and the possibility or impossibility of overcoming reification. Reification in this context stands for the divisiveness and fragmentation of modern society which is usually dated from the end of Greek antiquity! Herder, Fichte, Schiller, Hegel and Nietzsche are said to have defined the terms of this purported debate.[9] On inspection those terms have not included the word *Verdinglichung*. More specifically sociological descriptions of modernity which arose as a response to the development of capitalism in Germany, and which dichotomise history into, for example, *Gemeinschaft* and *Gesellschaft*, probably owe less to this earlier philosophical tradition than is claimed.

Unlike 'alienation' and 'anomie', 'reification' cannot be related to a contextual theory of human nature. In fact Marx's notion of man as a 'species-being' was intended precisely to avoid the presupposition of a fixed, eternal human nature. Marx presents the view that men make and remake their own nature and the societies in which they live through their productive activities and relations. 'Alienation' from this area of man's activity is one of the four famous aspects of alienation which Marx discussed.[10] Many commentators have equated reification with alienation usually by using the terms synonymously.[11] This has added nothing to the issue of whether there is a Marxian concept of human nature or to the analysis of the four aspects of alienation. It has merely compounded the terminological confusion which often accompanies the ostensibly most fastidious exegeses of Marx's work.[12]

Mitzman has launched an ambitious dichotomy between reification and alienation, designed to pick out different assumptions about individual personality and the development of modern society. Social theorists who 'value . . . the creativity of the personality' and the power of the will to dominate nature, see the 'threat' of modern society in 'the unified power of culture' (reification).[13] They are contrasted with social theorists who value the harmonious personality 'which seeks not mastery over, but reconciliation with, nature' and see the 'threat' to the personality in the 'divisiveness of modern culture' and the increasing estrangement of men from their own activity (alienation).[14] Mitzman considers that Nietzsche, Simmel, Weber and Sombart were concerned with reification rather than alienation. In both cases he defines 'the threat' as the increase in 'goal-oriented activity' and in 'rationalisation'.[15] However, the distinction between the two types is too rigid and it frequently breaks down in Mitzman's discussion. His inability to assign Marx to one side or the other illustrates the problem.[16] Most of the theorists whom Mitzman discusses presupposed both activity and harmony, defined the divisiveness and solidity of society (*Gesellschaft*) in terms of each other and recommended some sort of struggle in order to attain communality (*Gemeinschaft*). The two types turn out to be very similar, both presupposing the loss of the possibility of exercising human abilities.[17] Mitzman is in fact most concerned to establish the status *sui generis* of 'the sociology of reification'. Weber's sociology provides him with the ideal-type of this sociology,[18] but he has no hesitation in assimilating the work of many other theorists to this ideal-type:

> Sombart's analysis of the world created by the capitalist spirit, Tönnies view of *Gesellschaft*, Weber's perception of inescapable bureaucratization, and Simmel's notion of *objektiver Geist*, in their suggestion of reified structures hostile to the emotional and aesthetic qualities of the human spirit, are all fundamentally of a piece with the young Nietzsche's brilliant *aperçu* into the desiccation of human emotion . . .[19]

Instead of making the concept of reification more rigorous, Mitzman inherits and accepts all the vagaries associated with the term and extends the use of the term in a way which adds a few more vagaries of his own.

Misattributions of 'Reification'

In English language and in German language works, reification is persistently attributed wrongly to Hegel and to Marx.[20] Lukács' famous article, 'Reification and the Consciousness of the Proletariat',[21] is the source of the error that Marx used the word *Verdinglichung* in his section in the first volume of *Capital* on the fetishism of commodities, and Herbert Marcuse's account of Hegel's philosophy in *Reason and Revolution* may be the source of the mistaken belief that Hegel used the word.[22] This widespread misattribution has contributed to the debasement of the term. At worst, it has enabled writers to use reification as a catchword for Marx's epistemology construed in the most general way so that reification becomes synonymous with objectification and does not even pertain any longer to a specific mode of production.[23] At best, some writers have used reification, following Lukács, in order to generalise Marx's theory of commodity fetishism,[24] but without making it their task to rehearse Marx's theory of value and thus to assess the various different ways in which the theory might be generalised.[25] This usually results in more or less uncritical and faint imitations of Lukács. In fact Lukács, Benjamin and Adorno each construed Marx's theory of value differently and although the differences may appear, *prima facie*, to be merely differences of emphasis, they disclose profound differences of principle.

The different interpretations of Marx's theory of value arise out of the various emphases that Marx himself put on that theory in *Capital*,[26] in *Theories of Surplus Value*[27] and in the *Grundrisse*.[28] At the beginning of *Capital* Marx analyses the commodity as a use-value or useful object and as a 'value'. He demonstrates that 'value' is not a natural property of the commodity but appears when products are exchanged.[29] This 'value' represents human labour in the abstract. Marx describes the illusions which accompany the capitalist production and exchange of commodities in several ways:

> Labour capacity has appropriated for itself only the subjective conditions of necessary labour . . . separated from the conditions of its realization [the objective conditions] – and it has posited these conditions themselves as *things*, *values*, which confront it in an alien, commanding personification.[30]

This quotation lists the different emphases that Marx later put on commodity fetishism. Sometimes he stresses that a relation between men appears as a relation between things,[31] sometimes that 'value' appears to be a property of the commodity and thus a thing,[32] sometimes that the commodity takes on a will and life of its own and becomes personified.[33] At least two of the four aspects of alienation are contained in the description of commodity fetishism: alienation from the activity of labour, and from the product of labour. Marx notes these aspects in the *Grundrisse* in the same place in which he states the proposition which contains the germ of commodity fetishism and which is repeated in *Capital*:

> The social character of activity, as well as the social form of the product, and the share of individuals in production here appears as something alien and objective . . . In exchange value, the social connection between persons is transformed into a social relation between things . . .[34]

The same proposition with an additional emphasis occurs in *Capital*. It is mistranslated in the standard English edition and this has obscured the additional emphasis. The standard English translation is ' . . . A definite social relation between men . . . assumes . . . the fantastic form of a relation between things'.[35] The German translated as 'the fantastic form' is *die phantasmagorische form*[36] which should be translated as 'the phantasmagoric form' in English. The epithet 'phantasmagoric' stresses the personifications as well as the strangeness of the form in which the relations between men appear. 'Phantasmagoria' means a crowd or succession of dim or doubtfully real persons. The word was coined in England in 1802 and was taken over later into German. In the sentences which follow, Marx develops the idea of commodities as phantasmagoric:

> In order, therefore, to find an analogy, we must have recourse to the mist-enveloped regions of the religious. In that world the productions of the human brain appear as independent beings endowed with life, and entering into relation both with one another and the human race. So it is in the world of commodities . . .[37]

Marx meant this literally. It is not easy to appreciate this when English language translators and commentators use the standard (incorrect) translation.[38]

Lukács started his discussion of reification from the way men's productive activity becomes alien and objective to them under capitalism which is why he earned the reputation of having anticipated the discovery of Marx's theory of alienation when the *1844 Manuscripts* were later found.[39] Benjamin was most interested in the phantasmagoric and personified form of commodities and the life they lead as such. Adorno was most interested in the way a relation between men appears in the form of a natural *property* of a thing.

Simmel and Reification

Simmel's highly syncretic work fuses aspects of the philosophy of Kant, Hegel, Marx and Nietzsche.[40] He developed a philosophy of culture from which he derived the principles of his historical sociology.[41] In turn, his work had a profound influence on Weber and Lukács and on subsequent phenomenological and Marxist sociology. Many of the problems which later attend reification as a sociological category in Marxist and non-Marxist sociology are discernible in his work.

Simmel deserves the reputation of being the first to claim to have generalised Marx and to have thoroughly sociologised Nietzsche in order to produce a general theory of social forms and of life as the will to create culture. His concept of form is complex and unifies his various philosophical and sociological studies. It depends on a notion of man as a subject who acts on the world so as to engender structures which attain an autonomy independent of his will.[42] Form is thus activity of various kinds; the only way men can be in the world; and the products of activity, which, once created, follows objective laws which pertain to them.[43] The dualism which Simmel states in various ways, as life/form, subject/object, is ideally resolved in the process by which the individual may attain 'culture'.[44] This process would depend on the 'indigenous drive'[45] of the individual and would 'lead the soul to itself'.[46] Most of Simmel's work consists of examining those historical features of modern society which render such a resolution of the dualism increasingly unlikely. Hence, although his ideal for the resolution of the divisiveness inherent in life and form depends on notions of drives and self-reference or self-creation, his analysis of the forces prohibiting this resolution gives rise to the simple, bowdlerised account of social institutions, such as art, religion, cognition, work, as 'spirit objectified'.[47] Simmel's sociology of form as human activity and as social products, is weakened by the over-simplistic subject/object dichotomy on which it depends, not, as has been frequently argued, because of its overly formalistic nature.[48] Simmel characterises 'values' in a similar way. A value is genuinely 'cultural' when it represents an interpenetration between 'supra-personal forms' and the development of the individual subject or soul. According to Simmel, however, this rarely occurs and 'values' acquire an existence in themselves. Although Simmel opposed this tendency, the process of creating values in this way was an integral part of the creation of objective forms.[49]

It is precisely this emphasis on the *sui generis* status of 'values' which makes Simmel's claim that his sociology of forms represents a generalisation of Marx disingenuous, since Marx disavowed the apparent independence of 'value'.

The Marxian schema of economic development: that in every

historical period, the economic forces produce a form of production which is appropriate to them, inside which, however, they grow to an extent which can no longer be accommodated in that form but burst it and create a new one – this schema is valid far beyond the economic sphere.[50]

Simmel saw that the realm in which his theory of forms had an affinity with Marx was in the realm of work and alienation. He drew from *Capital*:[51] '[the object] isolates and alienates itself from the working subject through the division of labour . . . The finished effort contains emphases, relationships, values which the worker did not intend',[52] and explicitly relates his theories to commodity fetishism:

> The 'fetishism' which Marx assigned to economic commodities represents only a special case of this general fate of contents of culture. With the increase in culture these contents more and more stand under a paradox: they were originally created by subjects and for subjects: but their intermediate form of objectivity, which they take on in addition to the two extreme instances, they follow an immanent logic of development. In so doing they estrange themselves from their origin as well as from their purpose.[53]

Simmel's further claim that he is generalising Marx's theory of commodity fetishism is dubious, since he explicitly rejects a labour theory of value which he construes however as a physical theory.[54] This argument illustrates his sociologically undifferentiated and individualistic notions of the subject and of the object. His challenge to Marx's theory of the value-form and the money-form in *Capital* is presented most fully in his *Philosophie des Geldes* (Philosophy of Money) where he develops his own theory of value, of changes in the division of labour, and a theory of money, and where he clearly repudiates Marx.

In this book on the philosophy of money, Simmel does not presuppose money as an object in itself, but as a social form to be derived from more basic social forms. The exchange form, and money as the means of exchange, is conceived as the social form by means of which the subjective value with which an object is endowed attains an objective expression.[55] He sketches an ideal theory of increasingly complex modes of possession which an advanced money economy may facilitate, such as control over objects which are not in immediate possession.[56] Possession is seen as the expression and enhancement of the individual will, as its realisation, but he also considers the concomitant negative aspects of possession.[57] However, this kind of possession presupposes that objects are increasingly detachable from their context, and more autonomous; money itself is the prime example. Simmel then examines the division of labour which has developed since the nineteenth century, for the role of money can only be understood in that context.[58] In fact the division of labour has caused the debasement of individual culture and personality, rather than its enhancement, a 'culture of things' has grown rampant.[59] Simmel analyses the separation of the worker from his product, the creation by the worker of only part of the product, and the impersonal way in which products are consumed.[60] He now considers the division of labour from the point of view of the worker or creator and not from the point of view of the possessor. The scientist as much as the factory worker is covered by the category of worker. Simmel's contention that *all* social activity involves the production of forms prevents him from distinguishing between worker and artist or scientist, and from distinguishing between the sellers of labour and the owners of capital, even though his work strains towards such a distinction. Thus he reaches divergent views when he considers an advanced economy from the perspective of possibilities of possession and from the perspective of work.

After outlining the separation of objective from subjective culture, which results from the increased specialisation of work in industrial society, and the subsequent poverty of inner life, Simmel reconsiders the role of money. He suggests that money may enable the inner, private life to flourish again by leaving men an exclusively personal sphere removed from the sphere of indifferent objects.[61] If this occurs, and that depends on men not on money,[62] then money could constitute a significant countertendency to the general one. On the other hand, money may continue to make men even more heteronomous, beholden to the rule of objects.[63] There are many indications that Simmel believed that the latter tendency would continue and that money would not play a liberating role.[64] It is the passage in which Simmel half-heartedly suggests that money might provide a counter-force which Lukács quotes in his essay on 'Reification and the Consciousness of the Proletariat'. It is the only passage which Lukács quotes in his essay in which an instance of the word 'reification' actually occurs.

> Thus Simmel has this to say about the ideological structure of reification in consciousness: 'And therefore once these counter tendencies are adopted, they may strive toward an ideal of absolutely pure separation: every objective content of life will become more objective and impersonal so that the non-reifiable remainder may become all the more personal and all the more indisputably the property of the ego [*damit der nicht zu verdinglichende Rest desselben um so persönlicher, ein um so unbestreitbares Eigen des Ich werde*]'.[65]

Lukács unjustly comments on this as if Simmel had proposed it as an invariant principle.[66] This is the only occasion on which Simmel uses the word 'reify' or its parts. The ambiguities in his notion of culture, which sometimes means 'spirit objectified', sometimes a relation between transcendent forms and personal cultivation, sometimes objects or things devoid of substantive significance, arise from a piecemeal social ontology which consists of things as well as objects considered as objectifications. These ambiguities prefigure ambiguities in reification as a sociological category, but there is no justification for implying that Simmel was concerned with reification as such. Simmel provides enough equivocations in his orienting concepts. There is no need to add more.

The Young Lukács and the Young Benjamin

Lukács, Benjamin and Adorno all reacted against their formal neo-Kantian philosophical training by immersing themselves in non-Marxist nineteenth-century criticisms of Hegel's philosophy or of romanticism before they adopted versions of Marxism, and each produced major works in the non-Marxist tradition. They each centred their later work on Marx's theory of commodity fetishism, construed in a way which displayed continuities with their earlier work and with the other critical traditions which they had inherited, but in a way which evinced a deeper grounding in Marx than is evident in Simmel's writings. In each case the discovery of Marx encompassed the discovery of society, that is, of the social determinations of human activity, and made it necessary for the writer to define his relationship with the sociological tradition. Each accomplished this and maintained continuity with his earlier work by revising the other critical philosophical traditions in a sociological direction. The most important continuity was the interest in culture rather than society. After the adoption of Marxism, 'culture' was predicated on the theory of commodity fetishism and hence on a specific mode of production or kind of society, but the notion of 'culture' retained the more general or universal connotations. In each case, too, 'reification' was elevated over the theory of commodity fetishism and made to do more general sociological work in a way which had important theoretical consequences. It meant that the distinction between abstract and concrete labour, on which the theory of value and of commodity fetishism logically depends, received no emphasis and thus no theory of surplus value was adopted. The theoretical foundations for a theory of class conflict or for a Marxian theory of power and the state were thereby attenuated or abandoned.

Lukács and Benjamin were also schooled in literature and aesthetics. Literary criticism was not a discrete discipline but inseparable from the basic questions of epistemology and philosophical experience and, conversely, philosophical questions could not be considered apart from cultural forms. Lukács was profoundly affected by Simmel's theory of the

relationships between the 'soul' and cultural form as affording partial
possibilities for recapturing an inherently split and uncapturable totality.[67] The interest in 'totality' and in culture continued after Lukács had
adopted Marxism. In *Soul and Form* the connection with Simmel is more
one of vocabulary than of approach, for Lukács was toying equally with a
Kierkegaardian irony in his examination of aesthetic forms. In some of
the essays a debate between different philosophical theories of 'form' and
totality is clearly and dramatically presented.[68] As Lukács became more
interested in Marx and in sociology he also tried to use Simmel's sociology
more intensively as a way of unifying these perspectives. In an article
published in Hungarian in 1910, 'Theory of the History of Literature',[69]
Lukács grappled with 'form' in the attempt to unite aesthetic and
sociological perspectives. 'Form' is now seen as that which makes
literature a social fact;[70] while sociology, according to Simmel's definition
of it as the science of the forms of sociation (*Formen der Vergesellschaftung*),
and, as in Simmel's *Philosophy of Money*, an eminent example, 'is
responsible for everything which Marxism calls ideology'.[71] The second
of three essential points of contact between sociology and philosophical
aesthetics which Lukács makes in this article informs the structure and
concerns of his *Theory of the Novel*,[72] namely, the question of which literary
forms are possible in which epochs.[73] The theme is still treated in the book
in a predominantly philosophical vein. An article published in 1920, 'The
old culture and the new culture',[74] and written from an explicitly Marxist
viewpoint, reveals clearly the limitations in Lukács' fusion of Marxism
and the Simmelian notion of culture which was to dog his later work. The
old notion of culture as a value in itself, as everything which is not
'tainted' by the material processes of society, is preserved in Lukács'
argument that culture will only be possible when capitalism has ended
and culture can become 'autonomous' again. Lukács owes the idea of the
fragmentation of products under capitalism to Simmel's criticism of the
'culture of things'.[75] This position is quite different from Benjamin's and
Adorno's analysis of capitalism as precisely creating the conditions which
make culture 'autonomous' by severing cultural forms from other social
institutions. In the latter case 'culture' is not a designation reserved for
what is 'a value in itself' but always designates a relation between a mode
of production and cultural forms.

Adorno was deeply impressed by Benjamin from his youth.[76] After the
Second World War, it was largely Adorno's editing and publishing of
Benjamin's work which created the reputation of Benjamin's *œuvre*[77] as a
philosophical endeavour consisting of commentaries on and criticisms of
literary texts.[78] Adorno's interpretation of Benjamin's work was more
sensitive after Benjamin's death than it was at the time when Adorno was
searching for his own intellectual identity in relation to Benjamin.[79]
Adorno always overstressed the unity and continuity in Benjamin's pre-

Marxist and 'Marxist' writings.[80] He construed the pre-Marxist writings, especially *Origin of German Tragic Drama*,[81] in a tendentious quasi-Hegelian way, depending on notions of mediation and an essence/appearance dichotomy and he tried to force these perspectives on Benjamin's 'Marxist' writings.[82] Benjamin was never a Hegelian. He developed his ideas on the basis of a critique of Kant before he had read Hegel.[83] On the other hand, the most apparently 'Hegelian' aspects of Adorno's materialism, such as his concern with the 'concrete' and with 'identity' were always too imbued with Benjamin's ideas to make sense from a Hegelian perspective. Missing from Adorno's work is the Hegelian notion of 'self-reference'; missing from the Marxism of both men is any notion of human activity or praxis.

Benjamin's early work shows an increasing integration of sociological concerns into philosophically defined interests, prior to the explicit adoption of a Marxian position. In his doctoral thesis, *Der Begriff der Kunstkritik in der deutschen Romantik* (The concept of art criticism in German Romanticism),[84] he considered the Romantic theory of art to be a theory of artistic form as the medium of reflection, and assessed the relation of the fragmentary work of Novalis and Schlegel to the systematic philosophy of Fichte.[85] Benjamin was never impressed with the Romantic response to Kant's philosophy, which depended on notions of consciousness and self-reflection,[86] and he attempted instead to revise Kant's notions of experience and knowledge in his own manner.[87] He did this partly by taking Goethe's notion of *Urphänomenen*, which Goethe applied to the realm of nature, and applying it to the realm of history,[88] and also by taking Nietzsche's notions of myth and of the eternal return of the same. These Nietzschean themes, and the notions of *Ursprung* and *Urgeschichte*, provide the unity between Benjamin's pre-Marxist and his Marxist work: his search for an historical hermeneutics. *Ur* as a prefix in German means 'original', 'primeval', and hence 'archetypal', 'archaic'. Benjamin used the notion of the 'origin' or the 'idea' to mean the essential attributes of a thing. He sought to avoid the conventional notion of 'concept' and of 'essence' which imply the abstraction of attributes common to phenomena. Instead the 'origin' or 'idea' might be found by examining antithetical exemplars of a genre, such as *Tragödie* and *Trauerspiel* in drama:

> The history of philosophy as the science of the origin is the form which, from distant extremes and from apparent excesses of development, permits the emergence of the configuration of the idea as a totality characterized by the possibility of a meaningful juxtaposition of such antitheses inherent in these opposing extremes.[89]

In the book *Origin of German Tragic Drama* Benjamin argues that Greek tragedy and Baroque *Trauerspiel* are each determined by their time in the sense that they present the predominant myth of the time.[90] *Trauerspiel* means a 'melancholy' or 'mourning' play; 'funereal pageant' would be a less literal rendering. The myth comprises the history of the significance which the society of the time has given to nature,[91] and, as a myth, presents that significance as eternal. Benjamin calls this *Naturgeschichte* (the history of nature).[92] In seventeenth-century German drama, historical events are the subject of the plays which are thus apparently secular.[93] However, Benjamin shows that the historical life of the time is presented through the contemporary theological situation and that the emblems of ruins, relics, death-heads, have an allegorical or religious significance:

> This is the kernel of the allegorical view, the baroque, earth-bound exposition of history as the story of the world's suffering; it is only significant in the stations of its decay.[94]

The melancholy portrayal of objects and persons in baroque drama conveys the prevalent attitude to the natural world at the time. In the case of baroque drama the world is seen by dramatists as the history of its fall and thus the seemingly secular drama is a religious allegory or myth. Benjamin took up in this work Lukács' question of which literary forms are possible in which epochs, but avoided any historicism in the way he handled his answer.

Adorno, too, became involved in Marxism and in sociology as a result of dissatisfaction with academic philosophy. A generation younger than Lukács and Benjamin, his education in philosophy included the early works of Scheler, Husserl and Heidegger. These philosophers sought to break away from traditional philosophical idealism, both the nineteenth-century tradition and the early twentieth-century neo-Kantian schools. They did not do so by developing a social criticism of philosophy, either Marxist or sociological, or by a radical critique of the philosophical system in the manner of Kierkegaard or Nietzsche, but by founding a new kind of pure philosophy – ontology. Adorno found in the pre-Marxist work of Lukács and of Benjamin an alternative to the new philosophy. He was especially impressed by Benjamin's notion of *Naturgeschichte* and combined this with motifs from Lukács' *Theory of the Novel* in the early 1930s. He was, though, already critical of their early work. Although he later took over the term *Verdinglichung* from Lukács into his own Marxist work, he sought to transform it on the basis of insistent opposition to the Marxist work of both Lukács and of Benjamin. Nevertheless the themes on which Adorno alighted in their pre-Marxist work in a lecture, *Die Idee der Naturgeschichte* (The idea of the history of nature),[95] which he gave in 1932, dominated his work after that date.

In that lecture, Adorno attempted to redefine 'nature' and 'history'.
'Nature' did not have any connotations of physical nature but meant
'myth' or 'what human history bears as fatefully structured, pregiven',[96]
while 'history' refers to the sphere of human behaviour in which change
occurs.[97] These notions of nature and of history were developed to avoid
the formality of Heidegger's notion of historical Being (*das geschichtliche
Sein*).[98] The second half of Adorno's lecture consists of an attempt to
explicate a boldly-stated chiasmus which stands exactly at its mid-point:
historical being should be understood as nature-like; nature should be
understood as historical being.[99] Adorno draws on the ideas of Benjamin
and of Lukács in order to elaborate this proposition and at the very end of
the lecture claims that he was undertaking an exposition of the elements
of a materialist dialectic.[100] He is, however, severely hampered because
he has no concept or theory of society or of a mode of production. Instead
he fastens on to a notion of 'second nature' as the world of convention,
which Lukács reformulated in *The Theory of the Novel* and argues that
Benjamin's notion of *Naturgeschichte* illuminates the issue. Adorno quotes
a very Simmelian passage from Lukács' book in which Lukács explains
how men encounter a world of things created by themselves but lost to
them, because they have 'lost their obvious roots in superpersonal ideal
necessities'.[101] This is the world of convention or second nature. It has
significance, but the significance has 'become rigid and strange, . . . it no
longer awakens interiority; it is a charnel-house of long-dead interiorities'.[102] Adorno comments that Lukács has seen how the 'historical,
as what has passed, is formed into an apparent nature' and how 'rigidified
history is nature', but that he offers no way to decipher this.[103] Benjamin
does – by defining nature itself as transitory, as passing, and therefore as
intrinsically historical. Adorno generalises Benjamin's theory of
seventeenth-century *Trauerspiel*, so that all history is the history of
the fall of nature. Each generation sees this history on the face of
nature.[104] By 'nature' is meant the significance which is given to objects,
which Lukács called 'second nature' or the world of convention. The
allegorical meaning given to emblems of death and decay in the
seventeenth century is applicable to what Lukács described as 'a charnel-
house of long-dead interiorities'.[105] The meaning is the return of the
primeval theme of history (*urgeschichtliche Motive*): the fall and decay of
nature. Adorno was attracted to Benjamin's way of defining nature as
intrinsically historical since it offered a radical alternative to historical
ontology – Heidegger's notion of history as the ground of the structure of
Being (*Dasein*).[106] He was repelled by the idea of the return of the archaic
or mythical in history and by all the static, platonic aspects of Benjamin's
ontology.[107] Nor could he fully accept Benjamin's strange recasting of the
idea of nature. Nature for Benjamin is not the antithesis of culture, nor is
it defined according to men's interest in mastering the world. Nature is

culture itself, the history of the significance which has been given to the world. At the end of the lecture, Adorno suggests that any archaic or mythical theme only attains significance if it is seen as part of a specific historical process and that myth might therefore be redefined as 'historically produced illusion'.[108] For Benjamin's notion of myth as the return of the archaic, he substitutes the idea of reconcilement as the 'decisive, transcending theme of myth'.[109] Eventually Adorno rejected both the notion of history as the return of the archaic and the Hegelian-Lukácsian notion of history as the possibility or promise of reconcilement. His subsequent criticism of Lukács' and of Benjamin's theoretical development of the concept of reification turned on the same issues.

Against Lukács and Against Benjamin

Adorno judged that the concept of reification which was predominant in the explicitly Marxist work of Lukács and of Benjamin and grounded in Marx's theory of commodity fetishism assumed the theoretical role which (second) nature had played in their earlier works. He rejected their use of reification but sought to develop a concept of reification which would avoid the theoretical weaknesses which he discerned in their work. According to Adorno, Lukács' concept of reification presupposes the reconcilement of subject and object and thus relapses into idealism, and fails to found a truly materialist dialectic; while Benjamin's concept of reification designates the phantasmagoric form of commodity fetishism as the mode of the return of the archaic in the modern age. It thus loses the historical and theoretical specificity on which it was founded.

Lukács' concept of reification presupposes a subject/object dichotomy in several senses. He criticises the division of labour under capitalism and the consequent fragmentation of the commodity into an 'alien thing', in a way which, according to Adorno, verges on a criticism of 'thingness' as such.[110] As a critique of philosophical consciousness, it implies that the dichotomies of bourgeois thought can be simply eliminated.[111] As a theory of class struggle, it claims that the proletariat is the subject/object of history and the privileged carrier of such knowledge.[112] Adorno charged Lukács with thus accepting the idealist vision of reconcilement as the goal of history, but also as its origin. For when the subject/object dichotomy is posited as characteristic of capitalism, it implies that in pre-capitalist society a non-coercive harmony prevailed.[113] Adorno seems to think that Lukács' theory of capitalism has more in common with nostalgic *Gemeinschaft/Gesellschaft* antitheses than with a typology of modes of production. Lukács himself, in his 1967 'Preface' to the new edition of *History and Class Consciousness*, concedes that the book is marred by his having equated objectification with alienation.[114] 'Alienation' does not occur much in the book, but Lukács is presumably referring to his use of reification. Nor is Lukács' recantation necessarily to be given much credit. However, he does veer in the book from a simplistic subject/object ontology to a more complex theory of mediation. In any case the point supports Adorno's argument. Adorno considered that a further effect of Lukács' dichotomy was that reification appears to be a fact of consciousness, and that Lukács' approach is grounded in philosophical subjectivity.[115] Above all, Adorno feared that the work was haunted by the old ambition of philosophy: to tolerate nothing which is unassimilable to its concepts – the will to identity.[116] Adorno's differences with Lukács were political as well as theoretical, but they can all be derived from the difference in their concepts of reification.

The core of Adorno's criticism of the concept of reification in Benjamin's work is to be found in their renowned correspondence of the 1930s.[117] In that correspondence, which mostly concerns Benjamin's writings on the *Paris Arcades* and his study of Baudelaire, Adorno often induces Benjamin to be more theoretical. As Adorno's later essays on Benjamin reveal, he was well aware that Benjamin's work was highly theoretical, and in the earlier period he was in effect prevailing on Benjamin to change his theory.[118]

Benjamin had set out the aim of his work in an outline written in 1935. Its task was

> to show how reference to the reified representation of culture, to new creations and forms of life especially determined by the production of commodities . . . is a reference to the ensemble of a phantasmagoria.[119]

He defined phantasmagoria as 'the image that it [society] produces of itself and which it generally inscribes as its culture . . . when it abstracts from the fact that it is producing commodities'.[120] Benjamin called these images 'dialectical images', and the methodological task was to interpret them. He did so by conceiving them as allegories of modernity in his analyses of Baudelaire's poems and in his imaginative recreation of the experience of the *flaneur* in nineteenth-century Paris. The bazaar, the collector, the prostitute, the experience of hashish, were 'dialectical images' – aspects of modern society which constituted its phantasmagoria. Benjamin used the ideas of Jung and Klages to interpret the collective consciousness as the archaic which returns in the new mode of production.[121] Adorno told Benjamin that he had made reification into a static concept by concentrating on things and not deciphering them, that he had produced archaic not dialectical images, and that he was leaving his work 'on the crossroads between magic and positivism'.[122] Adorno informed Benjamin sternly that his Baroque book was better Marxism than his 'deduction of phantasmagoria from the behaviour of the

feuilletonists'.[123] In the earlier book Benjamin had had no concept of
society, but Adorno believed that the perspective on nature as (the)
history (of society) came closer to revealing 'mediation through the total
social process' than his later work.[124]

Although Benjamin took Adorno's advice regarding one article,[125] he
stood up for his interpretation of commodity fetishism as producing
hallucinations of identity (*Gleichheit*) out of which appear the phantasmagoria of men and commodities as weird, personified types.[126] Adorno
never granted this enterprise validity. He realised that Benjamin was the
allegorist of commodity fetishism: revealing the return of the primeval
theme of history in the petrified objects of the nineteenth-century, as the
seventeenth-century allegorists had done with the emblems of their
time.[127] He maintained that Benjamin had 'sworn loyalty to reification
instead of flatly rejecting it',[128] and contended that 'the liquidation of
phantasmagoria can only be accomplished with true profundity if they
are treated as an objective-philosophical category and not as a "vision" of
social characters'.[129] As a '"vision" of social characters', Benjamin made
reification into a 'content of consciousness', that is, into a subjective
category.[130] This, as far as Adorno was concerned, was to increase the
illusion that commodities are immediate use-values, when they are values
in exchange.[131] Such an approach hides and does not reveal the mode of
production. Yet Benjamin represented to Adorno the most radical failure
in the attempt on the part of twentieth-century philosophy to break out of
traditional philosophy and to turn to the 'concrete'. Adorno rejected the
way Benjamin tried to accomplish this, his *Urgeschichte der Moderne*
(primeval history of modernity).[132] The theoretical reasons for Adorno's
rejection of Benjamin's mode of analysis and description of society
inhibited him from producing any direct analysis or description of society
himself. Adorno made it clear later that his article on fetishism in music[133]
was a response to Benjamin's article on art and mechanical reproduction,[134] but *Minima Moralia* can equally well be read as a response to
Benjamin's *Passagenarbeit*.[135]

Thus Lukács' concept of reification was too general and Benjamin's
was too circumscribed. Adorno believed the very different philosophy of
history which the concept served in each case to be wrong. He accepted
the aim to base the analysis of cultural forms on the model of commodity
fetishism in a way which would make any crude distinction between
substructure and superstructure otiose. He thus sought to use the concept
of reification in an alternative way.

Analytical

Adorno and Reification

After 1923 many different neo-Marxist writers used the term reification sporadically and casually in their writings. It appears in the work of Bloch, Brecht,[136] Wittfogel[137] and Grossmann[138] (and Heidegger).[139] It does not, however, play any systematic or major role in their work,[140] but usually implies an unexamined reference to commodity fetishism combined with the standard dictionary connotation of 'to reify' – to convert mentally into a thing. In Adorno's work, on the contrary, it abounds. After 1932 it is the centrifuge of all his major works and of his many shorter articles.[141] The obsession is evident in his published correspondence with Ernst Krenek,[142] and in his posthumously published lectures.[143]

Prima facie, Adorno seems inconsistent and eclectic is his appeal to the concept of reification. In one place he proclaims that 'The dialectic means intransigence to all reification',[144] while in another he avers that 'the causes of human suffering are . . . glossed over not denounced in the lament over reification'.[145] In places he uses reification in the over-extended manner examined above as a feature of all human activity and of all kinds of societies.[146] He misattributes it to Hegel.[147] However, Adorno's concept of reification is consistent and original. Many of the apparent confusions arise from his quest to avoid grounding thought in the traditional ways and from the stylistic procedures which he adopted to achieve this. Adorno's theory of reification was based on commodity fetishism in a way which depended not on Marx's theory of work or the labour-process (alienation) but on Marx's theory of value, especially on the distinction between use-value and exchange-value. He was particularly concerned that reification should not be conceptualised as a 'fact of consciousness', a subjective or socio-psychological category. He indicted many critics of reification for this mistake, and tended to be even harsher with those writers who had tried to define and oppose reification in their work than with those non-dialectical writers who 'endorsed' it. He tried, too, in his sociological work, to make reification into an empirical category.

In what follows, the literal core of Adorno's theory of reification is extracted, largely from *Negative Dialectic*, the book which contains the most direct statement of his theories, and from the essays on sociology. Much interpretation and reconstruction has therefore been necessary in this attempt to transcribe Adorno's central ideas.

Negative Dialectic

> Theory . . . must transform the concepts which it, as it were, brings in
> from outside into those which the object has by itself, into that which
> the object would itself like to be, and confront it with what it is.[148]

Adorno emphasises this idea of 'conceptuality prevailing in the object
itself'.[149] This seems to imply that the object can be known independently
of theoretical concepts, which are then to be transformed into 'those
which the object has by itself'. What does it mean to say that an object has
concepts 'by itself'? How can we know that it does, and how can we know
what they are? In sum, what is Adorno's notion of 'the concept', and what
is his notion of 'the object'?

In English, a concept is taken to be that which a person possesses when
he grasps the sense of a word. This is the universal. In German *Begriff* may
mean the *referent* of a predicate, or what we in English would call a
property, this is, a real attribute. This is not to say that the question of the
status of concepts is unequivocally decided by language. Nevertheless the
'real' notion of concepts is, in German, as natural an understanding of
'concept' as the understanding more familiar to the English-speaking
world. Thus when in German it is said that 'an object falls under a
concept', the English equivalent might be to say that 'an object has a
property'. A concept, on this view, is what a predicate stands for.
Concepts, like properties, pertain to objects. This is important for
understanding what Adorno means by 'concept' and 'object'.

According to Adorno, there are three ways of thinking: identity
thinking, non-identity thinking, and rational identity thinking.[150] The
first, *identity thinking*, occurs when we use a concept paradigmatically to
pick out those particulars it denotes.[151] It is the relation between
universal and particular. Adorno is not concerned primarily with this
aspect of identity thinking. He is not proposing a theory of meaning.
More importantly this aspect of identifying is the *pragmatic*, nature-
controlling function of thought. However, concepts also refer to their
objects, and by this he means to the conditions of their ideal existence.
This is the *utopian* aspect of identifying. For the concept to identify its
object in this sense the particular object would have to have all the
properties of its ideal state. Adorno calls this condition *rational identity*
(*rationale Identität*).[152] But identity thinking, which is our normal mode of
thinking, implies that the concept is rationally identical with its object.
However, given the present state of society (the capitalist mode of
production), the concept cannot identify its true object. The consciousness which perceives this is *non-identity thinking* or *negative dialectic*. Adorno
claims that the possibility of thinking differently from our paradigmatic
mode of thinking is inherent in that very mode of thinking:

. . . cognition of non-identity lies exactly in that it also identifies, but to a greater extent and in a different way from identity thinking. This cognition seeks to say what something is, while identity thinking says under what something falls, of what it is a specimen or representative, what it thus is not itself.[153]

For example, 'the judgement that someone is a free man refers to the concept of freedom'.[154] This is rational identity, the utopian moment, the condition when the 'free man' would really have the property of being free, when the concept would be identical with its object. 'The concept does not only say that it can be applied to all men defined as free'.[155] That it applies, however, to all men defined as free is not denied by Adorno. Such defining or identifying is identity thinking, the paradigmatic mode of thinking. To see that the concept says more than this is to see the non-identity in the concept as it is currently applied. This is not to deny that objects subsumed under a class have definitions not contained in the definitions of the class. It does not deny that the concept is a universal, what a person possesses when he grasps the sense of a word. It is to affirm that the concept is more than is predicated of any man. The concept is the *referent* of the predicate – that set of properties which would make it identical with its object. It is important to understand that this is not a semantics, nor does it involve any denial or criticism of the laws of identity and non-contradiction.

Therefore to say that concepts 'must be transformed into those which the object has by itself, into that which the object would itself like to be, and confront it [the object] with what it is',[156] means, if the object is society, that society as it is now is an object which does not fulfil its concept. The concept is not equal to nor congruent with the object which it identifies. But that concept is what the object has 'by itself', that is, the properties it could potentially have. These properties are what it 'would like to be'. The personification of the object entailed by 'like to be' is a stylistic way of presenting the objective, utopian moment. This would be the condition of *rational identity*. To confront it, present society, with what 'it is', that is, to *compare* it with the condition of its rational identity, is to *see* the non-identity in the relation between the concept and the object. Thus Adorno is *not* saying that the object can be *known* independently of our concepts. Furthermore, given that the object is *ex hypothesi* what really fulfils its concept, 'It is pointless to ask whether these essential re-lationships are real or simply conceptual constructs',[157] because by definition, the real is identical with, or 'not yet' identical with, its concept. The real is *conceptual* but not a *construct*. Now, there is no logical objection to a definition of the concept as the object and of the object as the concept. However, the charge that such concepts are arbitrary and thus 'constructs' is still pertinent. The basic question of what the object is also remains to be considered.

Reification

Adorno's concept of reification can be grounded in Marx's criticism of merely apparent freedom and in his theory of value. To avoid the static implications of 'grounding' the concept, Adorno called Marx's theory of value variously the *Urphänomen*, the *Urgeschichte*, and the *Urmodell* of reification.[158]

Identity thinking is reified thinking – not only our paradigmatic mode of thinking, but also the mode of thinking of non-dialectical sciences. Identity thinking makes unlike things alike. To believe that a concept really covers its object, when it does not, is to believe falsely that the object is the equal of its concept. According to Marx, emancipation, for example, is not real, human emancipation, if it is merely political emancipation.[159] Adorno reaffirms this. To claim that the concept 'emancipation' correctly describes a state of affairs, when it is not real emancipation, is to make unequal things equal.[160] Adorno construes the process of commodity exchange as involving an analogous mechanism:

> The exchange principle, the reduction of human labour to its abstract universal concept of average labour-time, has the same origin as the principles of identification. It has its social model in exchange and exchange would be nothing without identification.[161]

Marx considered that to make individual qualities of labour into 'homogeneous human labour, . . . labour-power expended without regard to its mode of expenditure'[162] in the process of commodity exchange and hence in the equalisation of commodities to a monetary value or price,[163] is to make unlike things alike. Value appears to be a natural property of the commodity; but only use values are properties. As Marx said,

> It is through its own properties, its own qualities that a thing is use-value . . . as values commodities are social magnitudes, that is to say something absolutely different from their properties as things. Where labour is communal, the relations of men do not manifest themselves as 'values' of things.[164]

It is the way unlike things appear to be identical or equal, and the mode of thinking which can only consider them as equal, which is reification as a social phenomenon and as a process of thinking for Adorno. The general feature of Marx's theory of commodity fetishism whereby 'a definite social relation between men . . . assumes the phantasmagoric form of a relation between things',[165] is not the most crucial aspect to be stressed. The idea that value appears to be the property of a commodity, or the idea that the object is thought to fulfil its concept when in fact only use-values are properties, or the concept has a different object, is more important. Yet, as Marx said, 'exchange value is the only *form* in which the value of a commodity can manifest itself or be expressed'.[166] This is the origin of reification. It is thus unnecessary to construe the theory of reification as a compounding of Marx's theory of commodity fetishism and Hegel's ideas on the development of consciousness. Reification is a social category. It refers to the way in which consciousness is determined.

Thus, to say that something is reified is not to emphasise that a relation between men appears as a relation between things. It is to emphasise that a relation between men appears in the form of a property of a thing. To be non-reified, then, is really to be a property of a thing, or, by analogy, to be a use-value. In Marx's terms, 'it is through its own properties, its own qualities that a thing is a use-value',[167] or in Adorno's terms, something is non-reified when the concept is identical with its object. Now, which concepts does the object have 'by itself'? It has the reified concepts of non-dialectical sociologies and philosophies by means of which the non-reified concepts can be derived. In capitalist society, reified concepts are the only form in which non-reified properties can appear. Adorno ascribes this to bourgeois society in which 'All categories are objectified and become independent . . . They are cut off from the living subjects which constitute the substance of concepts'.[168] The non-reified concepts of critical theory are derived from the reified form in which they appear. These reified concepts originate, as Marx said of the origin of value, from the living subjects who labour to produce use-values: 'A use-value or useful article therefore has value [in exchange] only because human labour in the abstract has been embodied or materialised in it'.[169] In capitalist society a concept such as (exchange) value can only appear in that form. Reified concepts describe social phenomena, the appearance of society, as if it has the properties to which the concepts refer.

As this elaboration of Adorno's theory of reification indicates, the theory is grounded in Marx's theory of value in a highly selective fashion. It does not mobilise Marx's distinction between abstract and concrete labour, nor does it lead to any theory of the extraction of surplus value. Furthermore, Adorno's theory of reification does not apply to all concepts. Some concepts, whether theoretical such as 'value', or non-theoretical such as 'money', have no non-reified application and no utopian moment accessible to non-identity thinking. For example, Adorno calls the concept of value a 'heteronomous' reification when it occurs in discussions about value freedom in sociology. By this he means that 'value' does not have the possibility of the autonomous status which obtains when the concept is rationally identical with its object. The distinction between concepts which do have a non-reified application and those which do not is presumably based on the traditional distinction in Kant and Hegel between the fundamental categories and ordinary concepts. Adorno is not clear on this but he entitles the central section of *Negative Dialectic* 'Negative Dialectic Concept and Categories'.

The thesis of 'rational' identity is not empirical, nor is it an historical prediction. If it were a theory of history, it would relapse into the idealist assumptions of reconcilement and of the identity of thought with the world. The 'utopian' aspect of thinking, or 'rational identity', stress that concepts as ordinarily used are 'formations' (*ein Gewordenes, ein Entsprungenes*).[170] The model of the historical mechanism by which they are formed is provided by the distinction between use-value and exchange-value, or, in Adorno's terms, by identity and non-identity thinking. 'To want substance in cognition is to want Utopia'.[171] 'Utopia' is another way of naming the thesis that non-dialectical thought is closed thought, because it implies that the object is already captured. To see that the object is not captured is to see 'utopia'.

How is Critical Theory Possible?

Adorno states repeatedly that society and consciousness of society have become increasingly reified. In places, he says that they have become 'completely reified'. To say that society is 'completely reified' is to say that the domination of the exchange process has increased to the point where it controls institutions, behaviour and class formation in such a way that it prevents the formation of any independent and critical consciousness. To say that consciousness is 'completely reified' is to say that it is capable only of knowing the appearance of society, of describing institutions and behaviour as if their current mode of functioning were an inherent and invariant characteristic or property, as if they, as objects, 'fulfil their concepts'. Therefore, to say that consciousness of society is completely reified implies that no critical consciousness or theory is possible. It is to say that the underlying processes of society are completely hidden and that the utopian possibilities within it are inconceivable. The mind (*Geist*) is impotent; the object is inaccessible. The thesis of complete reification is therefore unstatable, because if it were true it could not be known, and Adorno employs strategies to avoid such a paradox. He states the thesis at different degrees of intensity. The most extreme statement is 'complete reification': the concept's apparent identity with its object has become unbreakable. On the other hand, he reaffirms that there must always be a possibility of non-identity or critical thought: 'No matter to what extent the mind is a product of that type [reified], it implies at the same time the objective possibility of overcoming it'.[172] Adorno presents these conflicting theses in order to induce in his reader the development of the latent capacity for non-identity thought – the perspective that the concept is not identical with its object. This is an attempt to prevent the complete reification which is imminent. He also presents conflicting theses in order to avoid 'grounding' the concept of reification in any of the ways in which he is criticising philosophy and sociology for grounding their concepts – as first principles, as static, invariant or indubitable and for thereby producing concepts which are dependent on the mind and thus subjective. Reification is not a 'concept', like, for example, society, subject, freedom. To see 'reification' involves a 'change of perspective' of the sort which Adorno had discerned in Benjamin's notion of *Naturgeschichte*. As a social process, 'reification' determines consciousness but, like commodity fetishism, it is not in origin a fact of consciousness. Adorno considered that most reactions to reification, whether philosophical, sociological or artistic, were reified, often because they grounded the concept.

Adorno does expound the thesis of total reification or total control in terms of a change in the relation between use-value and value in exchange. The thesis that human needs are now totally controlled is equivalent to saying that the 'use-value of commodities has lost its last spontaneous [*naturwüchsig*] self-evidence'[173] or

> if commodities consist of exchange-value and use-value, then in advanced capitalist society an illusion of pure use-value, as displayed by cultural goods, has been substituted for pure exchange-value. This exchange-value has deceptively taken over the function of use-value.[174]

Adorno believes that there is no satisfactory theory of advanced capitalist society because there is no longer a satisfactory theory of value.[175] The difficulties in grounding the formation of classes without a theory of surplus value are prohibitive.[176] There is no free market and hence no genuine exchange in the sense of Marx's description of 'fair' exchange: 'Everything is one [*Alles ist eins*] . . . today the forces of production and the relations of production are one . . . material production, distribution, consumption are ruled together'.[177] *Prima facie*, a Durkheimian model of society emerges. 'The still unindividuated tribal spirit of primitive societies, pressed by the civilized ones to reproduce itself in them, is planned and released by postindividual collectivism'.[178] The 'total control' of social relations implies that exchange relations no longer depend on 'freely alienable' forces of production. Such a totally controlled society would conform more to the model of a primitive or customary status society.[179] Identity thinking, as described by Adorno, has affinities with Durkheim's insight into the way society endows us with concepts and imposes their hold on us.[180] However, Adorno stresses that it is quite different to postulate total control in pre-individualistic and post-individualistic society:

> I am not maintaining anything similar to the tendency in cultural anthropology to transfer by means of a specified system of coordinates, the centralizing and total character of many primitive societies to western civilization. Even when one cherishes so few illusions as I do about the gravitations towards total forms and the decline of the individual, the differences between a pre-individual and a post-individual society are still decisive.[181]

The proposition that reification increases according to the increase in the dominance of exchange-value over use-value is intelligible, but it does not have the explanatory force which Adorno seems to claim for it. If commodities are increasingly produced on the basis of technological or political imperatives, which no longer depend on freely-alienable forces of production, labour and capital, then it should still be possible to reveal the social relations underlying the organisation of commodity production and the interests which determine the concomitant political organisation of society. Otherwise the whole notion of a mode of production based on a theory of value has, in effect, been abandoned, and the political organisation of society has become an autonomous force.[182] Adorno introduces a politically diffuse concept of control, unpacks it to show a reference to the exchange mechanism, and, as he admits, offers no alternative theory of value nor a theory of the operation of power. This constitutes another way in which he tries to designate the fundamental process which determines society, a change in the relation between use-value and exchange-value, without grounding the process in a subject – an agent or carrier, whether class or individual.

The status of the proposition of increasing reification as an historical thesis is also very difficult to assess. It is deeply entwined with Adorno's theories about the development of art and the 'culture industry'. As a kind of historical thesis, it has more in common with Weber's thesis of increasing rationality in the organisation of capitalism than with any dateable or empirically quantifiable thesis. For Weber too did not date or specify the rate of increase in (goal) rationality but posited its increase as endemic in the development of a specific mode of authority.

However, a historicist approach, whether teleological or relativist, is not encouraged by Adorno. The thesis of *total* reification is presented and undermined as an 'ongoing intervention' as much as a thesis which explains social change. Adorno chose a hard path between Benjamin's view of history as the corruption of the world, and Lukács' view of history according to which reconcilement between subject and object can be 'imputed' as the end of history. Adorno's position is encapsulated in the aphorism 'Universal history must be construed and denied'.[183] It must be construed because it is the only perspective from which the socio-historical formation of society and thought can be grasped; it must be denied because the world has no *telos* and capitalism has developed new means of enslavement, not of liberation.

Adorno tried to break out of the paradox of reification, but he also applied it ruthlessly to his own work. For Adorno there is a genuine interplay between knowing society by means of theory, and cognition by means of analysing reified concepts and theories. For Marx, to know 'theoretically' meant to know how social relations in capitalist society are determined by the production of commodities, and to endorse this analysis as the potential perspective of a universal class – the proletariat. Cognition by means of the analysis of the theories and concepts of classical political economy was indirect by comparison. Such cognition involved deriving the state of society from its appearance in those theories and concepts.

According to Adorno, theoretical knowledge in the former sense, to know how social relations are determined by the exchange mechanism, is now almost impossible. The theoretical perspective remains in his writings as a series of images and metaphors which intrude, often dramatically, into the main analyses of philosophies, sociologies, literature, and music. This notion of theory will be further discussed in Chapter Five. Thus Adorno does not accept Marx's ideas as an *a priori* theory of society, but *presents a dialectic*: he shows how various modes of cognition, Marxist and non-Marxist, are inadequate and distorting when taken in isolation; and how by confronting them with each other precisely on the basis of an awareness of their individual limitations, they may nevertheless yield insight into social processes. This approach, the analysis of reified theories and concepts, Adorno calls the 'immanent method'. Such a method is not analogous to the traditional Marxian understanding of art, law, and the state as superstructural phenomena. But it is analogous to the Marxian tradition of criticising ideology (*Ideologiekirtik*). For Marx, political economy both revealed and distorted the true social relations of men, while his thought and ultimately that of the proletarian class had a chance of understanding the true relations. For Adorno there is only one ideology, bourgeois ideology, which both reveals and distorts those relations. Hence, to return to the themes of Chapter Two, even an all-embracing ideology is not a 'lie' *tout court*.

Chapter 4

A Changed Concept of Dialectic

The Critique of Philosophy

For Marx, and many later Marxists, the critique of philosophy was equally the critique of society. This was not accomplished by relating the claims of philosophy to their social origin and thereby undermining their validity in a relativist fashion, but by demonstrating that the philosophy in question was wrong: self-contradictory, fundamentally inconsistent or antinomical and thus inherently self-defeating. A new notion of theory as the analysis of society was developed and the relation between philosophy as theory and philosophy as a form of practice defined. Adorno took this task upon himself, seeking to show that philosophy is impossible but essential – as theory – but that even as theory of society, it is bound to be self-defeating.[1]

Adorno used the term 'philosophy' in a deliberately equivocal sense. On the one hand, he used the term to refer to the philosophy of, *inter alia*, Husserl and Heidegger, and these flourishing philosophies were the targets of his criticism. On the other hand, he used it elliptically to refer to the 'liquidation'[2] of philosophical concerns in the realm of the individual social sciences, and the aim of his work was to reverse this separation. He sought to show that latter-day philosophy which raised the traditional claims of philosophy, albeit in new forms, was as inherently antinomical as classical German philosophy had been. He believed, however, that the new philosophy did not raise substantive and moral issues as profoundly as the classical tradition had done, and that this was partly because of the development of individual social sciences which had taken over some of the traditional concerns of philosophy. He thus also sought 'Stringently to transcend the official separation of pure philosophy and the substantive or formally scientific realm . . . ',[3] and to produce theory which would reunite philosophical and sociological concerns, that is, criticism of society. Yet Adorno realised that such criticism must be as antinomical as the philosophies which he criticised, 'entwined in its own impossibility'.[4] This is because as long as philosophy or theory raises claims apart from any praxis, it is bound to be self-contradictory; while if philosophy or theory understands itself as a form of praxis or intervention, its aims are then partly indirect, and the presentation of them as philosophy or theory will give rise to contradictory features. Adorno subscribed to both of these positions and this contributes to the complexity of his criticism of philosophy.

Adorno's criticism of philosophy is to be found largely in two forms. His short essays, the first one given as his inaugural lecture as a *Privatdozent* in the philosophy faculty at the University of Frankfurt in 1931, entitled *Die Aktualität der Philosophie* (The Relevance of Philosophy),[5] and, the last one posthumously published, entitled *Kritik*,[6] were addressed to the proposition 'Why more philosophy' (*Wozu noch Philosophie*), which was also the title of one of them.[7] In these pieces Adorno discusses some of the philosophy which was being produced in Germany at the time and asks what sort of philosophy, if any, should be produced. He always tried, on the one hand, to delineate the 'philosophical need' which informed new philosophies, including his own, and, at the same time, to pick out those features of society which made such philosophy self-contradictory and impotent. The other form in which Adorno's criticism of philosophy appears comprises major studies of individual philosophers, such as Kierkegaard, Husserl and Heidegger. He also published his studies of Hegel's philosophy with the intention 'of preparing a changed concept of dialectic'.[8] This ambition attained its most mature statement in *Negative Dialectic*.

In spite of the attention paid to Lukács' *History and Class Consciousness* in the socialist and communist camps when it was first published[9] and the *succès d'éstime* which it enjoyed among certain philosophically-inclined Marxists,[10] the book's renown did not assuage the general dissatisfaction with prevailing schools of neo-Kantianism within academic and extra-academic philosophical circles in Germany in the mid-twenties. Certain minor philosophers sought a philosophy of 'Being' which the anti-metaphysical proclivity of neo-Kantianism precluded, and they seized on the intuitionist aspects of Husserl's *Wesenschau* (intuition of essence), while others proposed to construct a philosophy of 'totality' which would 'overcome the duality of mind and matter'.[11] Adorno discerned three stages in the development of this philosophical confusion. First, 'Bergson's generation – also Simmel, Husserl and Scheler – yearned in vain for a philosophy receptive to objects, a philosophy which would substantiate itself'.[12] They wished to 'disavow idealism'[13] and were thus 'carriers of philosophical modernism'.[14] A working definition of idealism is offered by Adorno's description of it as any 'philosophy which tries to base such notions as reality or truth on an analysis of consciousness'.[15] Secondly, after 1925, this 'yearning' resulted in the dissemination of a philosophical jargon drawn from the works of these philosophers, which Adorno examined in his book *Jargon of Authenticity*.[16] Thirdly, a new concern is added to

> The anti-relativism that goes back to Husserl . . . [it] blends with an aversion to static, thing-like thought [*dinghaftes Denken*]. The philosophical need . . . has turned into a need to resist the reification of the mind which society has carried out and categorically dictated to its members.[17]

Heidegger is the prime representative of this opposition to static, ahistorical thinking.

The 'ontological need' thus amounts to the desire by philosophers of a specific period to break out of traditional philosophy, especially its neo-Kantian revival, but this outbreak did not involve a reinvigorated Hegelian attack on neo-Kantian philosophy nor a Marxian one. It did involve an attack on philosophical subjectivism and on philosophical and psychological relativism, and it did aim to found an objective reality. All these aims were paramount to Adorno. The 'outbreak' resulted, however, in the founding of 'ontology', not dialectical materialism, and Adorno devoted much of his criticism of this philosophy to showing that it relapsed into the very idealism which it was designed to avoid. It was an outbreak 'into the mirror',[18] a dramatic pun on the idea of breaking out of the philosophy of reflection. He does relate this philosophy to the socio-historical situation in Germany, especially when considering the 'jargon', but his most important arguments attend to the internal construction of the philosophies for the lacunae, and antinomies therein reveal the missing dimension of social criticism.

Many of the stylistic features discussed in Chapter Two can be discerned in Adorno's criticism of philosophy. The texts are not based on ironic inversion and anecdotal illustration of obverse themes, as is *Minima Moralia*, but on antinomical construal of the ideas of the philosophy under examination. An antinomy is a conflict of two arguments or doctrines, each of which taken in itself is cogent, but they cannot both be valid, and one cannot establish superiority over the other. Adorno presents whatever philosophy he is discussing so as to expose its basic antinomies. He then shows that only a dialectical approach can resolve the antinomy, often by turning it into a chiasmus, and that this must involve a reference to society. He calls this 'following the logic of aporias',[19] or the 'immanent method', and it justifies his rough and tendentious treatment of the texts of others'. They are, as he explains in the preface to his study of Husserl, 'the occasion not the goal' of the debate.[20]

Although Adorno retains an Hegelian vocabulary – subject, object, mediation – his reception of Hegel's philosophy is structured by his reception of Nietzsche's philosophy as well as that of Marx. It is striking that in his discussion of Hegel's philosophy, Adorno does not start from Hegel's moral and political philosophy as, for example, Marx did. He does not criticise Hegel's theory of the state or religion at all. This is because Adorno had adopted features of Nietzsche's philosophy, and developed a sociologically diffuse concept of power which seemed to absolve him of any further examination of the political process. His adaptation of Nietzsche's criticism of the traditional philosophical subject determined his own criticism and reintroduction of the term. Nietzsche rejected the philosophical system 'on the grounds that the totality of the world is not appropriate to our forms of consciousness'.[21] This reason for rejecting the philosophical system is equivalent for Adorno to judging that any such system attributes a role to the subject which it cannot assume.[22] Adorno's criticism of identity thinking means that he has rejected an Hegelian notion of the subject as the unity of the universal and the particular. Nevertheless he reinstates the term in his criticism of philosophy, especially of philosophy which eliminates any notion of the subject. He thus reintroduces a concept of the subject in his attempt to give priority to the object, to make 'being a subject' part of the meaning of 'being an object'.[23]

Criticism of philosophy for Adorno is criticism of various forms of identity thinking, of reification. As discussed in Chapter Three, Adorno was concerned not to reground his criticism in a theory of reification which would make the theory of value into a theory of consciousness or a relativist principle to which all his points could be referred and interpreted.[24] He thus, quite consistently, avoids intruding the theory of value or commodity fetishism as a principle of interpretation, but aims to show that the modes of thinking which he examines conform to the pattern of thinking outlined in the theory of value, especially in the way in which they are abstract and ahistorical.[25] As he admits in the preface to *Eingriffe* (Interventions), the phrase 'reified consciousness' occurs like a catchword in his articles,[26] but this almost loose use of it has a most stringent underpinning. In all of his discussions of individual philosophers too, Adorno indicts their thought for its reified structure, and in what follows the weight of this charge will be examined and assessed. It always designates some kind of dislocation in the philosophy under examination in the relation between the subject and the object: a denial of one pole of the relation, and/or a founding of the philosophy on the primacy of one pole, or, an attempt to avoid the subject/object dichotomy altogether.

In his criticism of philosophy and in his theories of the development of literature and music, Adorno is battling to redefine the Marxian problematic of the relation between 'being and consciousness' or thought. Thought, for Adorno, is not self-grounding in either an Hegelian or a Lukácsian sense. It is not simple reflection of social existence with no autonomy of its own. It is not simply activity, or 'mental labour' separated from physical labour. As identity thinking, it is the analogue of Adorno's construal and generalisation of Marx's theory of value. Both poles of the analogy, social exchange and thought, are real. The relation is not one of determination but of two processes with the same internal structure. As non-identity thinking (or negative dialectic), or rational identity thinking, thought attains a certain autonomy, not in the sense that it is outside the social process, but in the sense that it *is* the social process as the immanently demonstrable truth of identity thinking, which reveals the underlying social processes and the utopian possibilities, or impossibilities, just as the theory of value does. Adorno's philosophical ambition was to redefine the subject and the object, and their relationship, without presupposing their identity, and to show that this can only be accomplished if the subject and the object are understood as social processes and not as the presuppositions of pure epistemology. He is far more successful in demonstrating the impossibility of philosophy than in demonstrating that the various subject/object relationships which he criticises can only be interpreted as social criticism. This makes for better criticism of philosophy but for less convincing elucidation of the relationship between philosophy and society.

Hegel

Adorno's thought, like that of many Marxists, has a self-conscious and uneasy relation to Hegel's philosophy. In some respects the issues which preoccupy him are the conventional ones: the distinction between Hegel's method and his system; the criticism of the relation between the individual and society in Hegel's political philosophy; the rejection of Hegel's philosophy of world history. In other respects the issues are less familiar: the obsession with how to read Hegel's texts; the concentration on Hegel's theoretical philosophy at the expense of any engagement with his moral or political philosophy; and the attempt to turn Hegel's criticism of Kant against both latter-day empirical sociology and philosophical ontology. However, even where the more familiar issues are concerned, Adorno gives his construal of them and his answer to them an original twist.

Two of the three parts of Adorno's book on Hegel are concerned with how to read Hegel's texts, especially the *Phenomenology of Mind* and the (greater) *Logic*. One of these parts is entitled *Skoteinos oder Wie zu lesen sei*.[27] *Skoteinos* is a Greek word which means 'dark, dusky, obscure or blind'.

Oder wie zu lesen sei means 'or how to read'. Another part is entitled *Erfahrungsgehalt*[28] which means 'the substance of experience', and it equally concerns the way in which Hegel's texts should be approached. Adorno argues that Hegel's philosophy is not constructed on a first principle or on transcendental subjectivity;[29] that it is presented in a form which reveals the self-cognition of the object,[30] and that this results in texts which defy our usual habits of reading.[31] The reader is both merely 'looking on' (*blosses Zusehen*)[32] and entering into a new intellectual experience (*geistige Erfahrung*).[33] This experience involves the realisation that the subject is part of the object to be apprehended, but that the subject does not construct that object. This experience is negative in the sense that it does not consist of individual judgements by the subject, but of the process of becoming aware of the limitations of such judgements, and the gradual cognition of totality.[34] Unfortunately much of Adorno's discussion of Hegel's philosophy consists of general statements of its metaphysical intent which remain far removed from any detailed reconstruction of the process of any one or other of Hegel's texts. This is because Adorno is more interested in finding in Hegel's thought a basis for distinguishing between theoretical and empirical thinking than in finding in it a basis for distinguishing between theoretical and practical philosophy or praxis.

Adorno echoes Engels' description of the conflict in Hegel's philosophy between 'the whole dogmatic content of the Hegelian *system* [which] is declared to be absolute truth, in contradiction to his dialectical *method*, which dissolves all dogmatism'.[35] Adorno makes a series of similar points when he praises Hegel for establishing a notion of truth as process, but also criticises him for stifling this insight by creating a philosophical system;[36] when he argues that Hegel opposed the grounding of truth in a transcendental subject, but yet ultimately depended on a notion of truth grounded in subjectivity as *Geist*;[37] when he demonstrates that Hegel's notion of cognition implies a critical perspective on any given reality, but results in the legitimation of that reality.[38] Adorno considers that these features of Hegel's thought reveal fundamental antinomies in the latter's philosophy, but, unlike most Marxists, Adorno goes on to introduce his own position as a series of antinomies in relation to the ones discerned in Hegel's thought. Thus, while any system must stifle thought, it is essential to appropriate the power of the system;[39] the categories of the philosophical system have been 'absolutised', but those categories must be used in the critique of the system.[40] This self-conscious presentation of his own thought as antinomical was a way to avoid the inconsistent position into which he would fall if he presented all thought except his own as inherently antinomical. Another way in which he sought to avoid these paradoxes was by presenting his own thought in fragments, because although 'Dialectical theory, abhorring anything isolated, cannot admit [fragments] as such . . . They insist, in opposition to Hegel's *practice* and yet in accordance with his *thought*, on negativity'.[41]

At the very beginning of his book on Hegel, Adorno justifies his interest in Hegel in a way reminiscent of Marx's *Critique of Hegel's 'Philosophy of Right'*, by accrediting Hegel with insight into the inevitability of contradictions in bourgeois society and the problem of how they may be reconciled.[42] However, Adorno judges this to be an important *theoretical* achievement since it arises on the basis of a speculative perspective, and not merely on the basis of an empirical perspective. The 'speculation' which yields a perspective which is both empirical and critical is that of the original, self-splitting and reuniting identity of subject and object.[43] This theme informs much of Adorno's discussion of Hegel. Adorno finds Hegel's theoretical philosophy more radical than his practical or political philosophy. Whenever he refers to Hegel's *Philosophy of Right*, his aim is to contrast classificatory with dialectical thinking, or to contrast the value of public opinion with truth, or to distinguish between grounding moral philosophy in pure subjectivity and a notion of subject as mediated or determined by social processes. He never discusses Hegel's theories of the state, property or religion, or criticises Hegel's theory of the bureaucracy as the universal class as Marx did.[44] Thus, for example, he quotes the following passage from the *Philosophy of Right*:

> To consider particular laws as they appear and develop in time is a purely historical task. Like acquaintance with what can be logically deduced from a comparison of these laws with previously existing legal principles, this task is appreciated and rewarded in its own sphere and has no relation whatever to the philosophical study of the subject . . .
> A particular law may be shown to be wholly grounded in and consistent with existing legally established institutions, and yet it may be wrong and irrational in its essential character, . . . But even if particular laws *are* both right and reasonable, still it is one thing to *prove* that they have that character – which çannot be truly done except by means of the concept – and quite another to describe their appearance in history or the circumstances, contingencies, needs and events which brought about their enactment . . .[45]

For Adorno this passage evinces a sacrifice on Hegel's part of the unity of the historical and systematic approach in favour of the systematic.[46] Yet Adorno too drew on the distinction between the 'prescientific registration of mere unconnected facts, data, opinions',[47] and the perspective of their connection given by a view of the historical splitting and reuniting of subject and object. He was always trying in his discussion of Hegel's philosophy to find a basis for taking over the Hegelian contrast between merely empirical thinking and 'comprehensive' thinking, without taking over Hegel's assumption of identity or totality as reconcilement in history.

In the first and best essay in his book on Hegel, *Aspekte*, Adorno claims that Hegel's thought is reified by demonstrating how a central antinomy in Hegel's philosophy of mind (*Geist*), 'imitates a central antinomy of bourgeois society'.[48] He does this by turning the antinomy in Hegel's philosophy into a chiasmus: put simply, the antinomy is between Hegel's definition of the mind as activity or process and as absolute or free. Thus, Hegel separated abstract activity as logical coercion from concrete labour: society is separated into abstract exchange and concrete activity (that is, Hegel's philosophy presupposes (wrongly) that society is (inherently) divided: society is in fact, at present, divided and this appears immortalised in Hegel's philosophy. The relation between the antinomy and the chiasmus is established by showing that Hegel's thinking proceeds in a manner analogous to the model of social processes explicated by the theory of value. Adorno's exposition of Hegel's thought is logically prior to the reintroduction of such concepts as subject and object (also essence/appearance, universal/particular) in the second part of *Negative Dialectic*.

The exposition of the antinomy depends mostly on the chapter on the master and slave in Hegel's *Phenomenology of Mind*. The thesis laconically stated in *Negative Dialectic*, is elaborated here,

> . . . Hegel, in his chapter on the master and the slave, develops the genesis of self-consciousness from the relation of work, and he shows this by the way in which the ego adjusts to its self-determined goal as much as to heteronomous material. The origin of the ego in the non-ego is thereby disclosed. It is looked up in the real process of life . . . Thereafter, Hegel hypostatizes the mind, but in vain.[49]

Adorno argues that Hegel turns the pre-conscious experience of work into a form of reflection, into the pure activity of mind, its produced unity.[50] The particular abstract quality of work in a society based on commodity exchange is transformed into a notion of mind as the form of logical coercion. The work-process reappears as the achieved unity of the mind.[51] Adorno makes his case by close analysis of the vocabulary which Hegel uses and shows how it abounds in verbs and adjectives pertaining to work (labour), production, domination and coercion.[52] The vocabulary of domination reveals the social principle underlining Hegel's thought as much as the vocabulary of work.[53] In this way Adorno demonstrates that Hegel modelled the theory of mind on work, but that, at the same time, he separated the activity of mind from its real origin. Adorno claims that this mistake is analogous to the one delineated by Marx of judging work to be the origin of wealth. For 'Nature is the origin of use-value' and work is only the origin of use-value and thus of wealth when men own the means of production on which they work.[54] In capitalist society, this is not the case. Similarly, Adorno argues, Hegel mistook work, defined as opposition to nature, for an absolute origin.[55] Then Adorno develops the chiasmus. He says that this 'absolutising' of work is both correct and incorrect.[56] It is correct because labour is a universal and abstract principle in capitalist society, but it is incorrect because this philosophical expression of labour does not disclose the specific mode of production which gives rise to the kind of labour in question.[57] This is how 'mind' comes to be seen as free and self-determining in Hegel's philosophy, whereas 'mind' is in fact under the coercion of labour. It is also the basis on which Hegel's dialectic of the subject and the object is grounded in the subject which reappears as domination.[58] Adorno sought to redefine the subject/object dichotomy in a way which would avoid these implications. The dichotomy cannot be simply rejected because it does correspond to a real social process.

Adorno's most fundamental criticism of Hegel's philosophy consists in his criticism of Hegel's theory of identity. Adorno expressed this in many different ways, some of which are intelligible, others of which miscarry. Thus to deny the possibility of reconcilement of subject and object in history and to charge Hegel with transmuting the 'negation of the negation' into an acceptance of the *status quo*,[59] are intelligible but simple and unoriginal criticisms of Hegel's philosophy. However, Adorno's own theory of identity, non-identity and rational identity thinking cannot be intelligibly construed as a reformulation of Hegel's logic.[60] It is easy to misunderstand *Negative Dialectic* on this issue, because Adorno does present the idea of negative dialectic in two different and fundamentally irreconcilable ways. Sometimes he suggests that he is trying to express the 'ineffable',[61] the 'non-conceptual', the 'concrete'.[62] This longing is particularly evident in the 'Introduction'. It is Adorno's concession to 'the ontological need' and closely related to the same theme as he discerned it in Heidegger's and in Benjamin's work. It has nothing to do with Hegel.

The notion of the 'concrete' conflates philosophical and sociological connotations. Adorno uses it in at least four distinguishable ways. One sense of 'concrete' is the Hegelian-Marxian one: 'The concrete is concrete because it is the sum of many determinations, and therefore a unity of diversity'.[63] In this case, the 'concrete' refers to the individual as 'the actual starting point' of conceptualisation, and, secondly, as the result of considering the individual in relation to all its determinations. A second notion of 'concrete' in Adorno's writings is more loose, and merely involves a reference to society. To see an object 'concretely' is to see it as a social object or fact rather than as a pure philosophical or mental construct.[64] A third notion of 'concrete' which Adorno employs comes from Benjamin's writings and has two aspects. The first is that the 'concrete' is whatever is irreducibly material, that which resists any assimilation to our concepts or our consciousness, 'blind, intentionless material'.[65] The second aspect of Benjamin's notion of the 'concrete' is his theory of 'ideas' or 'origin'.[66] 'Ideas' as given by the names of things present the 'concrete' in his first sense. These 'ideas' are not concepts, for 'concepts' depend on the distinction between the general and the particular and describe phenomena. Benjamin compares 'ideas' with Platonic forms, since they are more real than phenomena which appear and which can be assimilated to our consciousness. He preferred, however, to think of Adam who first gave things their names, not Plato's theory of forms, as the analogue of his notion of 'ideas'.[67] Although Adorno was extremely critical of both of these aspects of Benjamin's notion of the 'concrete',[68] the first part of *Negative Dialectic* depends on the idea that concepts cannot capture the concrete in Benjamin's sense of the world as material. However, in the central part of the book Adorno adds a fourth, 'utopian' sense to this: a concept would be 'concrete' if it really covered its object (rational identity).

In this central section of *Negative Dialectic* Adorno explicates his notions of identity. His concern is with the relation between concept and object under the conditions of identity and non-identity thinking and the relation of these kinds of thinking to each other. The idea of rational identity, when the concept would be fulfilled by its object, is logically essential to Adorno's theory but is tempered in that no society need be conceivable in which that kind of identity would hold. Adorno's account depends instead on a structure analogous to the theory of value in which the central process of society is explained, the distinction between use-value and (exchange) value, without any reference to a posited future society. Thus even the notion of rational identity is not a restatement of Hegel. Adorno's idea of what constitutes an adequate relation between concept and object is nonsense from an Hegelian perspective.

This central part of *Negative Dialectic* is called 'Negative Dialectic: Concept and Categories'. After Adorno has explicated his theory of identity, he does reintroduce certain quasi-Hegelian categories, *inter alia*, subject/object and mediation.[69] He sought to provide a philosophical and sociological basis for establishing the priority of the object and the mediation of the subject and the object, without relapsing into a position which gives priority to the subject. However, it is difficult to give 'priority to the object'; sociologically, this would mean considering the social process as containing as well as conditioning our experience of it. The problem is partly conceptual:

An object can be conceived only by a subject but always remains something other than the subject, whereas a subject by its very nature is from the outset an object as well. Not even as an idea can we conceive a subject that is not an object; but we can conceive an object that is not a subject. To be an object is part of the meaning of subjectivity; but it is not equally part of the meaning of objectivity to be a subject.[70]

Adorno relied on the notion of mediation to reformulate the relation between subject and object, but 'mediation' should not be misunderstood as an external relation, as a third term, nor, conversely, in a way which re-establishes the identity of the subject and object. For a relation of mediation is not one of identity:

> What mediates the facts is not so much the subjective mechanism of their preformation and comprehension as it is the objectivity heteronomous to the subject, the objectivity behind that which the subject can experience.[71]

Adorno's criticism of post-Hegelian philosophy (and his criticism of sociology) consisted of demonstrating that any philosophy (or sociology) which did not involve a notion of subject and object and their mediation falls into antinomies which can be derived from the social processes which underlie the theoretical thinking in question. Such philosophy depends too on identity thinking (reification).

Kierkegaard

Adorno was interested in **Kierkegaard**'s philosophy for several reasons. Kierkegaard attacks Hegel's philosophy in his work and discredits academic German Idealism.[72] His approach was quite different from Marx's, but, like Marx, criticism of philosophy was only part of his endeavour and like Marx, a large part of that endeavour was to redefine the realm of the real. Kierkegaard's notion of *Existenz* had been adopted by twentieth-century German existentialist philosophy especially by Jaspers and by Heidegger. Although the notion plays a different role in their thought, it was inherited from Kierkegaard's writings. Adorno considered that the later existentialist philosophy was a dominant non-Marxist but materialist philosophy of his time, just as the work of Kierkegaard represented an important criticism of classical philosophy of its time, but in a quite different way from Marx's contemporaneous criticism of that tradition. Adorno was also interested in Kierkegaard's restriction of the realm of aesthetics and his major work on Kierkegaard is subtitled *Construction of the Aesthetic*.[73] In this book Adorno demonstrates that Kierkegaard's restriction of the realm of the aesthetic and the concomitant stress on 'inwardness' (*Innerlichkeit*) result in a mode of thought which has no object and which depends on an 'abstract' notion of the individual. Adorno's case rests on drawing out antinomies in

Kierkegaard's central concepts and then showing that these antinomies can be interpreted as antinomies in society, and that the mode of reasoning which gives rise to the antinomies has the same structure as the theory of value. In the article 'On Kierkegaard's Doctrine of Love',[74] Adorno stated his general approach:

All Kierkegaard's gloomy motives have good critical sense as soon as they are interpreted in terms of social critique. Many of his positive assertions gain the concrete significance [which] they otherwise lack as soon as one translates them into concepts of a right society.[75]

The antinomies in Kierkegaard's notion of the individual reveal the 'decisive character features of the typical individual of modern society'.[76]

Philosophy constitutes a negative stage in Kierkegaard's development of his theology[77] which is founded on belief rather than reason (*Vernunft*).[78] Within philosophy, the aesthetic stage is accorded no genuine cognitive value.[79] It is defined as the sphere in which men live in the present, 'in which [man] is immediately what he is',[80] and in which men relate to objects, to works of art, that is, aesthetics in the narrower sense of the term.[81] The realm of the aesthetic is based on a subject/object dichotomy but Kierkegaard rejects a subject/object dialectic as the basis of an Hegelian progression to absolute knowledge.[82] Adorno argued that Kierkegaard's 'objectless dialectic'[83] relapsed into many of the assumptions it was designed to resist, as any thought will if it seeks to eliminate any notion of the object. Adorno was most sympathetic, however, to Kierkegaard's refusal to posit identity between thought and reality and to his deposing of the 'autonomous *ratio*' as the foundation of knowledge.[84]

Adorno argued that Kierkegaard's notion of the individual, and of the individual's inwardness and existence, turns out on examination to be abstract, absolute and invariant. The subject is the scene (*Schauplatz*),[85] not the basis of Kierkegaard's dialectic, which takes place between inwardness and its meaning (*Sinn*)[86] – the act of faith.[87] This meaning is not immanent to the individual, it is not the individual's object, but qualitatively different from him, although it can only be attained by 'the reflection of inwardness'.[88] The world of things and of objective mind (*Geist*) is irrelevant to Kierkegaard's inner dialectic,[89] but Adorno shows that a notion of history and of mankind were essential to Kierkegaard and that therefore his notion of the individual is abstract. Becoming a Christian is not absolute in Kierkegaard's thought, but a never-ending process. The individual's inner history is the (philosophical) basis of the leap or act of faith.[90] The individual has a history because he is a member of the human race, of mankind. Mankind is defined by original sin.[91] Kierkegaard's notion of history is therefore aporetic. On the one hand, it means the uniqueness of the individual in history and his sin;[92] on the other hand, it presupposes an extra-historical notion of sin as the first event of human history.[93] But Kierkegaard did not wish to endorse this second notion of history because it presupposes the sin of each generation and thus robs the inner dialectic of the individual of its significance.[94] He had therefore to concede that there are qualitatively different periods of history in order to grant the individual the significance of his own inner history.[95] But this implies a notion of real or external history and thus contradicts Kierkegaard's intention to describe a dialectic with no reference to the objective world. Since Kierkegaard refuses any category of mediation to solve the paradoxes of his thought, the individual can only have the status of an abstract pole of his dialectic,[96] and appears wrongly to be absolute and immediate.[97] This is wrong in the sense that Kierkegaard rejected any absolute, and the categories of immediacy and mediation were irrelevant to him. The individual is 'absolutised' by Kierkegaard because the latter's philosophy depends on notions to which Kierkegaard cannot admit, and is thus irredeemably antinomical.

Adorno argues that this 'absolutising' of the individual corresponds to a real social process by which the individual is 'absolutised', and he attempts to set out the correspondence. He offers a weak, second-order argument according to which Kierkegaard's apparent neglect of the external world or of social reality should be interpreted as a rejection of society as a whole, due to the development of early capitalism and to the effect which this development was having on the individual.[98] A closer statement of the parallel between Kierkegaard's notion of the individual and the theory of value occurs in Adorno's discussion of Kierkegaard's doctrine of love. Kierkegaard's explication of the command to 'love thy neighbour' excludes any attention to the particular qualities of the individual involved and any expectation of reciprocity of love.[99] The other person as such 'becomes a mere "stumbling block" to subjective inwardness', for 'the substantial quality of love is "objectless"'.[100] The 'neighbour' according to Kierkegaard is the first man whom you see 'When you open the door behind which you have prayed to God and walk out . . .'.[101] The 'neighbour' is thus abstract and 'given', and loving him does not alter the world in any way whatsoever. Kierkegaard considers that individual men are objects, that is, finite, and thus barriers to love which must be infinite. He thus redefines individuality as absolute equality, as lack of differences between men, and in this sense individual men are not objects (of love, and so on). Adorno argues that Kierkegaard's initial position and his redefinition amount to a denial 'of reification':[102] that men as social actors are objects. Absolute or abstract equality is a basic principle of social relations under the capitalist mode of production. The exchange of commodities depends on labour in the abstract, while the idea of (abstract) equality in the market is part of the ideology of capitalism.

Kierkegaard's notion of the neighbour is in marked contrast with the 'neighbour' of the Gospels which

> . . . implies fishermen and peasants, herdsmen and publicans, people whom one knows and who have their established locus in a life of simple production which can be realized adequately by immediate experience . . . Kierkegaard has [taken] the abstract concept of man of his own period and substitutes it for the Christian neighbour who belongs to a different society.[103]

Kierkegaard's notion of the individual, whether it refers to he who loves or he who is loved, is abstract. It abstracts from individual qualities of men and thus 'absolutises' them by making them completely equal. *Pari passu*, the formal equality of a mode of production which separates men from a nexus of immediate relations with each other of the kind which obtains in a life of simple production, isolates them and 'absolutises' them as abstract individuals.

Adorno's discussion of Kierkegaard's thought and his theory of the individual incidentally reveals two different concerns in Adorno's own theory of the changing relationship between the individual and society. He criticises 'abstract equality' both on the grounds that it masks real inequality and on the grounds that it amounts to a mode of domination which turns men into the mass of individuals and (somehow) destroys the 'individual' as such. This becomes more than a difference of emphasis and will be considered further in Chapter Five.

Husserl

Adorno's book on Husserl is subtitled *Matacritique of Epistemology (Zur Metakritik der Erkenntnistheorie)*. In this book Adorno explains what he understands by epistemology and why any philosophy which depends on a first principle or ground (*das absolute Erste*) is illegitimate. He alludes to the social basis of this criticism of epistemology and introduces the reasons for his circumscribed but eventual defence of epistemology. The bulk of the book consists of unremitting exposures of antinomies in Husserl's philosophy, but it also lays the groundwork for Adorno's attack on Heidegger's philosophy and this is partly accomplished by qualified support for Husserl's enterprise. Where Husserl's phenomenology is concerned Adorno has to establish in the first place that it is justifiable to assimilate it to epistemology, since phenomenology does not propose a *theory* of knowledge but claims to apprehend acts of cognition as they occur in themselves.[104]

A mode of thought is 'epistemological' if it depends on an *Ursprungsphilosophie*, a philosophy of origin, that is, an indubitable, self-grounding, first principle. Adorno demonstrates that in any given case such philosophy will involve a subject/object dualism which will be resolved by giving priority to subjectivity; by basing the reality of being (*Sein*) and of meaning (*Sinn*) on the subject. This is equally true whether the philosophy in question is an *Immanenz* philosophy, that is, based in the realm of possible experience, or a *Transzendenz* philosophy, that is, establishes its grounds beyond the realm of experience. It is equally true even when the philosophy in question is empiricist or ontological and thus disposes *prima facie* with any first principle and with any notion of subjectivity.[105] Adorno's shows that the central concepts and propositions of these philosophies contain antinomies, and that the philosophies rely on identity thinking (reification). Again, Adorno presents his own position in antinomical fashion: epistemology is inherently self-contradictory; epistemology is nevertheless necessary. Although Adorno reveals that all non-dialectical philosophies are in some way grounded in subjectivity, he argues that those which have an explicit notion of the subject are superior to those with no ostensible notion of the subject. Epistemology of the former kind is 'necessary' in the sense that, as socially produced illusion, it is more accurate than any kind which has no notion of the subject.[106]

Adorno uses three different arguments to prove that any mode of thought justified by a first principle is always self-contradictory. These arguments are taken from traditional philosophy and are transformed into principles of social criticism by use of the figure of chiasmus: arguments which expose illegitimate abstraction in philosophy reveal principles of abstraction in society; arguments which expose the illegitimate dominance of the subject in philosophy reveal modes of social domination. Adorno indicts philosophy for these inversions with the charge of reification. He also offers a general but brief interpretation of the social genesis of the raising of these invalid philosophical claims, that is, of *Geist* (mind).[107]

It is not accidental that Adorno uses the term 'antinomy' rather than the term 'amphiboly' or 'paralogism'. Each of these terms names a section in the 'Transcendental Dialectic' of Kant's *Critique of Pure Reason*, in which Kant exposes an illusion of pure reason, and each may be taken to mean loosely a conflict of two equally cogent arguments. Adorno refers particularly to 'the antinomy of pure reason' because in that section Kant shows that

> The search for the simple first, the absolute cause, results in an infinite regress; the infinite cannot be posited with validity as given, while such positing appears unavoidable to the total mind.[108]

However, Kant does ground his philosophy in an absolute first principle:

the transcendental unity (or identity) of the ego, and in the irreducible givenness of the categories.[109] Similarly, Adorno argues, Husserl's philosophy relies on a notion of 'givenness' and bases truth on a transcendental structure and thereby restricts it in effect to the (immanent) constructions of a subject.[110] Although Adorno does not endorse Kant's distinction between the understanding and pure reason, he draws on Kant's demonstration of the logical absurdity of the inference contained in the proposition

> That if the conditioned is given, the entire sum of conditions, and consequently the absolutely unconditioned . . . is also given.[111]

as one of the arguments against first principles in philosophy.

The second kind of argument used by Adorno draws on Hegel's criticism of an absolute or immediate beginning or principle in philosophy. Adorno concedes that Hegel's theory of mediation is quite irrelevant to Husserl's phenomenological reduction,[112] and reaffirms the necessity of criticising philosophy in its own terms, that is, of 'immanent criticism'.[113] It is the importance of the notion of 'givenness' (*Gegebenheit*) in Husserl's philosophy (and in empiricist and rationalist epistemology generally) which affords the basis for Hegelian criticism. For any philosophy which posits 'givenness' (that is, what is given) as immediate is mistakenly positing it as a substantial concept when it is a relational one, or, in other words, when it is mediated.[114] Empiricist epistemology which posits 'givenness' as its principle thereby contradicts the empiricist requirement that there can be no general first principle, while rationalist epistemology reduces 'givenness' to the mind which it posits as its first principle. Neither *Geist* (mind) not 'givenness' can provide an independent basis for epistemology because they are relational concepts which mediate each other.[115] Husserl's philosophy was an explicit attempt to 'reconquer the objectivity of truth as against relativist psychologism',[116] that is, not to base truth on an empirical-psychological analysis of consciousness. Adorno shows by examining Husserl's notion of givenness that the latter's thought did nonetheless presuppose the unity of consciousness.[117]

The third kind of argument which Adorno uses in his metacritique of epistemology is a Nietzschean argument against first principles in philosophy, which is designed to reveal the idealist implications of ontology. Adorno quotes Nietzsche to the effect that 'true Being' is a mental construct on the basis of which our belief in an external world of things is erected.[118] In view of this position, Husserl's distinction between descriptive psychology and transcendental phenomenology is negligible, for all ontology is idealist.[119] Nietzsche's strictures against the systematic debasement in traditional philosophy of what is dynamic or changing, and against the elevation of static, self-grounding concepts to the realm of thereby abstract and empty 'truth', are marshalled against Husserl's predilection for an *a priori*, invariant philosophy,[120]

> ... the last and the first are confused ... the 'highest concepts', that is, the most general ... are placed ... at the beginning, *as* the beginning ... Moral: everything of the first rank must be *causa sui*. The origin out of something else is regarded as an objection, as a sign of questionable value.[121]

This violent act (*Gewalttat*) on the part of philosophical method arises from the social division of mental and physical labour.[122] *Geist*, or metaphysics as transsubjective being, mistakes itself for an absolute. Adorno does not use the distinction between mental and physical labour in order to stress that mind is a form of labour, but in order to stress the mistake on which philosophy is predicated: that thought is a discrete, self-contained activity when it is in fact a societal activity. This, Adorno suggests, is a reflex on the part of the mind due to its actual impotence and uncertainty. For it does not contribute to the real reproduction of life, nor to the real domination of men, but provides methods – the means of domination – for those who dominate.[123] In this book Adorno had not yet developed the theory of negative dialectic fully, that is, the theory of the interconnection between modes of thinking and the specific mode of production.

Although Adorno demonstrates that Husserl did not succeed in breaking out of traditional epistemology, he begins and ends the book with a defence of Husserl in opposition to the subsequent development of ontology, especially the philosophy of Heidegger. Husserl's attempt failed because he used the categories of the idealist analysis of consciousness, such as 'transcendental ego', in his attempt to reject the assumptions of 'constitutive subjectivity', of *Immanenz* philosophy.[124] He did indeed start the turn to ontology. Adorno defends Husserl for his initial retrieval of a notion of philosophical truth which was opposed to empiricist psychologism, that is to philosophical relativism.[125] He defends him ultimately in spite of, or because of, Husserl's relapse into idealism, for attempting nevertheless 'to destroy idealism from within'.[126] Adorno argues that a philosophy which depends on a subjective *ratio* is more coherent and more desirable than one which rejects such a notion completely. He thus defends Husserl's formalism against Heidegger's 'search for the concrete', and he defends Husserl's idea of innovation in philosophy against Heidegger's.[127]

The three central chapters in the book concentrate on Husserl's earliest phenomenological work, *Logical Investigations* (1900). In the first two chapters Adorno follows closely Husserl's *Prolegomena to Pure Logic*[128] and the second *Investigation*[129] (respectively) and exposes antinomies in Husserl's early statement of logical absolutism and in his notion of 'species'. In the third chapter *Zur Dialektik der erkenntnistheoretische Begriffe* (On the dialectic of epistemological concepts), Adorno casts his net more widely and demonstrates repeatedly that Husserl's notions of immediacy are either irrevocably antinomical or that they are categories of reflection. This means that in Husserl's attempt to develop a transcendental philosophy and thus abolish any gap between knowing and what is known, Husserl confected notions which are either contradictory, because they presuppose what they set out to prove, or which, in order to have any meaning, presuppose that there is a gap between knowing and what is known, and thus still need a theory of mediation (categories of reflection) to bridge the gap.

Adorno deals with Husserl's notions of 'givenness' and of 'intentionality' in both of these ways. Husserl separated psychic acts from logical norms, that is, the realm of the real from the realm of the ideal.[130] Logical truths and their meaning are 'given' in inner experience. Unlike in Kant's philosophy, 'phenomena' do not result from the combination of the categories and sensuous intuition.[131] For Husserl, phenomena are the objects of transcendental acts; they are the 'intentions' of such acts.[132] Hence, what is 'given' becomes the achievement of intentionality, and the idea of 'givenness' collapses into a pre-Kantian notion of identity with the subject.[133] On the other hand, Adorno argues that Husserl's various ways of distinguishing between the act of cognition and its content, such as *noesis/noema*, or the earlier distinction, perception/sensation (*Wahrnehrung/Empfindung*) still imply that ideas are 'reflections' of objects.[134] For example, what is purely self-given is distinct from the act of knowing it. But it is only by virtue of being known that what is given acquires meaning. Hence what is given is mediated, if only by the act which bestows meaning, and what is mediated – even if the mediation is part of its constitution – must in some sense exist before the act of mediation.[135] 'Intentionality' is used to abolish the gap between subject and object, since 'being' becomes a predicate of intentional meaning. Husserl's notion of 'givenness' does not remain a simple and immediate notion, but is integrated into a theory of knowing, that is, into an epistemology.[136] Adorno describes 'intentionality' as an extreme case of 'reification', that is, of reducing existence to the epistemological subject, but he does not unpack the charge of 'reification' sociologically, in this book, and for good reason.

Adorno does indict Husserl's philosophy for abdicating criticism of the sort associated with philosophy which depends fundamentally on the subjective *ratio*. For example, Husserl's philosophy is not critical in the Kantian sense of exposing the illusions of unfounded dogmas which disport themselves as genuine knowledge, but capitulates to the predominance of whatever is 'given' because, in Husserl's mature work, every universal qualifies equally for the status of *noema*.[137] Of the major philosophies which Adorno criticised, Husserl's contains the least social content, although it has had a great effect on sociology, mainly through the work of Alfred Schutz. Adorno does not discuss anything written by Husserl after 1931 and the works by Husserl which he does discuss do not include even peripheral remarks about society to which Adorno might attach more central theoretical importance, nor do they contain any sustained moral or practical philosophy, and this is why Adorno is sociologically cautious. To attain a perspective on 'the social preformation of the contingent experience of the individual',[138] it would not be sufficient to expose Husserl's abstract and pure subject as an empirical one, nor to solve the overly-privileged position of the subject by a commensurable or prior notion of the object, nor indeed by posing the subject/object dichotomy as general and invariant. All these solutions would substitute another form of identity for the one rejected.[139]

Heidegger

Adorno was strongly impressed by Heidegger's philosophy, especially by the latter's major work *Being and Time*.[140] He respected and even shared some of Heidegger's philosophical interests. For Heidegger, too, was opposed to traditional epistemology and aimed in his own work to give priority to a living object and to historical reality. Furthermore, his philosophy was designed to reveal its author's awareness of its intrinsic limitations. Nevertheless Adorno subjected Heidegger's philosophy to the most serious and unsympathetic criticism. He argued that Heidegger's ontology also relapsed into a kind of idealism by showing that its seminal notions are antinomical. However, in the case of this philosophy, Adorno had strong social and political objections to the particular form of identity thinking which it evinced. He analysed the language of Heidegger's work as a particularly distinguished representative of one of the ideologies which prevailed in Germany after 1930. This ideology, found by Adorno in the works of many writers of this time, turns out to be another version of a philosophy of private virtues ('authenticity' (*Eigentlichkeit*), and 'inwardness' (*Innerlichkeit*)) which is presented as if it represented the realisation of public virtue and political action.[141] Adorno interprets this ideology and the philosophy on which it is partly based, as amounting in effect to a particularly pernicious sanction and legitimation of an authoritarian *status quo*.

Adorno did not write a book specifically on Heidegger. His main criticism of Heidegger's philosophy appears in the first part of *Negative Dialectic*,[142] and his main criticism of the ideology of 'authenticity' appears in his book *Jargon of Authenticity*. However, Adorno discussed

Heidegger's work, briefly or at length, in all of the articles or books in which he examined the state of philosophy generally, and in all those in which he examined, at least ostensibly, the work of individual philosophers. He also took issue with Heidegger's interpretation of Hölderlin's poetry in one of his 'notes' on literature.[143]

According to Adorno, Heidegger sought to base his philosophy on concrete, determinate, existing being (*Dasein*), in opposition to Husserl's preoccupation with a realm of essences which are established in a way which is indifferent to the realm of the natural world of existence; and in opposition to all post-Socratic philosophy which, due to its emphasis on the theory of knowledge, has not granted priority to the question of being (*die Frage nach dem Sein*).[144] *Dasein* is Heidegger's term for 'the entity which each of us is himself and which includes inquiring as one of the possibilities of its Being'.[145] *Dasein* takes priority over other entities in the question of Being. That question is the question of the meaning (*Sinn*) of Being. Heidegger redefined the problem of meaning in opposition to Husserl's theory of intentional meaning, and in a way which would also avoid basing the analysis of meaning on the relationship of being and consciousness.[146] Adorno argued that to make the question of Being irreducible and to grant it ontological primacy was to found another *Ursprungsphilosophie*, an absolute first.[147] For Heidegger, Being is not only 'present-at-hand' (*vorhanden*) but belongs to historical reality. History provides the basic structure of Heidegger's ontology,[148] thereby resisting the eternal and static presuppositions of Husserl's thought. According to Adorno, Heidegger's notion of 'historicality' as the presupposition of *Dasein*, and his notion of 'facticity' as the realm of facts, are 'ontologised' notions, that is, notions pertaining to a *theory* of the ontical.[149] They thus become notions of essence, of the attributes of history as such, and fail to capture empirical or contingent history.[150] Nor do they provide a theory of the relation between history and nature (*Dasein*) as they seem, germinally, to promise.

Adorno demonstrates that Heidegger's attempt to develop a new kind of philosophy 'beyond subject and object, beyond concept and entity',[151] 'to delimit zealously his version of ontology from objectivism, and his anti-idealist stand from realism, whether critical or naive',[152] also relapsed into idealism. It is idealist according to Adorno because it ultimately displays absolute principles, abstracting procedures, and notions which presuppose the priority of subjectivity. However, the particular kind of identity thinking which Adorno discerned in Heidegger's work did not depend on any concept of reason (*Vernunft*), and thus did not offer even an inverted or greatly circumscribed criterion of critical rationality.[153]

Adorno has three criticisms of Heidegger's conviction that Being has a 'meaning', and of the search for that meaning. The first criticism is that

Heidegger is not able to establish that the meaning of Being is beyond entity and thingness:

> Under no circumstances is Being to be a thing, and yet, as the metaphors keep indicating, it is to be the 'ground' and something solid.[154]

This not only indicates that Heidegger relied on connotations which betrayed the 'meaning' assigned to Being, but also that he based his philosophy on an absolute principle:

> He [Heidegger] . . . says that neither the subject nor the object are immediate and ultimate; but he . . . reaches for something immediate and primary beyond subject and object.[155]

The second criticism is that Heidegger's attempt to show that the meaning of Being is nonconceptual makes Being meaningless: Heidegger said that 'Being, precedent to each abstraction, is no concept',[156] yet

> We are to conceive Being as the absolute, but it is the absolute only because we cannot conceive it.[157]

Heidegger demands that we think without a concept, and this can only evaporate into 'a know not what', into a pathos of invocation.[158] The third criticism is that if Being has a meaning, it must depend on abstract thought, and thus the meaning of Being reverts to categories of essence. It is abstract because to establish the meaning of Being by stripping it of all reference to entities, 'strips Being of everything other than pure thought',[159] and such thought is 'blind to the moment of synthesis in the substrate',[160] blind, that is, to the complex process of mental abstraction and synthesis necessary in order to be able to conceive of 'Being'. Heidegger resolves the problem that there is no Being without entity by making existence, that is, the being of entity, into the essence of Being:[161] 'The essence of *Dasein* lies in its existence.'[162] Hence Heidegger's Being is antinomical: if it is immediate, primeval and non-conceptual, it is meaningless; if it acquires a meaning, it is not immediate, primordial and non-conceptual, but is (equal to) its essence, and is thus a concept of reflection. Adorno was especially interested in the particular form of identity (reification) on which Heidegger's concept of Being and other concepts in his philosophy such as 'authenticity' depend. Heidegger's notion of Being displays identity thinking:

> The knowledge that 'is' can be neither a mere thought nor a mere entity [is transformed] into something transcendent in relation to those two definitions.[163]

No judgement can be made of this Being, that is, nothing can be predicated of it. Thus no non-identity can be perceived, even in the simple, grammatical sense that subject and predicate are never completely identical with each other.[164]

Just as in Husserl's philosophy, no distinctions of relative validity can be made between *noemae*, so in Heidegger's philosophy, no distinctions can be made between different kinds of entities or existences. However, Adorno believed that Heidegger's approach had less heuristic validity than Husserl's. The identity thinking embraced by Heidegger's notion of 'authenticity', and the presuppositions pertaining to subjectivity which underpin the notion, amount, in Adorno's view, to an extremely quiescent social philosophy.

Dasein, according to Heidegger, 'belongs to itself'; it is ' "in each case mine" '.[165] The distinction between authenticity and inauthenticity 'depends on whether this element of being, *Dasein*, chooses itself, its mineness'.[166] Adorno objects that Heidegger's principle of 'choosing oneself' is empty. It does not contain any reference to the social and political organisation of the world as the realisation of the ego (or will), which thereby refers to, or chooses, itself.[167] The principle has no object, that is, no theory of what the self is, and thus provides no criterion by which to judge that the self has been chosen.[168] Furthermore, this approach reaffirms the *status quo*: '. . . the ego posits itself as higher than the world and becomes subjected to the world precisely because of this'.[169] For,

> Such a philosophy need no longer be concerned with how far society and psychology allow a man to be himself or become himself, or whether in the concept of such selfness the old evil is concentrated one more time. The societal relation, which seals itself off in the identity of the subject, is desocietalized [*entgesellschaftet*] into an in-itself.[170]

Dasein presupposes absolute unity of subject and reality. In this it is like the traditional absolute ego, but it is unlike it in having no theory of rationality in the practical or moral sphere. *Dasein* is said to be twofold: 'ontic, namely, determined by existence and "ontological", because existence is thus determinative for it'.[171] This distinction might be equivalent to a distinction between concept (or subject) and reality, but it has been reneged by the definition of *Dasein's* existence as essence which thus presupposes the absolute identity of the subject.[172]

Adorno charges Heidegger with 'reifying' his concepts and unpacks this charge to show the analogy with the theory of value. He believes that Heidegger's concepts imply a social theory which represents and reaffirms an authoritarian social structure. Heidegger's notions, such as 'Being', 'choosing oneself', presuppose something which exists 'in-itself'. They are not relational categories. But

> He who accepts the world of commodities as the in-itself, which it
> pretends to be, is deceived by the mechanisms which Marx analysed in
> the chapter on fetishes. He who neglects this in-itself, value in
> exchange, as mere illusion, gives in to the ideology of universal
> humanity.[173]

For example, the notion of authenticity (although Heidegger does not
analyse it socially) implies a social condition in which relations to others
and thus to oneself are simple and transparent.[174] To advance such a
position in a society in which social relations are not simple and
transparent lends support to the mode of domination in that society.
Adorno suggests that the absence of any theory of action in Heidegger's
philosophy corresponds to the real social impotence of the individual in
society.[175]

Instead of developing a theory of action, Heidegger uses language in a
way which pre-empts the need for any social or political action. Adorno
calls this use of words a 'jargon':

> . . . the jargon acquires its defining character by the way it imputes its
> truth. It does this by making an intended object present – as though
> this object were Being without any tension towards the subject.[176]

'Jargon' is thus a particularly strong type of identity thinking. In fact, it is
a kind of rational identity thinking, 'Everyday or philosophical language
is spoken here and now as if it were the sacred one'.[177] Adorno's theses of
the three kinds of thinking pertain to concepts and objects, not words or
language. Yet words can be used in ways which reinforce identity
thinking:

> . . . jargon obliterates the difference between [the] more for which
> language gropes and the in-itself of this more . . .[178]

But they can also be used in ways which detract from the concept's
apparent identity with its object:

> Language becomes a measure of truth only when we are conscious of
> the non-identity of an expression with what we mean.[179]

Adorno discerns a particular 'jargon' in the writings of Karl Jaspers, Otto
Friedrich Bollnow and Ulrich Sonnenmann during the period 1930 – 60,
which had ramifications in many other kinds of minor writing and public
addresses. He sees the philosophical foundation of this jargon in

Heidegger's work. The choice of seminal words and the way in which such words are used in these works reinforces an 'ideology of universal humanity', by invoking a condition of rational identity as if it obtained in present society. For example, Adorno quotes from Bollnow's book *Neue Geborgenheit* (The New Security)[180] to show how

> . . . security, as an existential value, turns from something longed for and denied into a presence which is here and now, and is independent of what prevents it from being.[181]

The notion of 'inwardness' performs a similar function in Jaspers' writing:

> [it transposes] a historical state of affairs into the pure essence of Man [which] becomes affirmed and eternalized at the same time. In this way the jargon plunders the concept of Man, who is to be sublime because of his nothingness. It robs him of precisely those traits which have as their content the criticism of states of affairs, which preclude the divine right of souls.[182]

Thus when Adorno says 'Man is the ideology of dehumanization',[183] he means that to imply that humanity is realised in the present society is to reinforce and reaffirm all those features of that society which prevent the realisation of man. He shows too how this is frequently accomplished by appeals to archaic images of social relations.[184]

Although Adorno offers no explicit thesis about the extent of its prevalence or political influence, this jargon is another case of the peculiarly strong cross-fertilisation in Germany between philosophical culture and general culture. Adorno revealed the ways in which this philosophy reinforced a parapolitical ideology and this is one of the reasons why he wanted to pitch the case for his alternative as a rival to the underlying philosophy.

A Changed Concept of Dialectic[185]

Any philosophy which systematically denies one pole of the dialectic, the subject or the object, or which, conversely, is grounded in one to the debasement of the other, will fall into antinomies, will reify its concepts. Adorno sought a perspective from which the separation of the subject and object could be seen to be a characterisation of the object and not constituted by the subject:

> For there could no more be truth without a subject freeing itself from illusions than there could be truth without that which is not the subject, that in which truth has its archetype [*Urbild*].[186]

Only social theory guarantees this perspective, a theory furthermore of a specific society. The *Urbild* is the model of social relations explicated by the theory of value, and by Adorno's extrapolation of that theory into a theory of modes of thinking. He was most opposed to Husserl's theory of intentional meaning and to Heidegger's theory of the meaning of Being. Neither of these theories were able to see that the mind is at work in the meanings which confront it, but that it does not constitute those meanings by itself. Adorno generalised the theory of value in a way that would satisfy these criteria. He sometimes called this approach 'natural history', which is the history of the interaction of specifiable kinds of societies with nature, of their culture as a mode of domination.

Adorno's critique of philosophy is not always convincing. The philosophical weaknesses which he exposes have often been discerned by critics writing from quite different positions. He succeeds in this sense even though he never takes the philosophy with which he is engaging entirely on its own terms. It is difficult, however, to judge the move from revealing irreconcilable antinomies in central concepts to establishing the social origins of those antinomies. This is partly because the move is always accomplished by means of chiasmus and analogy, and partly because there are no criteria by which to judge that this move is the only one which can account for the antinomies discerned, nor any reason why the subject/object relation should be considered uniquely as a social relationship. The only partial criterion is the internal cogency of the analogy. The most successful strategy draws out the antinomies into which philosophies fall when they try to establish indubitable and absolute first principles. The sociological decoding is only convincing when the philosophy in question is examined 'immanently' in this way. Yet, even at its most 'immanent', this form of critique succeeds at the expense of transforming all philosophy into epistemology, even when such philosophy consists of a radical attempt to renounce epistemology.

There is a gap between Adorno's critique of philosophy and his social critique which is only filled in by his aesthetics or sociology of art. In this he develops an alternative theory of the social structuring of meaning (illusion) which can be seen as a Marxian and sociological answer to the philosophical theories of meaning which he abhorred. Adorno's well taken revelation of a gap between Heidegger's moral and political philosophy is embarrassing, for there is a similar gap in Adorno's own thought.

Chapter 5

The Dispute over Positivism

The Critique of Sociology

Adorno carried on his search for a changed concept of dialectic by criticising sociology. The various non-dialectical notions of 'constitutive subjectivity', or denials of subjectivity at the epistemological level in sociology display the same inability discerned in philosophy to apprehend the way in which the social process 'constitutes' any cognition of society. At the more substantive level, Adorno sought to show that only a theory based on the critique of such sociology could understand the way in which specific social processes constitute the individual. This theory was not to be sociological in the narrow sense of a strict empiricism, nor in any sense which would forsake those themes also essential for an adequate conception of 'the subject' and which Adorno considered to be intrinsically philosophical, such as, 'totality', 'nature', and essence/appearance. Hence Adorno not only exposed antinomies in theoretical and empirical sociology, but attempted himself to adumbrate a theory of the individual and social change, and to conduct empirical research. However, although this body of work is less oblique than most of his other work, the redefining of sociological concepts and theories and the empirical research is not as substantial as might be expected from its status as complementary to the critique of philosophy on the one hand, and to the sociology of art, on the other.

The connection between the various approaches classed together as an academic discipline under the name of sociology is at best a highly abstract one: namely, that they all, in one way or another, deal with social phenomena. They are unified neither in their object nor in their methods.[1]

Adorno stressed the lack of homogeneity in sociology, and he discussed some of the different kinds of sociology in detail, but he also developed a general argument which delineates what counts as reified sociology:

> For sociology has a double character: as the subject of all knowledge, precisely as society, the bearer of logical universality, it is at the same time the object. Society is subjective because it refers to the men who form it. Its principle of organization refers to subjective conscious-ness . . . Society is objective because of its underlying structure, because its own subjectivity is not transparent to it, because it has no total subject and because its organization prevents the formation of one. This double character alters the relation of social scientific cognition to its object, but positivist sociology [non-dialectical or non-critical sociology] does not perceive this. It treats society as if it were an object which can be defined from the outside even though it is potentially a self-determining subject. Such sociology thereby makes into an object that which causes objectification and by which objectification may be explained. This substitution of society as subject by society as object constitutes the reified consciousness of sociology.[2]

Adorno does not merely propose that it follows from the double nature of society as subject and as object of knowledge that any sociology which operates solely on the basis of society as object, takes what is, in effect, a determining process to be a predetermined object. The thesis that the object is not transparent to subjectivity is a thesis about a specific society, capitalism, whose particular objectivity and subjectivity are structured by the production of value in exchange. The theory of value which explains the underlying law of capitalist society explains too how sociology fails to see itself at work in the object which it cognises. For such sociology describes the appearance of society correctly. It is incorrect in attributing the properties which it classifies to society as if they were natural and invariant properties instead of examining the processes of their formation. It is on the basis of a theory of change in the production of value in exchange that Adorno sought to base his theory of change in social organisation and the individual.

Adorno judged that the 'intrinsic tension'[3] of sociology is between

> . . . the philosophical idea, without which sociology is unable to apprehend its object, society, and the empirical determination of fact, without whose resistance to wild ideas and mythology, thought is condemned to impotence in society. . . .[4]

Adorno means at least four things by the proposition that 'society' is a philosophical idea, but they involve only differences of emphasis: first, that the concept 'society' is one which is not identical with its object and which therefore requires non-identity thinking in order to examine it; secondly, that a correct view of the mediation between subject and object is needed; thirdly, that these notions cannot be translated, *tout court*, into empirical terms because, fourthly, they depend on a notion of totality and 'a view of the totality is necessarily philosophical'.[5] The concept of 'totality' occurs a lot in Adorno's writings on sociology. It adds little or nothing, however, to the theory of value (reification) and to the theory of identity and non-identity thinking. It is simply another way of stating the basic characteristic of non-identity thinking. The critical perspective of totality 'seeks to save or helps to bring forth what does not obey the totality, what contradicts it or what first forms itself as the potential of individuation which does not yet exist',[6] that is, to perceive the mediation of the individual by the totality (or, of the appearance by the essence) is to perceive how the existence of individuals, or the façade of society, does not fulfil its concept, how unequal things are made equal by the prevailing form of commodity exchange and by the corresponding conceptual apparatus of that society.[7] 'Totality' in Adorno's usage is neither a 'comprehensive principle of explanation',[8] nor is it 'ontologized', made into primeval reality,[9] 'an arbitrary globalism'.[10] It should not be confused with his substantive thesis that capitalist society has become more total, that it increasingly controls and constrains individuals,[11] nor with the concomitant thesis that philosophy and sociology can no longer grasp the totality, neither the whole of existing society nor all its possibilities.

The concept of nature and the phrase 'the domination of nature' occur frequently in Adorno's criticism of sociology. 'Nature' is always a relational term for Adorno. He does not discuss any issues pertaining to the technological domination of the natural world,[12] nor the question of the relation of society to nature in a free society which has appeared in the work of some Marxist writers as the 'apotheosis' of nature.[13] Adorno does distinguish his approach from

> A science which hopes to extract and crystallize 'the social' by abstraction from the problems entailed in the relationship of social forces to the process of society's own self-preservation, [and which] is compelled to fetishize what remains as 'inter-personal' relations,[14]

by stressing 'the functions, and essential contradictions, of these relations in the human metabolic interchange with nature'.[15] But he is more interested in the history or formation of whatever a specific society regards as 'nature'. This is what he calls 'second nature'. In capitalist society, 'value [in exchange]' structures the appearance of things as 'in themselves', 'as nature'.[16] 'Nature' refers to the cultural forms which result from a specific mode of social interaction, while 'the domination of nature' refers to the mode of domination of men structured by the same underlying mechanism.[17] Adorno's concept of 'nature' is philosophical, because it is used to encapsulate the perspective of the transmutation of historical processes of formation into 'apparent' nature. It is also, notoriously, a systematically ambiguous notion, and Adorno exploits its ambiguities:

> Mankind commits more of a sacrilege by permitting its claim to supremacy to repress all thought of its nature as a species [*Naturwesen*], and by thus perpetuating the blind spontaneity of nature [*Naturwüchsigkeit*], than by reminding itself that it is a part of nature [*Naturhaftigkeit*]. 'Sociology is not a cultural science [*Geisteswissenschaft*]'.* To the extent that the hardening [*sic*] of society reduces men increasingly to objects and transforms this condition into a 'second nature [*zweite Natur*]', methods which testify to this are not sacrilegious. The unfreedom of the methods bear silent witness to the unfreedom that prevails in reality.[18]

Adorno turns a point about different methods into a point about different objects. A sociology which considers the methods of natural science inappropriate for the study of society will proceed differently from one which considers the methods of natural science appropriate. He then moves from the idea of treating man, according to the methods of natural science (as 'a piece of nature [*ein Stück Natur*]'[19]) to a substantive theory of man as a species in a Marxian sense. 'Perpetuating the blind spontaneity [or growth] of nature' refers to the underlying processes of production and reproduction by which a society maintains itself, and which may make a specific social formation appear to be 'a piece of nature', 'second nature'. These processes would be more fully obscured by a sociology which opts for an interpretative approach than by a 'naturalistic' sociology, in spite of the latter's limitations. *Geisteswissenschaft*, which Adorno is here attacking, may refer to an object of study or to a method of study.

Adorno's criticism of sociology and the empirical sociology which he conducted or to which he contributed do not exhaust his sociological writings. The justification for discussing them together is that Adorno's criticism of empirical social research can best be understood if compared with the kind of empirical sociology which he devised himself or with other people, and, conversely, this empirical work can best be understood in the light of Adorno's criticism of 'conventional' social research. Adorno's criticism of theoretical sociology and of empirical social research is collected in Volume 8 of the collected works. His empirical work on authoritarianism, on Fascist agitators, and on astrology, is contained in the two parts of Volume 9, but the radio research which he conducted under the auspices of the Princeton Radio Research Project when he first arrived in the United States (1938–9) and which so greatly coloured his subsequent opinions about social research is not included in either of these volumes.[20] The essays on sociological theory deal with three sorts of issues: topical controversies in sociology, for example, social conflict, the individual and organisation; the interpretation of Freudian theory for sociology; and empirical social research and questions of objectivity in social science.[21]

These articles were mostly written to introduce or summarise conferences, as radio broadcasts, as introductions to books containing articles by various authors, and as contributions to polemics. They are short and slight, and are among Adorno's stylistically least accomplished or composed pieces, although they often depend on stylistic devices, such as chiasmus, to establish their seminal point. However, this part of Adorno's work is consistent with the rest of his thinking and it does add to the ideas which are crucial throughout his work, even if not as much as it might. Adorno considered it more important to practise his kind of sociology in the realms of music and literature than to criticise current sociology. He paid particular attention to the sociology practised in Germany in the fifties and was well informed on this and on the sociology which he had encountered in the United States. Most of his articles criticising sociology were written in the fifties. In the sixties he was increasingly preoccupied with major projects such as *Negative Dialectic*, and, especially in the mid- and late sixties, with his work on aesthetic theory. Tiedemann maintains that Adorno's writing on sociology in the sixties was a 'distraction' from the latter's main work, although welcomed by Adorno as a 'healthy corrective'.[22] The distracted but passionate inspiration of this work is evident.

It is thus regrettable that this part of Adorno's work has received the most widespread attention in Germany as part of a *Positivismusstreit* (dispute over Positivism), as a result of the controversies arising out of the conference on the logic of the social sciences which was held by the German Sociological Association in Tübingen in 1961 and of the volume published much later (1969) which collected and republished polemical articles written in response to the conference.[23] It looks as if similar attention may be paid to the English translation of this volume.[24] For even within his criticism of sociology, Adorno was not most interested in engaging with positivist philosophy of social science, and the lack of any sustained engagement with positivist epistemology in his criticism of latter-day philosophy is striking too. His contribution to the book consists of one essay on empirical social research, and one on the logic of the social sciences and the infamous 'Introduction'. They are all shot through with the peculiar features of Adorno's thought. These features receive their best treatment in *Negative Dialectic*, and that text can be used to throw

light on the cryptic and elliptical references to identity and non-identity
thinking and to reification which abound in the articles by Adorno which
appear in the book. The criticism of empirical social research is best
understood in terms of Adorno's own ambitions in empirical sociology
and in relation to his aim to develop a theory of the relation between the
individual and society.

Durkheim and Weber

Adorno construes the major methodological precepts of the sociology of
Durkheim and of Weber as an antinomy, and argues, by the use of
chiasmus, that the antinomy arises from the structure of society.[25] His
interpretation of these precepts is one-sided and tendentious, and
depends on transcribing the relevant concepts in Durkheim's and in
Weber's work into concepts of reason (*Vernunft*). Unlike other neo-
Marxist critiques of Weber's sociology, Adorno does not indict Weber's
notion of goal-rationality for being an apology for the instrumentality of
capitalist society.[26] Instead he takes Weber's definition of sociological
inquiry at the beginning of *Economy and Society*, as the interpretation of
subjectively meaningful social action (*Verstehen*) to be a substantive and
prescriptive thesis that social action should be intelligible as the
realisation of men's will, as rational. Weber's instruction to unpack social
institutions so as to reveal the individual's orientation to them is not
merely a methodological device but a theory of what constitutes
autonomy.[27] Men are free and social institutions are rational to the extent
that they express men's will and are understood to do so, to the extent that
they are transparent. In a society in which social relations between men
are determined by the production of value in exchange, the social
institutions which arise cannot be intelligible in the sense specified
because of commodity fetishism.[28]

Durkheim's definition of social facts as external constraint in *The Rules
of Sociological Method*, and of the realm of sociological inquiry as starting
from such facts, is construed by Adorno not merely as a methodological
device, but as a substantive thesis, the converse of Weber's, that social
institutions are not intelligible to men because they do not represent
men's will and are thus 'impenetrable [*sic*]' by their reason.[29] Durkheim
prescribes that the realm of men's heteronomy should be the concern of
sociology. He recognises correctly that men are not free and that social
institutions are not transparent, but he does not interpret this as arising
from the features of a particular kind of society.

Durkheim's rule that one should treat social facts as things [renounces]
in principle understanding them. He was convinced that society meets

each individual primarily as that which is not identical, as 'coercion'. To that extent reflection on society would begin where intelligibility [or comprehensibility, *Verstehbarkeit*] ends. The method of natural science defended by Durkheim registers the . . . 'second nature' into which society congeals against its living members. This antithesis to Weber is as one-sided as the latter's thesis [that society is comprehensible]: it takes comfort in incomprehensibility as much as Weber takes comfort in comprehensibility. Instead incomprehensibility should be comprehended, which would be to derive relationships which have grown independent and impenetrable . . . from the relations between men.[30]

Since social action in such a society is not the expression of the free individual nor intelligible as such, society is not identical 'with the individual', that is, not rationally identical with the concept of the individual. Adorno judges that Weber's position is correct but unrealistic, given the nature of capitalist society, while Durkheim correctly describes the appearance of society, but sanctions that *status quo*, 'society as a mechanism of collective constraint'.[31] This is partly because at this level of primary methodological structures, neither Durkheim nor Weber grant any role to theory. Weber emphasised *Verstehen*, the interpretation of social action by the reconstruction of ends-means ideal-types, but society cannot be explained by 'singular acts or by ideal-type constructs, with no regard for the totality of society from which the phenomena to be understood alone receive meaning'.[32] Durkheim's emphasis on social facts, and on their collation and comparison, prevents him from developing any theory which would explain those facts, their formation and the mechanism of coercion.[33]

Where the question of value judgements in sociology is concerned, the positions of Durkheim and of Weber are also antinomical, although on this issue they reverse positions:[34] that is, Durkheim comes closer to a substantive notion of rationality. Any sociology which separates judgements of fact from judgements of value is bound to be inconsistent. Adorno's point is not that these judgements are inseparable. It is that the very question of their separability or inseparability is illegitimate. This follows from the basic characteristic in identity thinking: 'The claim to truth and the rejection of untruth of the simple logical judgement is already constituted in the procedure which the cliché allots to values separate from their base'.[35] Non-identity thinking is not a separable form of evaluation but 'a concrete process of cognition where what is decided by the confrontation of the thing with what it claims to be according to its concept, is thus decided by immanent criticism'.[36] Weber had a notion of reason (*Vernunft*) to the extent that he stressed that social action should be intelligible, and he also recognised the necessarily subjective component of objectivity in cognition. It was thus inconsistent of him even to raise the question of values, since these precepts imply a substantive position that makes such an issue irrelevant.[37] In spite of Durkheim's emphasis on facts and his lack of any notion of the social subject, he believed that 'There are not two ways of thinking and judging, one for establishing existence and one for its estimation'.[38] This position is possible for Durkheim because of the peculiar nature of his positivism, the stress on social facts which goes together with 'the normative hypostasis of the collective mind'.[39] Durkheim raises the question of value judgements, but he interprets it as a question of ideals and their corresponding value systems.[40] He specifically rejects a Kantian separation of the ideal and the real.[41] The desire and the will for an ideal to be real are intrinsic to the ideal: 'Concepts are equally constructions of the mind and consequently ideals . . . all judgements bring ideals into play. There cannot be more than one faculty of judgement'.[42] Durkheim's position on this issue is nearer to a notion of substantive reason than Weber's, that is, to the view that men realise and recognise themselves freely in social institutions and social life. For Durkheim 'takes over collectively sanctioned values, equates their collectivity with their objectivity, and thereby dispenses with the question of their moral possibility.'[43]

Durkheim's sociology, nevertheless, is riddled with the antinomies which arise when the attempt is made to reconcile a positivist notion of 'social facts' as the moral norms of a given society, with an idealist notion of a collective consciousness which transcends the consciousness of individuals.[44] For Durkheim's central concepts are designed in a way which prevents examination of processes of social formation and of any but the simplest relation between consciousness and social reality, and which preclude any notion of the individual or subject. On the one hand, Durkheim stipulates that the collective consciousness cannot be reduced to the sum of individual consciousnesses or to the statistical average, yet on the other, he also depends on the statistical average as an indicator of the collective consciousness.[45] He has no way of resolving this discrepancy because he has limited himself to registering the moral facts of society and to affirming the objectivity of the totality which they form: '[Durkheim's theory] moves the objectivity of the collective consciousness into the place of the objectivity of the underlying social life processes',[46] and thus can make no distinction between what a society appears to be and what it really is, nor, therefore, can he examine the processes of mediation by which the totality comes to appear to the individual or subject to be the essence of society. Adorno is interested in those propositions of Durkheim which indicate a critical dimension to the latter's notion of collective consciousness, but which he cannot sustain. For example, Durkheim considers the possibility of innovation by the individual in changing the morality of society and concludes that 'in any instance, we cannot aspire to a morality other than that which is related to the state of our society',[47] although

> the individual may escape the existing rules of society so long as he desires society as it is and not as it appears to itself . . . and not to justify an historically outmoded state . . . The principle of opposition is thus the same as that of conformity.[48]

Durkheim reaches this position by 'opposing to the collectivity . . . the collectivity itself, one, however, more or less conscious of itself'.[49] But Durkheim has no way of conceptualising a collectivity 'more or less conscious of itself'. The collective mind can only be a factual and static one for Durkheim, not one which can undergo any process of 'becoming more conscious of itself'.[50] This is partly because of the insufficiency of the kind of relationship which Durkheim posits between the individual and society. Increasing self-consciousness could only come about via the consciousness of individuals, but Durkheim will concede no such possibility.[51] Durkheim 'reifies the collective mind', by which Adorno means that he makes it into a notion of a social subject *sui generis*, in-itself.[52] Durkheim cannot develop a theory of the mediation of the individual and the collective consciousness for fear of abandoning the factual perspective. He thus personifies the collective mind 'which thinks, feels, wills',[53] and then simply equates the universality (the ideal humanity) of the collectivity with the universality of the individual, which is distinguished from the individual's 'empirical, sensuous' being.[54] He is unable to develop any more complex perspective of the mediation between the collectivity and the individual which would not depend on this egregious dichotomy, nor on such a simplistic equation.

Adorno maintains that in *The Division of Labour in Society* (1893), Durkheim did have a notion of social life-processes and that he derived civilisation from the struggle for existence and examined the problems of different kinds of social cohesion arising out of different forms of the division of labour. However, he did not develop, nor did he sustain this insight into historically different kinds of society, nor into the division of labour as a process underlying the formation of social institutions and which has to be continuously maintained. Instead he concentrates in his later work, *The Elementary Forms of the Religious Life* (1915), on the forms of collective consciousness and on social institutions. He did not treat them historically but as primeval phenomena (*Urphänomenen*), and he became increasingly preoccupied with primitive relations as prototypical for all social relations, as the 'elementary forms'.[55] Thus

> The developed [*gewordenen*], overpowering relations, . . . 'second nature', becomes first nature to him; history becomes what it certainly

also is, natural history, although [to him] a history of the mind.[56]

Social relations are then posited by Durkheim as invariant, and natural, regardless of whether a given society is based on a simple or an advanced division of labour. This approach is particularly inadequate for analysing a society based on commodity exchange, since it attributes inherent properties to institutions which those institutions only possess because of the specific mode of production. This approach thus makes 'second nature', that is, institutions which arise from the production of value in exchange, into 'first nature', that is, makes them appear to be institutions which would exist in a society which only produced use-values. Durkheim furthermore turns 'natural history', the formation of social relations by the underlying mode of production in any historically specific society, into the story of the collective consciousness ('the mind').

Adorno was interested in Durkheim's work because, *prima facie*, many of their positions were similar. But Durkheim's original commitment to positivist methodology and to granting sociology an unique object in relation to other social sciences, resulted in a sociology which had weak conceptual poles and which was incapable of generating theories to examine the social relations structuring the societies which Durkheim observed.

Class and Organisation

The results of Adorno's discussions of sociological theories of class and organisation are elusive, and *prima facie*, not very original. Marx's theory of class provided a theory of the appearance or early formation of the proletariat, but not an adequate theory of the later integration of the proletariat into capitalist society. Adorno sought to examine the formation of the 'masses' in 'post-individualistic', 'post-market' society,[57] but he also shied away from theories of 'mass society' and sought to develop a relational notion of the masses, namely, the relation between the mode of domination and the formation of the individual. Adorno's fusing of a theory of reification and a theory of domination or mode of organisation has little in common with Lukács' comparisons between the alienation of industrial work and the alienation of bureaucratic work, or between the formal rationality demanded by the capitalist economy and that demanded by legal-rational bureaucracy.[58] In spite of Adorno's stress on organisation rather than on class, his theory has even less in common with Dahrendorf's theory of the central importance of relations of authority for the explanation of class cohesion and class conflict in capitalist society.[59] Adorno does not raise the question of the legitimacy of a mode of domination, or the question of bureaucracy as a legal and rational mode of organisation. Production has become an end in itself, that is, the production of value in exchange, not value for use. Adorno states that the relations of production predominate over the forces of production, and that they are incapable of generating revolutionary social change.[60] He means that the production of value in exchange is still the underlying mechanism of society, but in a society in which there is no real market, the result is an impersonal, anonymous mode of domination, and no distinction can really be maintained between forces and relations of production.[61] He produced no theory of science and technology as new forms of control as Marcuse has done,[62] nor any theory of the changed role of political power as Habermas has done.[63] He was concerned to dissolve notions of agency, while retaining the notion of a mode of production and used Freudian theory to accomplish this.

Adorno discussed Marx's concept of class in an unpublished essay which he wrote in 1942.[64] Marx's concept of class only ever convincingly designated a formal or 'negative' unity of function.[65] Just as the idea of the equal right and the equal chance of all to compete in the market was a fiction, so is the idea of the bourgeois or proletarian class as a real unity arising out of the equal position shared by the owners of the means of production, or by the sellers of labour-power.[66] Real unity within, for example, the bourgeois class, can only arise out of a relation of domination within the class:

> . . . the law of equal exchange and its legal and political forms of reflection . . . is the contract which silently rules the relation between the kernel of the class and its majority, the bourgeois vassals, in the sense of relations of power.[67]

Adorno does not specify the 'kernel' but elaborates this 'double character of [the bourgeois] class'.[68] On the one hand, its character consists of the 'negative' unity which has the function of oppressing the proletariat as well as the control of its own class. On the other hand it is a real unity in Marx's sense as long as the class is actively presenting its particular interests as the interests of the whole society. The unity is 'negative' in the sense that it hides the privileges of the rulers within the dominant class, and unites the proletariat only by oppressing its members. This is to affirm that the specific mode of production determines the basic class distinction but in a formal rather than a substantive way. In the early stages of the development of capitalist society unity within the bourgeois class and within the proletarian class is visible, the potential lack of unity latent. In late or monopoly capitalism, the lack of real unity between members of the same class is visible, but the underlying formal unity is not visible.[69] In other words, the mode of production still determines the central relation between oppressor and oppressed, but the majority of men are not able to experience themselves as a class. Adorno enlarges this

point by discussing Marx's prediction of the increasing impoverishment
of the masses:

> The prognosis of the theory of the few property owners and the
> overwhelming mass of propertyless is fulfilled, but instead of this
> resulting in the essence of class society becoming obvious, the essence
> has been mystified by mass society in which class society terminates.[70]

Adorno rejects a revisionist interpretation of the theory of increasing
impoverishment, for example, that 'relative impoverishment' persists
between classes.[71] He proposes that as long as 'liberalism' continued, by
which he seems to mean competition between workers in the market for
labour, Marx's prediction was correct.[72] The price paid to labour would
fall as long as the market system operated anonymously and without the
conscious direction of the bourgeoisie. Instead, domination has been
exercised outside the realm of the economy in order to incorporate the
proletariat into the system by transferring a part of monopoly profits.
Everyone has been 'impoverished' by being subject to this incorpor-
ation.[73] Having rejected a revisionist interpretation of Marx's theory, it
is odd that Adorno opts for such a figurative one. But Adorno suggests
that Marx's theory of alienation provided insight into the social basis of
the likely impotence of the proletariat.[74] The theory of the brutalising of
the worker by the nature of work, and of his separation from the
mechanised work process, made highly problematic the question of how
such a worker would become capable of political action which would
demand insight into the whole organisation of production and also
extreme self-sacrifice.[75] Marx quite rightly did not produce a psychology
of the worker and, in his critique of political economy, he rejected the
very notion of 'individuality' on which any psychology could be based.
The increased division of labour and the diminished role of the market
brutalises the worker less, but the social organisation of production is no
more intelligible than it was: 'This impotence results in revolution as little
as naked poverty did before'.[76] Adorno does not say that the increase in
the division of labour results in the splitting of the function of the
capitalist, for example, the separation of ownership and control, and of
the function of wage-labour, for example, an increase in white-collar
work. He is saying that the increasing concentration of capital has made
everyone into a function of capital.

Several points are unclear in this essay. The change from a market
economy to monopoly, in a society which is based on the production of
value in exchange, is ambiguous. Competition as 'free' competition in the
market was always an illusion; thus the nature of the change is not
specified, partly because Adorno only alludes to the theory of value as a
distinction between use-value and exchange-value and did not mobilise

any more of Marx's theory. Adorno depicts a change in domination which consists in a change from an earlier stage of capitalist society in which the agent of domination is conceivable and the class of dominators identifiable, to a later stage in which the agent of domination is not identifiable, and domination is only conceivable as a theory of the formation of the individual, not as a relation between classes. He accomplishes this by a theory which makes the agent of domination less easily identifiable than at the earlier stage!

In an essay on social conflict,[77] Adorno enlarges the notion of 'the double relation of the proletariat to bourgeois society',[78] to explain how it was reasonable to predict social conflict between classes in the early stages of the formation of the industrial proletariat, but how the early situation also contained the germ of the subsequent development which has not led to overt class conflict. The proletariat was recruited from 'exterritorials',[79] peasant farmers and craftsmen, who were objects of exploitation and never autonomous subjects of the total social process of capitalism: '[The proletariat] existed outside the concept of a society which sought to be free and emancipated'.[80] On the other hand, the proletariat were also, 'as the producers [productive labour] of social wealth, immanent to society, the epitome of its productive forces'.[81] This relation of labour to capital has been the crucial one. The influence of capital expanded into the spheres of mind and public opinion 'and always occupied the consciousness and unconsciousness of the fourth estate'.[82] Class consciousness has to be created, as Marx and many later Marxists realise. The objective basis of class antagonism has not disappeared, but the basis on which such antagonism would erupt has been neutralised and displaced.[83] Marx's prediction that social conflict would arise as the conflict of interests between classes became evident to the proletariat in the work place, presupposes that social relations would become more intelligible or transparent in the work place, in spite of commodity fetishism which distorts the appearance of social relations and makes them less, not more transparent. The increasing complexity of the division of labour makes individuals, whether workers or managers, into 'personifications, phantoms'[84] of capitalism, so that individuals and the social relations between them become more abstract and unintelligible. Social conflict is displaced to the relations between these abstract individuals, and concerns 'socially marginal phenomena'.[85]

In an essay on the individual and organisation,[86] Adorno says that organisation cannot be examined separately from the whole social process but nevertheless offers a definition of organisation as a 'consciously created association, oriented to a controlled goal . . . goal rationality is essential'.[87] He gives this definition a substantive twist by stressing the way organisation makes people into tools for the realisation of its own goals so that human relations are always mediated by the predetermined goal. It cannot, therefore, be 'consciously created', or, at least, not by those who are subjected to it. This, he affirms, is reification, that is, social relations between men are expressed as a goal which appears to exist for its own sake, while the underlying processes which give rise to these relations is neglected. The spread of organisation is interpreted as a spread in this kind of social relation, not as the spread of bureaucratic organisation as particularly suited to the goal-means rationality of capitalist society. Adorno confirms this by rejecting the thesis that the spread of organisation to all spheres of society is unavoidable. He interprets this thesis of the increase in bureaucracy as a symptom of what needs to be examined, as 'a scapegoat'[88] for the increase in economic and social integration, and as another expression of our inability to penetrate the anonymity of our society. Similarly, he rejects the thesis that 'the present state of organization . . . threatens men',[89] since it implies that there could be a notion of man apart from the formation of men by organisation. Adorno suggests that we abandon the traditional concept of the individual as, even in some circumscribed sense, autonomous. The increased fragmentation of the division of labour has not only continued to make men into parts of the machinery of capitalism but has induced them to become tools to themselves, to recognise and treat themselves as means rather than as ends.[90] This is what Adorno seems to mean by 'the extension of organization' but his use of the concept of organisation is extremely vague. It does not refer specifically to the work process, nor to the principles of bureaucracy. He intends it to draw attention to the problem of how to conceive of the individual in late capitalist society. He says:

> There is too little organisation where organisation should be necessary, in the forming of the conditions of material life and the relations between men depending on them, and too much organisation in the private sphere in which consciousness is formed.[91]

This proposition displays the equivocation in Adorno's discussion of organisation. In the first clause, organisation alludes to a bureaucratic ideal-type, in the last clause, to the social processes which form the individual. Adorno's concept of organisation is 'overdimensional',[92] as he himself assesses 'organization'.

These essays are marked by auxesis, and by the equivocal use of their key notions, such as domination, organisation. Adorno partly justifies this by using Benjamin's idea of 'constellation'.[93] To examine something by a 'constellation' means to juxtapose a cluster of related words or con-notations which characterise the object of investigation without implying that the concepts used are identical with their objects. Adorno cites Weber's use of ideal-types, not as mere methodological devices, but as a series of approximate presentations of an object which is not directly accessible . . . . . . by gathering concepts round the central one that is sought [for example, capitalism], they [ideal-types] attempt to express what that concept aims at, not to circumscribe it to operative ends'.[94] This is another way in which Adorno applies his own theses to his own endeavour:

> . . . the capitalist system's increasingly integrative trend, the fact that its elements entwine into a more and more total context of functions, is precisely what makes the old question about the cause – as opposed to the constellation – more and more precarious.[95]

'The old question about the cause' might be the question of the origin of capitalism, of its basic mechanism – the production of commodities – and of change in the relation between class consciousness and class conflict. To inquire instead into the 'constellation' which characterises latter-day capitalism might be to examine the set of conditions constituted by the same basic mechanism, by the formation of individuals to fit a highly complex division of labour, yet without positing class consciousness and without any theory predicting change.

Theory of the Individual

Adorno was one of the earliest writers to recognise the importance of psychoanalytic theory for certain philosophical problems and for sociological analysis. In his original *Habilitation*, on which he worked from 1924 – 7 but which he withdrew before it was examined,[96] he argued that psychoanalysis offered a theory which resolved the Kantian paralogism between the transcendental theory of the soul (*die Seele*, the psyche) and empirical psychology.[97] It answered the question of how, since the 'unconscious' is not an empirical notion, there can be an empirical science of the unconscious.[98] This interest in psychoanalysis predated Adorno's involvement with Marxism. However, he took up precisely this question of the empirical potential of psychoanalysis when he later conducted empirical sociological research within the aims and assumptions of critical theory.

Adorno always defended a strong, orthodox interpretation of Freud, against the later Freud himself, against the neo-Freudian revisionists, and against Talcott Parsons. He based his interpretation of Freud on the latter's earlier works not on his later, more explicitly socio-cultural works. Adorno circumvented the issue of whether Freudian theory analyses capitalist society specifically as patriarchal society, or whether it presupposes features of a specific society and generalises them to provide a general theory of society. Adorno claimed that Freudian theory provided concepts whose analytical power went a long way in uncovering the processes of socio-psychological formation in capitalist society, while in other respects, the theory presupposed features of the society which it sought to examine. He defended his interpretation of Freudian theory against the early revisions of it by psychologists who sought to give the theory a greater sociological content, but who, in his view, merely reduced the impact of Freudian concepts for any sociological analysis. He also defended it against Parsons' interpretation of the division between psychology and sociology and he criticised Parsons' adaptation of Freudian ideas for sociological analysis too.

Adorno used Freudian theory to illuminate two questions: first, how people come to accept any 'ideology which is contrary to their rational interests but adapted to reality',[99] for example, Fascist ideology. 'Contrary to their rational interests' means that the ideology in question, for example, plays on people's unconscious mechanisms and hence is not fully intelligible to them;[100] 'adapted to reality' means that such behaviour may be nevertheless goal-rational, that is, oriented to predetermined and prevalent social goals.[101] This question is inseparable from the other more general one of the change in the socio-psychological formation of the individual, 'the loss of autonomy', which Adorno sought to define sociologically. The definition of this 'loss' depends on a theory of autonomy. Freudian theory does not posit the individual as existing in himself, but conceives of the development of the so-called autonomous individual as an achievement, and thus offers a cogent basis for a theory of 'loss of autonomy' which does not idealise what counts as autonomy in the first place.

Adorno criticised ostensibly 'realistic' and 'sociological' revisions of Freudian theory,[102] especially Karen Horney's *New Ways in Psycho-analysis*.[103] Horney's basic contention is that 'character' is not formed by early erotic, inter-familial conflict but by the 'pressure of culture'.[104] Such a theory of the unification of culture and the psychology of the individual is not able to demonstrate the mechanism of unification, while a radical interpretation of psychoanalytic theory based on a theory of the erotic conflicts involved in the formation of the individual can show how 'the social principle of domination coincides with the psychological principle of the repression of drives'.[105] The revisionist theoretical neglect of sexuality thus amounts to a particular hostility to the complexity theory, to the distinction between essence and appearance, and thereby robs psychoanalysis of its critical impulse.[106] Adorno means that the revisionists abandon the complex relations between psychic entities postulated by Freud. As a result they establish simplistic correlations between the individual and society instead of examining processes which would involve using the more rigorous set of distinctions. For example, Horney diagnoses the cause of neuroticism in Western civilisation as the importance given to competition between individuals.[107] Adorno appeals instead to the loss of autonomy and spontaneity which the individual suffers owing to the reduction of competition. Competition, or lack of it, cannot be the basis of a theoretical explanation in any case because it has always been a phenomenon of the façade of capitalist society.[108]

Adorno finds the obverse, Parsons' attempt to make use of psychoanalysis in his sociology, equally inadequate. First, Parsons understood the province of sociology, namely 'the institutional structure'[109] of society, and the province of psychology, namely, 'the personality structure'[110] to be different, because of the different concerns of the disciplines in question and their relatively immature state.[111] Adorno derives the state of the disciplines from the state of society. For the realm of the psychological is increasingly split from the realm of the sociological, which means, loosely, that what is purely personal in the individual is diminished in relation to what is socialised, in other terms, the id, as the realm of drives, is increasingly governed by the ego:

> For what characterized the specifically social dimension is emancipation from psychology through the interpolation of abstract determination between people, principally the exchange of equivalents, and through the hegemony of a rational faculty [the ego] modelled on such abstractions from human psychology.[112]

Hence no psychological explanation can in principle be given for what does not derive from the individual psyche, and any science which based itself on the 'psychological' as such would have no object. Individual behaviour is commensurable because 'the actual process of socialization is based on the fact that as economic subjects they [individuals] do not relate to each other at all immediately but act according to the dictates of exchange value'.[113]

Parsons does use some psychoanalytical concepts 'at the level of abstraction' which he deems necessary for sociological analysis.[114] *Ex hypothesi*, he is thus assuming that there is no conflict between the 'levels' of the psychological and the sociological.[115] He employs the concept of the superego without the concept of repression. It is thus impossible to analyse the process of formation which the concepts were designed to analyse or to discern any lack of social integration or the presence of any kind of social conflict:

> According to Parsons, the integration of society . . . coincides with the schemata of the 'average superego'. This dove-tailing of the individual and the social system is elevated to the status of a norm without any investigation of the place both these 'measures' occupy in the overall social process and, above all, of the origin of the 'average superego' and its claim to normative validity . . .[116]

Adorno uses Freud's model of the psychology of the ego to explain the 'loss of individual autonomy' and to explain how the individual adjusts to social reality in a way which makes his action less intelligible to himself.[117] The model of the development of the autonomous ego is that the (male) child fears and hates his father, but identifies with him and therefore redirects this aggression against himself, takes over the role of the father, and thereby becomes autonomous. If the child, for some reason, does not aspire to become the father, he may continue to fear and submit to authority without introjecting it, identifying with it in such a way that it remains external to him, 'more powerful and less internalized',[118] and an autonomous ego will not be formed. This kind of development might occur, for example, if the father is experienced by the child as impotent but authoritarian, as might be the case in a society with a highly complex division of labour, but with a high degree of uniformity in the work process, and a low degree of market competition.

The concept of the ego is twofold: it is supposed to arrest the play of inner forces ('drives') and test them against outer reality.[119] It is thus 'psychic' and 'extrapsychic', 'a quantum of libido and the representative of outside reality'.[120] Adorno does not discuss the notion of the superego, but shows how the complex operations of the ego makes the question of what counts as social integration problematic. He does this by comparing the notions of ego and id with the notions of conscious and unconscious.[121] The ego is both, *qua* consciousness, the opposite of repression, and, *qua* unconsciousness, the repressive agency itself.[122] To be able to assert itself in reality, the ego has to understand reality and act consciously,[123] that is, internalise prohibitions and identify with them. Instead, Adorno claims, many of the renunciations are not intelligible to the ego,[124] that is, the ego does not identify with and internalise the prohibitions, but simply sets them up in the unconscious and thus remains largely confined to the unconscious, that is, to the heteronomous rule of the unconscious.

> The ego's cognitive activity, performed in the interest of self-preservation, has to be constantly reversed, and self-awareness forgone, in the interest of self-preservation.[125]

Freud himself showed that the renunciation demanded of the individual is not rewarded by such compensation as would on conscious grounds alone justify it,[126] and also that the ego is predisposed for its dual role, as conscious and unconscious.[127] Adorno is emphasising that situation in which the ego develops its potential for differentiation in relation to the id to the minimal extent and regresses to what Freud calls 'ego-libido',[128] for example, the individual may merely submit to external authority in order to satisfy the desire for instinctual gratifications with as little interference as possible. In his sociology Adorno examined 'the currently prevalent forms of regression'.¹²⁹ These were, firstly, fascism, as the prototype of those kinds of domination which do not give rise to the kind of identification which results in the development of a strong ego, but in this case, to narcissistic identification,¹³⁰ and, secondly, the 'culture industry', as the extension of the principle of exchange value into the organisation of leisure which creates and feeds the desire for instinctual gratification.

Adorno's engagement with psychoanalytic theory remains one-sided. Psychoanalytic theory provided the way to examine the mediation between the individual and society, an explication of the view that 'the individual is at the same time, universal and particular',¹³¹ without diminishing the reality of either the individual or society. He taxed both philosophies and sociologies for failing to do this. Heidegger, for example, did not allow adequately for the mediation of men by social institutions but established a theory of 'man' (*Dasein*) as such; while Durkheim, for example, concentrated on the reality of social institutions to the detriment of any theory of how they mediate the individual. Yet Adorno's emphasis on the formation or deformation of the individual did replace any further definition of the macro-factor, the form of domination. He might at least have detailed the mechanisms by which power has become diffuse but omnipotent, and how that is related to change in the organisation of production. Ideology, domination, and reification are simply equated with each other, and the individual is not satisfactorily reinserted into the socio-political context.

Sociology and Empirical Research

Adorno originally defined 'positivist' epistemology in social science as any mode of cognition which grants theoretical priority to 'what is at hand, what is given as fact'.¹³² In response to Karl Popper's objection to this as a designation of his position, Adorno redefined the issue as 'scientism', by which he meant any epistemology of social science which grants priority to its own cognitive procedures.¹³³ He argued that any philosophy of social science which founds its criterion of validity on the internal consistency of a set of theoretical propositions, or on the falsifiability of hypotheses will be inherently contradictory, and that this arises from the inability of such philosophy to apprehend the social constitution of the cognitive values espoused. He discussed Popper's version of 'scientism' in two articles, but wrote about empirical social research in at least seven pieces.¹³⁴ Empirical social research is narrowly defined and not placed in the context of an empirical sociology which might use empirical methods to examine hypotheses or to quantify over theoretical terms. This is partly because, for Adorno, such issues belong to the province of the 'scientistic' *interpretation* of empirical methods. It is also because he sought to develop a sociology which would use empirical methods, although not in a way which would aim to confirm or disconfirm hypotheses or theories by examining relations posited to hold between observables under specified conditions. Several traditions of empirical social research are relevant to Adorno's ambition. They are: the pre-Second World War tradition in Germany; the Frankfurt School tradition; the development of social research in America in the 1930s and 40s; and the development of empirical sociology in Germany after the war in the fifties.

The use of empirical research techniques predated the development of sociology in Germany.[135] As early as the late eighteenth century, social statistics was a substantive discipline which collected data on social and economic change.[136] By comparison, according to Adorno, the later attempts to adapt empirical research to the demands of the ideal of natural science narrowed the purview of social research.[137] For only those facts selected for their relevance in establishing hypotheses were of interest, whereas previously *all* available information had been gathered. The Frankfurt School in the early thirties continued, in a sense, the earlier tradition. Horkheimer explained, in the first edition of the *Zeitschrift*, why the Institute was called the 'Institute for Social Research'.[138] One reason was that social research was not going to be used solely in the service of problems conceived according to the domain of one discipline, empirical sociology, but for the cognition of the whole of society, which might involve the realms of psychology, economics, and so on.[139] Conversely, no one method could produce conclusive results concerning any object of investigation, but the results of several methods, qualitative as well as quantitative, would need to be collated.[140] Above all, empirical methods were not going to be used to eliminate inconsistencies and contradictions in theory by confining their operations to examining only whatever could be easily transcribed into empirical terms.[141]

Adorno distinguished three causes which contributed to the great extension and development of empirical social research in the 1930s and 1940s: large industrial enterprises needed increasingly to use it in order to plan their markets; governments used it to manage their war effort; and the new forms of mass communications utilised it.[142] Adorno called this research 'market and opinion research'. Although 'market research' might inquire into psychological motivation, 'opinion research', was limited to ascertaining people's manifest beliefs.[143] Empirical research, considered more generally, might correlate the beliefs held by members of a group with objective facts, such as occupation and income. 'Beliefs' may be broken down into 'consciously-held beliefs'; 'attitudes'; that is, 'sedimented' modes of perception, reactions; and behaviour. These aspects may not be consistent in the case of any one individual.[144] Adorno lists a great many different techniques which may be used to investigate 'beliefs'.

Adorno insists that empirical research as described and the techniques listed, must be distinguished from 'theory',[145] reserving 'theory' to mean a commitment to a view of the production of value in exchange as the underlying process in society in relation to which all other phenomena are to be understood. He deplores the use of empirical research apart from such theory. However, he lists techniques for ascertaining beliefs, attitudes, and behaviour, including those which he used himself, in isolation from theory. In some of his other discussions of sociology and empirical research,[146] he persists in presenting empirical sociology as hostile to theory, and as confining itself to ascertaining opinions. He tends not to discuss sociology which has used empirical methods to investigate theories, for example, the sociology of class or the sociology of organisations, although he was well informed about such work.[147]

One of the origins of Adorno's argument is his experience on Paul Lazarsfeld's Princeton Radio Research Project.[148] The aim of this project 'was to try to determine eventually the role of radio in the lives of different types of listeners, the value of radio to people psychologically, and the various reasons why they like it'.[149] Adorno judged that the project

> . . . was concerned with the collection of data, which was supposed to benefit the planning departments in the field of the mass media, whether in industry itself or in cultural advisory boards and similar bodies.[150]

He defined the work as 'administrative research' since it was expressly stipulated in the project's charter 'that the investigations must be performed within the limits of the commercial radio system prevailing in the United States'.[151] Adorno took this to mean that ' . . . the system itself, its cultural and sociological consequences and its social and economic presuppositions were not to be analyzed'.[152] The research took as axiomatic 'to proceed from the subjects' reactions as if they were a primary and final source of sociological knowledge'.[153] Adorno later drew on the procedure of this project as a general model of empirical sociology. Sociology, according to this model, merely concerns itself with ascertaining 'reactions', independent of any corpus of theory and makes the individual its ultimate point of reference and explanation. Adorno opposed to the approach of the Princeton Project one which would

> . . . determine how far the subjective reactions of the persons studied are actually as spontaneous and direct as the subjects suppose; and how far not only the methods of dissemination and the power of suggestion of the apparatus, but also the objective implications of the material with which the listeners are confronted are involved. And, finally, it had still to be determined how far comprehensive social structure . . . came into play.[154]

He firmly asserted that 'the apparently primary, immediate reactions [are] insufficient as a basis for sociological knowledge because they [are] themselves conditioned'.[155] However, he conceded that 'motivation-analysis' provided a means for 'penetrating the pre-conditions of the subjective reactions through additional detailed, qualitative studies',[156] although he remained sceptical that such studies could 'really proceed from the opinions and reactions of individuals to the social structure and the social essence'.[157] It is striking that he did not advocate empirical investigation of the 'pre-conditions' themselves. In fact he remained convinced that 'the structures of the total society resist direct empirical treatment'.[158] He did devise complex theories about the radio system which impressed Lazarsfeld, but neither men were successful in translating the concept of 'fetish' into empirical terms.[159]

Lazarsfeld introduced the first issue of the 1941 *Zeitschrift*, in which several pieces of the Project were published, by trying to summarise the difference between 'administrative and critical communications research',[160] associating the latter with Adorno and the Institute for Social Research. He suggests that administrative research would observe people's daily habits and the effect of the media on their lives;[161] critical research might ask whether people's attitude to reality was profoundly changed by the media, how the media are controlled and organised, and how 'in their institutional set-up, is the trend toward centralization, standardization and promotional pressure expressed? In what form, however disguised, are they threatening human values?'[162] He breaks down the 'operation' of critical research into stages:

a) A theory about the prevailing trends toward a 'promotional culture' is introduced on the basis of general observations . . .

b) A special study of any phenomenon consists in determining how it expresses these prevailing trends . . . and contributes to reinforcing them.

c) The consequences of b) in stamping human personalities in modern, industrial society are brought to the foreground and scrutinized from the viewpoint of more or less explicit ideas of what endangers and what preserves the dignity, freedom and values of human beings . . .[163]

This summary, although intended to be sympathetic, shows how little Lazarsfeld understood Adorno's position. There was no question of assessing 'values' as more-or-less discrete entities. More fundamentally, this attempt to give the critical procedure a deductive form was misguided. Adorno certainly proceeded from a theory of society and described 'observed data as mere epiphenomena upon the theory',[164] not as phenomena which 'express' or can be deduced from the general theory. Paradoxically, once he abandoned the attempt to quantify over alternative theoretical terms, such as 'fetish', he did not advocate such special studies of phenomena, but accepted the results of mere 'opinion research' as the basis for theoretical elucidation.[165]

Another influence on Adorno's assessment of the possibilities and limitations of empirical research was the development of sociology in Germany in the post-war period. The pre-war emphasis on more or less formal sociological systems was discredited and instead research techniques imported from the United States were undiscriminatingly espoused, 'to meet the tasks of planning which arose after total defeat'.[166] An example of this kind of work was a study into 'whether and to what degree the family resisted the uprooting of entire population strata in the post-war period'.[167] Adorno describes this work as atheoretical and aphilosophical, by which he means not that theories were not devised and tested, but that the research merely 'registers single facts' instead of 'thinking comprehensively' (*übergreifendes Denken*) in a way which would surpass registering facts and would therefore necessarily be critical.[168] 'Comprehensive thinking' is one of the many indirect phrases which Adorno employs to refer to the production of value in exchange as the fundamental mechanism of society which gives rise to systematically mistaken beliefs about it. Adorno often obscurely calls the process of the production of value in exchange 'the essence' of society, and the mistaken beliefs to which it gives rise, 'the appearance', that is, the form in which the underlying process appears to people. When he accuses the later post-war sociology, which was more theoretical and which examined, for example, changes in class consciousness among industrial workers, of being atheoretical too, he does not mean that such sociology lacks theoretical perspectives, but that it has eliminated any theory of society as a whole from its consideration.

Thus the apparent shift of emphasis in the sociology of industry to the individual unit, the enterprise, and to the group as the object of sociology, amounts to a change in principle not to locate industrial relations within the context of the forces of production and the social relations of production.[169] This sociology declares its intention of

. . . [separating] 'life processes' from 'work processes' in the economic organisation – as if the objective structure of work, and its character as a commodity, had nothing to do with the life of the worker.[170]

Adorno argues further that this approach supports 'the supremacy of existing relations'.[171] He never criticises the use of empirical methods on principle, but their being harnessed to such limited frameworks.

. . . the sociology of the enterprise [cannot] ignore the end of the

enterprise, which determines the objective functions of the workers . . . to reduce the object of the sociology of the enterprise to those
components of the worker's behaviour not immediately determined by
the end of the enterprise . . . means to eliminate from the object of
sociology the compulsion to which individuals must submit in order to
preserve their lives and the life of the society.[172]

Adorno also discussed the 'preference for subjective investigations . . .
confirmed by a survey of the voluminous literature on post-war German
youth'.[173] By 'subjective', he means that

> Very little significance is attributed to the objective life conditions of
> this generation: most of the works deal with the attitudes and
> behaviour of the young, and only rarely are these interpreted by
> reference to the social structure.[174]

This literature is quite theoretical: the absence of class consciousness[175]
and the presence of alienation are themes which pervade 'nearly the
entire literature'.[176] Alienation is 'described . . . in terms of the
"Labyrinth" of modern society, which makes very difficult an "inner
relationship" to the state'.[177] Adorno comments:

> It could be asked if modern society is in fact as opaque as the sociol-
> ogists depict it, above all as opaque as the sociologists themselves
> seem to find it? In the era of large scale organisations the tendency to
> eliminate complicated intermediate mechanisms has perhaps made
> many things simpler than when liberalism flourished; perhaps there
> are veiling mechanisms of a particular kind, which make society
> appear impossible to understand; and perhaps we ought now to study
> those mechanisms? The alleged labyrinthine character of society may
> well be interpreted as a projective image of the impotent, who are now
> unable to do that which was once termed 'making one's own way'.[178]

Instead of less competition (an 'intermediate mechanism') for example,
between workers making social relations more transparent, they have
become more opaque. Social relations have become more opaque partly
because in the sphere of consumption, they can *seem* more intelligible
than they are, 'an illusion of pure use-value, as displayed by cultural
goods, has been substituted for pure exchange-value. This exchange-
value has deceptively taken over the function of use-value'.[179] At the
same time, in the sphere of work, social relations have become less
intelligible, owing to the increased fragmentation of the division of
labour. Theory should show how the 'strong adaptive tendency of
youth'[180] may arise from the clash 'between work and leisure',[181] thereby

uncovering 'veiling mechanisms' which concern the very formation of the individual, but which cannot be discerned as long as analysis is confined to mere description of adaptive behaviour.

Adorno's more general critiques of sociology and empirical research and of 'scientistic' notions of objectivity can only be understood in the light of these contexts. Furthermore, his understanding of concepts and of 'experience' make it impossible for him to countenance a sociology which would quantify over clearly defined terms. He declined to define concepts because to do so would be to construct the object by the concepts of the science and to attribute static, invariant properties to it. He shuns investigating 'an object with an instrument which, through its own construction, decides in advance just what the object is – a simple case of circularity'.[182] Definitions are thus omitted, because to define a concept would be to stipulate what the object is, which would be to imply that the concept is rationally identical with its object. *Ex hypothesi*, empirical reality or experience of it cannot be specified apart from concepts. Experience of social reality is mediated by concepts, thus there is no independently definable reality to pit against concepts in order to 'test' them.[183] This notion of experience is complex, it both connotes the empirical, reality itself, and the possibility of knowing reality.[184] Adorno does not thereby debase experience. On the contrary, it is the basis of any cognition. But to stipulate *a priori*, that is apart from experience, what is to count as empirical evidence for a concept, is merely to register what the methodology is equipped to register.[185] The lamented hiatus between theoretical and empirical sociology is misconstrued according to this view: for theory and experience necessarily interact.[186] This does not imply that theory is supreme. A circle is unavoidable:

> . . . there can be no experience which is not mediated by – often unarticulated – theoretical conceptions, there can be no conception of any use which is not founded in experience and continuously judged by it. The circle cannot be concealed. . . .[187]

The distinction between essence and appearance delimits the role of theory and hypothesis for Adorno as well. There is no question of what Adorno calls 'appearance' being articulated so as to count as evidence for what he calls 'essence', in the way that observables may count as evidence for unobservable theoretical entities in standard philosophy of science. 'Essence' for Adorno does not refer to multiple, unique, Husserlian essences.[188] He uses several other elliptical phrases to refer to the production of value in exchange as the underlying process of society, among them: 'the underlying law of society' or 'the societal law';[189] 'the objective structure of the society'.[190] 'Appearance' sometimes refers to the mistaken beliefs which people have about society, sometimes to the behaviour of individuals, and sometimes to the institutions which arise on the basis of the underlying process of society and which are misunderstood by people. Theory investigates the basis of the deviation not the correlation between the 'essence' and the 'appearance' of society:

> . . . decisive structures of the social process, such as the inequality of the alleged equivalence of exchange, cannot become apparent without the intervention of theory.[191]

This position is incompatible with the idea of formulating and testing hypotheses.[192] It illuminates esoteric assertions, such as, 'concealed essence is non-essence':[193] 'essence' refers to the production of value in exchange; the production of value in exchange structures the appearance of society; exchange value appears to be a real attribute of commodities although it is not a real attribute; it is therefore not really an essence, but 'non-essence'.

Adorno's major criticism of scientistic sociology and of certain kinds of empirical research is that they reduplicate, instead of explaining what they observe. Any theory which stipulates what is to be tested will then pick out only what is thus more or less narrowly defined. Empirical research which simply ascertains people's opinions reproduces the mistaken beliefs which people hold, instead of explaining how they come to hold such beliefs.[194] However, such theories and such empirical work do have a cognitive status for Adorno: they provide the place where his analysis starts. He quotes Hegel's aggressive assertion approvingly 'Public opinion deserves to be respected and despised'.[195] For the scientistic approach describes the appearance of society more accurately than, for example, the *verstehende* approach, which cannot capture the apparently fixed, invariant, unintelligible appearance of society.[196]

Adorno's own approach is more helpfully called *Deutung* than 'theory'.[197] *Deutung* is translated as 'interpretation' in the English translation of *The Positivist Dispute in German Sociology*, but 'elucidation' would be better because Adorno distinguished his position so clearly from *Verstehen* which is often translated as (subjective) interpretation.[198] Adorno's procedure is best described as an 'indirect method',[199] or as the physiognomy of appearance',[200] since it involves the elucidation of the relation between the underlying process of society and the forms in which the process appears – people's perception of it, the methodologies of non-dialectical sociologies, and other cultural forms.

Towards an Empirical Sociology

Adorno devised his own empirical work and contributed to group projects in a way which was quite consistent with his criticism of empirical social research. In his major areas of research he established and examined typologies, for example, types of musical behaviour, and types of more and less authoritarian character. These typologies are not intended to provide classificatory schemata which could be tested, or ideal-types in the sense of refined concepts against which reality could be measured. The beliefs and behaviour of people in particular spheres of social action are observed to be rigid and stereotyped in a specifiable and limited number of ways. These 'types' are then shown to be determined by the underlying process of society, the mode of production. The production of value in exchange and the concomitant mode of domination in late capitalism give rise to 'typed' behaviour which tends to be generally or universally prevalent. 'Indirect methods' have to be used to demonstrate the mechanism by which such behaviour is determined and thus the question of how adequately concepts are translated into empirical terms and the question of circularity in the argument are irrelevant or need to be posed in a very different way. Adorno was always alive to 'the danger of a methodological circle'.[201]

> . . . that in order to grasp the phenomenon of cultural reification according to the prevalent norms of empirical sociology one would have to use reified methods . . .[202]

and that to translate concepts into empirical terms amounted to attempting to 'square the circle'.[203] He took care to try and avoid this inconsistency in his work.

Adorno's first major piece of empirical work was his collaboration on the Princeton Radio Research Project. In his capacity as collaborator he continued to elaborate theoretical themes on which he had published before joining the Project, especially the phenomenon of fetishism in musical production and reception,[204] conducted an analysis of radio symphonies,[205] and developed a typology of musical behaviour.[206] It was during the course of this work that he developed the notions of 'standardization' and 'pseudo-individualism' foreshadowing the notion of 'personalization' which 'later played a significant role in *The Authoritarian Personality* . . . '.[207] Studies of 'authoritarianism' constituted his other major research activity. In *The Authoritarian Personality* he was individually responsible for the 'qualitative' analyses, although he also helped to construct the 'Fascism (F) Scale'. He contributed the qualitative work to another major study of authoritarianism conducted after the war in Germany which used experimental methods but which was also a predominantly quantitative study, *Gruppenexperiment*.[208] He executed several further pieces of content analysis, among them one on the speeches of an American agitator,[209] another on the astrology column of the *Los Angeles Times*,[210] and another on television plays.[211] These studies used psychoanalytical concepts to examine how standardised and often commercialised techniques exploit certain contradictions in the mentality of their potential 'clients', which are themselves traceable to social contradictions, in order to reinforce standardised patterns of behaviour.[212] The collaborative projects always utilise a combination of qualitative and quantitative methods. It was thought that this plurality would prevent the research techniques from being given more importance than the phenomenon under investigation.

The joint project *The Authoritarian Personality* is well known as a piece of empirical sociology which claims that it measures the anti-democratic potential of the individual, locating a specified disposition by utilising a range of related interview scales. The major criticisms of the book, that the notion of 'fascist' or authoritarian personality is presupposed but not demonstrated by the empirical tests, and that it fails to explain authoritarianism at the macro-level, relying instead on depicting a psychological syndrome, are well known too.

Adorno responded in two ways to criticism of *The Authoritarian Personality*. He referred to the macro-theory which was published elsewhere,[213] and he explicated the idea of the role of empirical research on which the book had been based. This was somewhat disingenuous because the theory, a chapter in *Dialectic of Enlightenment*, although written between 1941 and 1945 in America, had been purposely published in German,[214] and the later replies to critics were all written in German too, although the book aroused most interest and controversy in the United States.[215]

The relevant chapter in *Dialectic of Enlightenment*, 'Elements of Anti-Semitism: Limits of Enlightenment' displays affinities with the 'Research Project on Anti-Semitism' which was announced and outlined in the *Zeitschrift* in 1941.[216] It consisted of an historical outline of anti-semitism and mass movements, and included a typology of 'Types of Present Day Anti-Semitism'. The chapter in the *Dialectic of Enlightenment* circles around the proposition that 'Bourgeois anti-semitism has a specific economic reason: the concealment of domination in production'.[217] The capitalist is judged to engage in productive labour, but, as Marx argued, profit, the return to capital, is not correctly regarded as a return to productive labour.[218] The Jews were, for a long time, excluded from owning the means of production but owned much of the circulation sector.[219] This role as 'middle man', as intermediary, is more visible to the worker in the sphere of commerce and consumption than the role of the capitalist, but less intelligible to him as an essential function of capitalism: it is easier to understand the immediate function of the production of goods, less easy to understand the intermediary function of commerce, advertising, financial techniques;[220] and it is easier to understand the relation between wages and prices than to understand the relation between the worker's own productive labour and the wages received for it.[221] Hence the 'economic injustice of the whole [that is, capitalist] class is attributed to them [the Jews]'[222] and they are regarded by the masses as non-productive parasites:[223]

> The merchant [the Jew] presents them [the workers] with the bill which they have signed away to the manufacturer. The merchant is the bailiff of the whole system and takes the hatred of others upon himself. The responsibility of the circulation sector is a socially necessary pretence.[224]

The growth of large organisations diminished the role of the intermediary, the sphere of circulation, since production and distribution come to be dominated and controlled by 'strong centralized agencies'.[225] Hence there was no longer any economic need for the Jews, but there was certainly a need to attribute to them the crises of the whole system, such as those of the interwar period, by reviving the image of the non-productive parasite.[226]

The rest of the chapter in *Dialectic of Enlightenment* develops a psychoanalytic theory of anti-semitism as a projection of the change in the mode of domination on to the Jews, as the projection of a new form of impotence, as Marx revealed religion itself to be a projection of social impotence. 'Projection' is not only a projection in Marx's sense of what is denied (power), but also a projection of what is desired and feared. 'Projection' is not only in Marx's sense a projection which controls the exploited, but it also expresses the needs and fears of the exploiters. The theory of projection is predicated on the general theory of the individual's loss of autonomy. Fascism is understood as an extreme case of such loss of autonomy, which Adorno explicated by means of the model of narcissistic identification.[227] Fascist propaganda mobilised 'unconscious, regressive processes' in a specific way which did not represent 'the return of the archaic, but its reproduction in and by civilization itself' in a planned and calculated way.[228] Adorno used Freudian theory to examine anti-semitism and fascist propaganda precisely in order to show that 'psychological' processes are not in themselves determining processes:

> In a thoroughly reified society, in which there are virtually no direct relationships between men, and in which each person has been reduced to a social atom, to a mere function of the collectivity, the psychological processes, though they persist in each individual, have ceased to appear as the determining forces of the social process. Thus the psychology of the individual has lost what Hegel would have called its substance.[229]

Adorno produced a 'negative psychology', as it were. His criticism of philosophies and sociologies which had no notion of the subject or of epistemological subjectivity and of those which granted complete autonomy to the subject was undertaken for the sake of a subject which 'has lost its substance', which has lost its autonomy. Sociologists fail to understand their own epistemological subjectivity for the same reason that they fail to develop a satisfactory theory of the individual. Adorno gave up the proletariat as the subject-object of history, as cogniser and carrier of history, but he was devoted to locating and analysing the fate of the individual, of the lost subject of society. Thus it was a serious misunderstanding, as far as he was concerned, when *The Authoritarian Personality* was accused by critics of offering no theory of anti-semitism, or of basing its explanation on psychological and subjective factors.[230]

It is clear from the 'Introduction' to *The Authoritarian Personality* that the prevalence of anti-semitic ideology is assumed, and that the question asked is, why and how do some individuals succumb to it more readily than others.[231] The question which interests the authors is not why is one kind of individual more susceptible than another kind, but the more general question concerning the nature of the widespread susceptibility to certain ideologies in our society, or the reasons for the prevalence of such ideologies.[232]

The empirical work was not intended to 'prove or disprove'[233] the theory. It was intended to aid the analysis of the underlying mechanisms which make individuals susceptible to certain ideologies. It used indirect methods, for the Fascism(F) Scale depended on taking indirect questions as indicators of potential susceptibility to Fascism. Although it was important that the F−scale correlated with the other scales which investigated beliefs more directly, this was never held to validate the F−scale as an indicator of Fascist potential. In fact it was judged that the correlation between the scales should not be too high, since it was expected that people would admit to certain beliefs more readily when their political content was less explicit.[234] The work with the scales explored ideas which were developed in the course of detailed case studies. Psychoanalytic concepts were employed to examine the relation between experience of authority and ego formation. The charge of circularity was not denied. It *was* denied that the research was narrowly limited to what the theory already presupposed, since the theory went far beyond the bounds of what could be validated by empirical work. It was admitted to be circular in the sense that different kinds of empirical work were brought together to throw light on central themes, to make them cogent.

> . . . a great many different insights converge from many directions
> upon the same principle themes, so that what is unproven by the

strictest criteria gains in plausibility . . . we never regarded the theory simply as a set of hypotheses but in some sense standing on its own feet, and therefore did not intend to prove or disprove it through our findings but only to derive from it concrete questions for investigation . . . and demonstrate certain prevalent socio-psychological structures. Of course, the criticism of the F–scale is not to be gainsaid, that to establish tendencies indirectly that cannot be got at directly owing to fear of censoring mechanisms coming into play, presupposes that one has first confirmed the existence of the tendencies that one assumes the subjects hesitated to proclaim.[235]

However, this does not imply that the theory and the results of the research were arbitrary. The whole range of scores was developed into a typology by Adorno.[236] The typology was understood to be real, 'Our typology has to be a *critical* typology in the sense that it comprehends the typification of men itself as a social function'.[237] 'There is reason to look for psychological types because the world in which we live is typed and "produces" different "types" of persons'.[238] However, Adorno only suggests what the social principle of stereotyping is. He distinguishes between the non-authoritarian and authoritarian personality and proposes that the authoritarian personality is more of a 'type' than the non-authoritarian personality:

The more rigid a type, the more deeply does he show the hallmarks of social rubber stamps. This is in accordance with the characterization of our high scorers by traits such as rigidity and stereotypical thinking. Here lies the ultimate principle of our whole typology. Its major dichotomy lies in the question of whether a person is standardized himself and thinks in a standardized way, or whether he is truly 'individualized' and opposes standardization in the sphere of human experience,[239]

adding a note to emphasise the substantive point which he is making:

It should be stressed that two concepts of types have to be distinguished. On the one hand, there are those who are types in the proper sense, typified persons, individuals who are largely reflecting set patterns and social mechanisms, and on the other hand, persons who can only be called types in the formalogical sense and who may often be characterized by the *absence* of standard qualities . . .[240]

This principle guided his interpretation of the interview material. He derives different types from the unintelligibility of the social structure:

Stereotypy misses reality in so far as it dodges the concrete and contents itself with preconceived, rigid, and overgeneralized ideas to which the individual attributes a kind of magical omnipotence. Conversely, personalization dodges the real abstractness, that is to say, the 'reification' of a social reality which is determined by property relations and in which human beings themselves are, as it were, mere appendages. Stereotypy and personalization are two divergent parts of an actually non-experienced world . . .[241]

Adorno even proposes that these equally inadequate ways of dealing with reality are due to the conflict between the unintelligibility caused by the increase in industrial standardisation with the illusion of intelligibility given by modern mass communications,[242] but, disappointingly, the explanation stops at this provocative point.

The problem with *The Authoritarian Personality* is also evident in Adorno's criticism of sociology. Inadvertently he undermines his commitment to objective, macro-processes (for example, 'the social principle of stereotypy', and 'reification') because he does not enlarge on the ways in which such processes determine different spheres of social life. As a result the overall perspective is easily lost. Adorno remains close to the sociologists whom he criticises for finding society so opaque, since although he provides a very general explanation of why society appears opaque, he does not make good his implicit offer to dissolve the opaqueness at the level of theory by examining its causes. His tantalising suggestion, also to be found in some of his articles, that in advanced capitalist society the work process is such that society appears less intelligible while the realm of leisure (culture) acquires an illusory intelligibility is developed only in the sphere of leisure and thus a promising antithesis remains latent.

Chapter 6

The Dispute over Modernism

The Sociology of Culture

Adorno explored change in the mode of production domination in the sphere of culture, especially music and literature, not in the sphere of work. 'Culture' does not merely designate the realm of consumption, nor the organisation of leisure according to the principle of commodity exchange. Adorno developed a general theory of culture predicated on his use of Marx's theory of value by transcribing the range of Marx's categories of production (composition), distribution (reproduction), exchange (the culture industry) and consumption (reception). 'Production' does not refer to the organisation of work or manufacturing; 'reproduction' does not refer to technology; 'the culture industry' does not refer to industry.

In this part of his writing Adorno steps outside immanent analyses of intellectual and artistic works to proffer explicit general strictures on method for sociology. These general prescriptions were, however, derived from his analyses of works. In this part, too, he wrote as a composer, as a critic, as a sociologist, and as all three together. For the task of the composer or writer is explicitly or implicitly analogous to that of the sociologist.[1] He chooses a form in which to work, and all form expresses society in a more or less critical way. The sociologist is explicitly or implicitly a composer. His method is more or less critical of society, and this is expressed by the form in which he chooses to write. The sociology of culture is inseparable also from criticism (aesthetics) because the social origin, content and function of a work of art can only be fully understood by examining the internal formation of a work, that is, the way its meaning is structured. Thus sociological examination of the text and context of a work of art cannot limit itself to questions of fact and absolve itself from questions of evaluation.

> I do not want to ignore the question of quality for the sake of the 'socially functional or dysfunctional question'. But, quite the contrary, I seek to show, in *opposition* to vulgar sociology, that the sociological question can be meaningfully formulated only *on the basis* of the question of aesthetic quality. In other words, sociology should not ask how music functions but how music stands in relation to the underlying antinomies in society: whether music confronts them, overcomes them, leaves them as they are or indeed hides them. *Only* an immanent question concerned with the form of works will lead to this.[2]

The 'question of quality' is the question of the form of a work. Form is constructed on the basis of a stance towards society which can be decoded in any given work.

Adorno's writings in the sociology of culture are here somewhat arbitrarily conjoined. Adorno republished some of his essays and review essays on music and literature in slim volumes which he subtitled 'Critical Models',[3] and he republished much of the rest of his writing on music and literature in the same format.[4] The essays deal with a wide range of cultural topics including education and the media, as well as consisting of pieces on cultural critics,[5] and more general theoretical rubrics.[6] The major writings on music consist of a series of monographs; on Wagner,[7] on Mahler,[8] on Stravinsky,[9] on Schönberg,[10] and on Berg.[11] The most famous of these are the ones on Stravinsky and Schönberg which were published together with a critical introduction as *The Philosophy of New Music*.[12] There are two volumes entitled aesthetics: the small aesthetics which consists of republished essays,[13] and the voluminous *Ästhetische Theorie* (Aesthetic Theory) which was unfinished when Adorno died and published posthumously.[14] He also wrote a series of introductory lectures on the sociology of music, and a series on aesthetics.[15]

Adorno also composed music for most of his life. He composed before he went to Vienna in 1925 to study under Berg and Eduard Steuermann.[16] He continued composing after his return to Germany in 1928, and his correspondence with the composer Ernst Krenek indicates that he continued to compose during his exile in England and America in the 1930s.[17] In Oxford in the thirties he was known as a musician,[18] and Thomas Mann confirms in *The Genesis of a Novel* that he was composing music in California in the 1940s.[19] He wrote several pieces after the war on the problem of composing music in the post-1945 period,[20] and he taught music at Darmstadt in the fifties and the sixties.

From the age of 17 (1920) to the year of his death (1969), Adorno wrote as a music critic for newspapers, music journals and for the radio. Most of these reviews were very short, occasional pieces which were never republished.[21] From 1928–31 Adorno was editor of *Der Anbruch*, a famous monthly journal published in Vienna, and the organ of 'new music'. In the 1920s in Vienna, *neue Musik* stood for the progressive Austro-German musicians, Schönberg and his school above all, but also Paul Hindemith and Krenek, as opposed to the more conservative faction headed by Hans Pfitzner. From the early twenties there had been a dispute over methodology, a *Methodenstreit*, as it were, between the schools. Schönberg's pupil, Berg, replied in *Der Anbruch* to Pfitzner's tirades against 'the new aesthetic' and against the possibility of intellectual and sociological analysis of music.[22] Adorno always associated himself with the school of new music, with creating and defining the new idiom as composer and as critic.

Adorno's writings on music and on literature are heterogeneous in style. The main analyses of individual works and *œuvres* are florid and dense, full of elliptical references to his general philosophical and sociological ideas, such as reification, identity and non-identity thinking, and the fate of the individual. Over the range of this large body of writing, including the more theoretical work, the distinction between easier and harder texts does not always correspond to the distinction between directly and indirectly written texts. For example, the introductory lectures on music[23] contain a straightforward, simply written account of how the sociology of music might proceed, in contrast to the monographs on music which demand a high level of expertise in the history of music theory in order to follow the details of Adorno's argument, although the broad points are clear. Yet the essay *Ideen zur Musiksoziologie* (Ideas on the Sociology of Music)[24] is much more complex and profound than the lectures, but it still contains a direct statement of Adorno's position in contrast to the essay *Musikalische Warenanalysen* (Analysis of Musical Commodities).[25] The latter proceeds in the manner of *Minima Moralia*, with short anecdotes ridiculing various social modes of reception (consumption) of classical and romantic music in order to illuminate the transmutation of such music into commodities, and is interspersed with theoretical conclusions.[26] In one book, entitled *Quasi Una Fantasia* after a piece of music by Beethoven, the essays are reorganised in sections in a way which imitates the organisation of a musical composition.[27] The first section is called *Improvisationen* ('Improvisations'), the second is called *Vergegenwärtigungen* ('Representations') and consists of essays which represent themes on which Adorno had already written, bringing his work on Mahler and Stravinsky up to date, while the third is called *Finale*.

Adorno sought to develop a sociology of artistic form.[28] Music, the most formal art because it is non-conceptual, interested him most. The notion of form is highly ambiguous. On the one hand, it refers to musical genres and the analysis of form would examine their relation to kinds of societies and their relation to social life, such as liturgical and secular music, or opera and chamber music. Sociological investigation of musical forms in this sense has affinities with Durkheim's approach to the elementary forms of religious life, with the way in which Durkheim argues that religious forms present (reinforce) and represent (interpret) society.[29] On the other hand, form refers to the internal organisation of music, to melody, harmony and even the tonic system itself. Analysis of form in this sense would examine the conjunction between particular features of musical technique and principles of social organisation in other areas of social life in a way homologous with Weber's examination of the increasing 'rationalization' of Western harmonic chord music and the relation between its rational and affective features.[30] These two notions of form are not always distinct:

> After the idea of a hierarchic [ecclesiastic] authority had been submerged by that of a community formed by individuals with equal rights, [the community forming] function was then transferred to [secular] society itself. From then on society 'represents' itself musically in a dual sense: it represents its own life processes in the forms of great music with their internal movement, and confirms itself as the authority which has replaced the old one, by means of the power and impressiveness of these forms.[31]

Different societies, for example, theocratic and secular, with different modes of social control and different musical forms, such as plainchant and symphony, respectively, are contrasted here with form as the 'internal movement' of music. Two notions of 'represent' are also contrasted. The first is that society represents musically 'its own life processes', that it expresses and interprets social reality, although it may convey that social reality is antinomical or contradictory. The second is that society 'confirms itself' musically as authority, that dramatising itself musically may have the function of legitimising existing social relationships, or it may undermine, criticise and disconfirm them. A contradiction in social reality is, for example, that bourgeois society forms a totality by virtue of the opposition of the interests of individuals and classes since it is based on the production of value in exchange, but

> The specific function of music, which secured its primacy during the nineteenth century, and which alone made possible a 'religion of art' in the Wagnerian style, consisted in the fact that in individualistic society, music more than any other medium appeared to reawaken the consciousness that, in spite of all the opposition of interests, this society was a univocal whole.[32]

This function of music might be interpreted as a longing for the past, an aspiration for the future, or a legitimation of the *status quo*, depending on the general conditions of production, exchange and reception of music.

Adorno's sociology of music depends on the assumption that social 'meaning' can be predicated of music but not as its 'content'. He opposed any sociology of art which assumes that the experience of any work of art is a primary datum,[33] or that such experience constitutes a subjective reflex to effects intended by the content of any work of art.[34] On the one hand, the sociology of art should investigate how the relation between society and art 'crystallizes'[35] in the work of art, on the other hand, it should investigate the mechanisms of distribution and control which determine the reception ('experience') of works of art.[36] Radical disjunction may occur between the composition and reception of works, and this can be given a sociological explanation. Therefore, the sociology of art must not limit itself to examining only those works which attain wide dissemination, because

> [If] works of art of the highest order . . . do *not* attain any important social effect, this is a social fact just as much as the opposite case.[37]

The social 'meaning' of a piece of music and its social function may diverge or contradict each other.[38] For example, given the prevalent conditions of (musical) production and distribution in a particular period, a piece of music may express aspirations for a changed society, but in another period, with different conditions of exchange and distribution, the same piece of music may come to legitimise existing social relations.[39] Under the same conditions of production and distribution, different musical forms may develop, some of which resist legitimising prevalent norms of communication and others which conform to and confirm such norms. Thus Adorno does not judge that the 'meaning' of the music under altered conditions changes. 'Meaning' in this unusual sense does not refer to the intentions of the composer, or to any ahistorical or fixed notion of the meaning of a work.

These general ideas provide the framework for detailed analysis of musical technique. Musical technique must be understood more sociologically than is usual in the conventional academic study of music, but more musically than the exogenous application of sociological categories to music might imply.[40] It is not a matter of discovering the social origins of musical technique in any period, but of determining how these elements are used in composition to make musical (and social) sense: 'The formal constituting [*sic*] of music[al meaning], ultimately its logic, must be made to speak sociologically'.[41] Adorno does not deny that music can be understood in terms of its own immanent, autonomous development because the traditional approach to the history of music demonstrates that it can.[42] However, the 'autonomy' of music must itself be understood as a social fact, as determined by a particular kind of society. Only if such a perspective is adopted will the stance of any music to society become discernible:

> The unsolved antagonisms of reality reoccur in the work of art as the immanent problem of its form. This, not the entry of objective moments, defines the relation of art to society.[43]

Adorno thus sought a theory of culture, of the status of culture in particular kinds of societies and of change in the relation between culture and society.

The Dispute over Modernism

The dispute over modernism refers here to some of the conflicting theories of culture and of cultural change and the related aesthetics, developed by a number of neo-Marxist writers largely on the basis of polemical interchange with each other, since the 1920s. For some of these writers the dispute had implications for their creation or composition of works, particularly for Brecht and Adorno. Lukács, Brecht, Benjamin and Adorno were most directly involved, but Bloch,[44] Horkheimer,[45] Marcuse,[46] Hanns Eisler[47] and Karl Wittfogel[48] made important theoretical contributions to the debate as well. This dispute is far more important than the dispute over positivism.

The issue which preoccupied these writers after the First World War, during their years in exile before the Second World War, and after the Second World War, was known originally as the 'dispute over expressionism and realism'.[49] The opposition of Naturalism to Expressionism in German aesthetics and literature before the First World War was fundamentally redefined by the engagement of neo-Marxists in the controversy in the 1920s. Put crudely, 'Naturalism', especially in literature, stood for a realist aesthetic, the accurate depiction of reality, and for scientific progress and social reform.[50] 'Expressionism' stood for the revolt against realism, against materialism and bourgeois society, and for an aesthetic which stressed the priority of the mind (*Geist*) and new forms of abstraction in art not beholden to representing the laws of nature;[51] ' . . . this type of anti-bourgeois revolutionism meant not only sharp rupture with socio-political institutions but also with all social agencies of change'.[52]

In the 1920s a dispute developed between Lukács and a group around him who supported the older, realist genre and were appalled by the new literary forms which they judged to be decadent and counter-revolutionary, and men like Bloch, Brecht and Benjamin who were excited by the new formal and technical possibilities in art and believed that they had progressive political potential.[53] In the late twenties, the controversy reached its most explicit statement in *Die Linkskurve*, the journal of the Union of Proletarian Revolutionary Writers, founded in Berlin in 1928, in which Lukács published articles denigrating Brecht's work.[54] The final edition of the journal in 1932 was devoted to a series of articles by various authors against dramatists and writers influenced by Brecht.[55] The dispute continued in journals published in exile,[56] focused on the question as to whether expressionism was an anti-fascist, revolutionary force, or whether it had helped to prepare the way for the triumph of fascism.[57]

The question of 'Expressionism' is thus highly complex. On the one hand, it meant the cult of the mind, and the disassociation of art from any social base or political responsibility, while, on the other hand, in the neo-Marxist camps, it meant the adoption and development of new forms of non-realist art in order to exploit their political potential for the mass age.[58] Adorno was critical of both of these positions and his own stance represents yet another alternative based on a rejection of 'realism'. These original parameters reappear in the later literature under many different labels. They have continued to structure much debate about the relation between society and art in the twentieth century and to influence the analyses of specific works.[59]

Adorno's criticisms of Lukács' and of Benjamin's notion of culture and of cultural change were the most germinal for his own ideas.[60] Their theories of culture are consistent with their respective philosophies of history and with their respective generalisations of Marx's theory of value (reification), and their detailed analyses of specific works are consistent with the theories of cultural change and modernity.

Lukács defined culture as products and abilities separate from the immediate maintenance of life.[61] Culture is only possible in a society in which 'production is a unified and self-contained process'.[62] The capitalist mode of production destroys the previous autonomy of culture by turning cultural products into commodities and by splitting up the work process.[63] In the twentieth century, 'the era of finance capital',[64] culture has collapsed because even the *apparent* basis in reality of the bourgeois ideology of freedom (free competition and so on) no longer exists. The possibility of culture, for Lukács, depends on conditions of 'organic unity' and the (now lost) ideal of harmony. He expresses this by saying that 'the form and content of cultural expression enter into contradiction with each other'.[65] For example, the form or ideology is that man is an end in himself, while the content or material (that which is formed) is that man, under the capitalist mode of production, is a means to an end.[66] Culture will only be possible again when the rule of the economy is abolished.[67] This theory of culture is at one with Lukács' theory of reification as primarily a thesis about the work process, and with his philosophy of history as the search for the basis of reconciliation, for restitution of the unity of subject and object. It is also the basis for his comparisons of old and new literary forms, and for his special concern for reconciliation in the novel.

Adorno rejects the view that culture is *Geist* (mind), understood as that which transcends the material reproduction of life.[68] Pre-capitalist society is not contrasted with capitalist in terms of the destruction of autonomous culture, instead the 'autonomy' of cultural forms is only achieved under capitalism.[69] When works of art are exchanged as commodities, they become detached from the context of social use and ritual and thus become 'autonomous'. Culture does not presuppose organic unity in a society, but always arises on the basis of the mode of production and concomitant social organisation of a society and expresses the contradictions of that society. 'Culture is the perennial protest of the particular against the universal as long as the universal is unreconciled with the particular'.[70] If, for example, the universal is reconciled with the particular when man is an end in himself, culture will express the reality that man is not àn end in himself. Thus Lukács' criterion for the destruction of the possibility of culture is Adorno's criterion for the possibility of its existence.

Adorno therefore rejects the idea that the increase in organisation at the expense of the ideology of freedom has finally 'destroyed' culture as the powers of fragmentation and specialisation take over from the wholeness and unity of culture.[71] Organisation 'represents . . . the universal against the particular',[72] that is, if the universal – the actual structuring principle of society – treats men as means, then it is opposed to the interest of the particular, man as an end in himself. The 'increase in organization' amounts to an increase in the power of the organising principle of society, and hence to an increase in unity not an increase in divisiveness. Culture is partly neutralised. It is less autonomous in the sense that it is reinserted into a social context of apparently immediate use and ritual. However, since the increase in unifying power is still founded on a contradiction, the production of value in exchange, culture partly resists integration in new ways.[73] The question is not whether culture has lost its unity, but whether the possibility of expressing disunity may have been lost.

It was Benjamin's ideas on the technological reproduction of works of art, especially photography and the cinema,[74] which led Adorno to develop his ideas on the ways in which change in the social relations of distribution, exchange and consumption would affect production and technique in the field of music.[75] Benjamin traced the changing social status of works of art in three kinds of society. First, works of art are ceremonial objects designed to serve in a cult,[76] and, as such, they have an 'aura' of magical authority. Secondly, art practices are emancipated from ritual and works are presented for exhibition, thereby attaining a semblance of autonomy.[77] As long as criteria of authenticity and uniqueness are applicable to them, they still retain the 'aura' of tradition and its authority. 'Aura' for Benjamin means the illusions created by the (realist) work of art which are based on the harmonious representation and reconciliation of social contradictions. Mechanical reproduction destroys this aura by detaching 'the reproduced object from the domain of tradition'.[78] It thus destroys the authority of the perception (illusion) of the uniqueness and permanence of objects and reveals 'the universal equality of things',[79] and it also destroys the semblance of their autonomy. Benjamin could not stress enough his belief that the entire function of art is thereby changed.[80] This new way of perceiving turns art into the service of the interests of the masses.[81] It helps them to understand their position and to emancipate themselves from tradition and authority: '. . . the total function of art is reversed. Instead of being based on ritual, it begins to be based on another practice – politics'.[82] Benjamin was aware that in fact the development of the cinema had proceeded differently, inducing the participation of the masses in new ways of recreating old illusions, 'the phony spell' of commodities.[83] But he was sanguine that new forms of collective experience and of progressive reaction would be achieved as 'To an even greater degree the work of art reproduced becomes the work of art designed for reproducibility',[84] that the new production and reception of works could and would coincide for revolutionary ends.[85]

These emphases on the magical and on the technological, on different relations to objects and on the masses as such, are further instances of Benjamin's interest in atheoretical ways of illuminating (reified) things afresh. His optimism about the new possibilities of the age of the masses is compatible with his view of history as the return of the archaic or 'original' in the wholly new forms of the present:

> To bring about the consolidation of experience with history, which is original [that is, a return to the origin] for every present, is the task of historical materialism/[It] explodes the epoch out of its reified 'historical continuity'./Yet this . . . results in the preservation and removal of the course of history in the epoch.[86]

This perspective is also evident in the attention which he pays to history and parable in his analyses of the works of Kafka and of Brecht.[87]

Adorno interpreted the changes wrought by the mechanical reproducibility of art in different terms. 'Reproduction' was not significant to him as a mechanical or technological change, but because it resulted in new modes of distribution of art and in new forms of consumption or reception of works, that is, in new forms of social behaviour.[88] He believed that these developments constituted a new form of social and political control, not a new possibility for emancipation.[89] He was not only interested in how ' . . . the work of art reproduced becomes the work of art designed for reproducibility', but how new forms of production (composition in music) develop, which do not succumb to the new dominant mode of distribution. The realm of the former so-called 'autonomous' art is the realm in which this occurs, in which significant change in *techniques* occur, as much as in the realm of mechanical reproduction.[90] Adorno thus disagreed with Benjamin that 'autonomous' works of art were defined by their possession of 'aura' and were necessarily counter-revolutionary.[91] On the one hand, he believed that Benjamin exaggerated the change brought about by technical reproduction; for example, the cinema relied on conventional realist effects and did not exploit its purported abstract, 'alienating' possibilities.[92] On the other hand, Benjamin underestimated the extent to which art forms in the tradition of autonomous art could abandon 'aura' and develop new techniques.[93] As an example, Adorno referred Benjamin to the music of Schönberg.[94] Adorno also considered that Benjamin was naïve to expect, in any case, that the proletariat would be immediately affected by the sheer perceptual changes associated with mechanical reproduction, and accused him of 'the anarchistic romanticism of blind confidence in the spontaneous power of the proletariat'.[95] Adorno himself expressed neither complete confidence in new techniques, nor complete despair in the new forms of mass exchange and distribution of art. He insisted above all that *avant-garde* art and popular art should be examined in relation to each other, since 'Both are torn halves of an integral freedom, to which however they do not add up'.[96] In his sociology of music and literature and in his aesthetic theory, Adorno used materialist concepts to examine the relationship of the 'torn halves' systematically, centred on the theory of commodity fetishism (reification).

Forces and Relations of Production

. . . the commodity character of music is not determined by its being exchanged, but by its being *abstractly* exchanged, in the way in which Marx explained the commodity form: hence not an immediate but a 'reified' exchange relation occurs. When you [Krenek] explain the way art 'has become autonomous' [*die 'Autonomisierung' der Kunst*] as the decisive change, that is really exactly what I mean by its commodity character. Only it is the same phenomenon described not from the side of the *relations* of production, but from the side of the *forces* of production . . . If by capitalism one understands more than mere 'for money', namely, the *totality* of the social process defined as a unity of exchange by abstract labour time, then, in an exact sense, capitalism has made art into a commodity *together with* men. The commodity character of art as the objective side, and the destruction of 'human dignity' as the subjective side are equivalent and cannot be torn apart from each other.[97]

Adorno stresses the abstract nature of the exchange of cultural commodities in opposition to the perspective put forward by Krenek,[98] and to that of Benjamin.[99] First, the relation which results from the exchange and the concomitant consumption of what is exchanged is not an immediate or an intelligible one in the same sense in which Marx contrasted the intelligibility of exchange in non-commodity producing societies with its unintelligibility in capitalist society. Where music is concerned, the illusion that exchange and consumption is intelligible is particularly strong due to its apparently immediate value in use.[100] Secondly, the abstract nature of exchange is emphasised as the premise for examining any other features of the relationship between society and music, for example production, reproduction, and consumption. This approach would do more justice to the objective preconditions of the 'subjective' modes of reception of art, and would avoid Krenek's too simple view that art is distorted by being incorporated into the process of capitalism,[101] and Benjamin's view that an enlightened consciousness would triumph from the immediate effects of new technology. Adorno employed the distinction between forces of production and relations of production because then exchange and reproduction fall on both sides of the distinction in a way that is analytically preferable to consigning them implicitly to one side of the distinction or to the other. Furthermore, the central thesis of his sociology of art is that there is a contradiction between the forces and the relations of production in the realm of culture. Therefore, Adorno starts from the commodity character of music, the fact that it is exchanged in a way which gives rise to fetishism, that is, the social relations between men which underlie the product appear to be the natural property of the object produced, that is, its value.[102] The development of means of mechanical reproduction increases the volume of exchange of cultural products and gives rise to new forms of art, but it does not alter in principle the commodity character of such products.[103]

As a force of production, mechanical reproduction may be considered in terms of the technology which produces the radio, the cinema, the gramophone, but as a relation of production it must be considered as a new mode of distribution which presupposes the dominant mode of production and exchange in society. Thus mechanical reproduction also permits the reproduction and larger distribution and exchange of works of art which formerly were not reproducible, according to the prevailing norms of exchange, thereby increasing their commodity character.[104] Change in the realm of 'production' of works of art also depends on the prevalent conditions of exchange, hence on the dominant mode of production of all other commodities in society.[105] Adorno does not say what that is in terms of the social relations of work, manufacturing or the buying and selling of labour-power. He divides 'production' of music into two types: composition, the development of new techniques designed to avoid the prevailing norms of exchange, distribution and consumption, and 'the culture industry', the producing of works for reproduction and mass consumption.[106] Composition, in this sense, is a force of production as much as mechanical reproduction. The 'culture industry', in this sense, is oriented to the prevalent relations of production, that is, to the widespread norms of reception and consumption of music in society.[107] This perspective is odd in several ways. Music is counted partly as production when in standard Marxist terms it would be counted as part of the superstructure and hence fall under the relations of production. Innovation in (artistic and musical) production is judged in terms of the significance accorded to the dominant relations of production, and the designation 'force of production' is really reserved for what resists those relations and not for new techniques or for new technology as such. Composition is not, however, a relational term in the way work or 'labour-power' are for Marx. In the realm of consumption, the 'culture industry' is a force of production in the sense that it constitutes a changed form of social domination and control, while considered under the relations of production, it is responsible for new kinds of social behaviour which Adorno examined by using Freudian categories.

Adorno's sociology of literature and music is devoted mainly to examining genres and individual works of art in the light of the thesis that a contradiction has developed between the forces and the relations of production. On the one hand, there will always be a disjunction between production and consumption of art in a society based on the production of commodities, that is, under the conditions which produce so-called autonomous art. For the criterion of artistic production (composition) that a work is authentic, will be more or less at odds with the demands of consumption (reception) that it should be intelligible.[108] On the other hand, in the present age,

> . . . the contradiction between the forces of production and the relations of production becomes flagrant: the forces of production are displaced into high, quasi-privileged spheres, isolated, and therefore, even when they incorporate true consciousness, are also partly false. The lower spheres obey the predominant relations of production.[109]

The contradiction is derived from the prevalent mode of exchange which combined with the new forms of distribution (reproduction) results in a dislocation in the realm of culture. This notion of contradiction, however, is odd. It implies displacement between production and consumption which determines the *status quo* but does not change it, and which appears to be a permanent rather than an inherently unstable situation. The notion of forces of production and the notion of relations of production are not really commensurable. By 'forces of production', Adorno means the specialist's skill of composition, whether for the market or not, and the techniques and technology which both determine and are the tools of composition. He does not refer to the general preconditions of buying and selling labour-power, or of the labour-process. But by the 'relations of production', he means something approaching the conventional Marxist notion, namely, life styles and habits of consumption, consciousness shared and differentiated according to class position. Although Adorno is only concerned with cultural goods, he implies that the relations of production which are generally dominant determine the consumption and reception of those products, but without specifying what those relations are. Conversely, he implies that the social control exercised by the production and distribution of such goods ('the culture industry') determines social behaviour in the sphere of the relations of production to a large extent.

The Notes on Literature

Although Adorno's analyses of literature are set within his theoretical framework, they concentrate on one side of the sets of relations posited, on the formation and structure of 'new' literature and not specifically on different genres, nor on their distribution and reception. His sociology of literature is therefore more schematic than his sociology of music, which encompasses both 'new' and popular music, has a more clearly defined and intensive historical range – from Wagner to Berg – and contains more detailed technical analyses to illustrate sociological theses. In music, the notion of a 'crisis in meaning' can be established more precisely in technical terms, while sociological interpretation of it is more speculative. Yet the performance, distribution and reception of music, which Adorno calls 'music life', are more amenable to sociological investigation. However, even though the writings on literature are less systematic, they offer a significant and important alternative to the work of Lukács, Benjamin, Brecht and Sartre in this field.

In a now-famous book which Lukács wrote after the Second World War, *Wider den missverstandenen Realismus* (Against misunderstood Realism),[110] he continued to join battle on the themes which had dominated his dispute with Brecht during the years of exile, expressed in terms of a distinction between 'realism' and 'modernism' (not 'realism' and 'expressionism' as in the earlier dispute), and summed up by the choice dramatically urged by Lukács upon his readers in the central essay of the book, 'Franz Kafka or Thomas Mann',[111] as representatives of the two poles of his distinction. Adorno wrote a very hostile essay on Lukács' book, '*Erpresste Versöhnung*' (Extorted Reconciliation),[112] which, together with his own essay on Kafka[113] and the documents of his collaboration in the 1940s with Thomas Mann on the latter's book ·*Doctor Faustus*, amount to a substantial challenge to Lukács' position.

Lukács defended 'realism' against 'modernism' in the novel. The difference is one of style, and of underlying ideology which is the 'formative principle' of style.[114] Since Lukács considered that pre-occupation with style was one of the symptoms of 'modernism', he derived social meaning – a 'view of the world'[115] – from characteristics of style and called it 'content': 'style . . . is the specific form of a specific content'.[116] 'Realism' is committed to a view of man as an essentially social and political being, formed by his society and striving to attain understanding of its contradictions in order to act on it.[117] Texts written in this tradition portray the lives of individuals, firmly rooted in specified and identifiable space and time, and the complex tissue of their interaction with their environment, in a way which is universal and concrete.[118] By 'universal', Lukács means typical and also harmonious in the sense of transcending a particularist view;[119] by 'concrete', he means according to the real possibilities of people in the given situation.[120] 'Realism' in this way aims at 'a truthful reflection of reality'.[121] 'Modernism' is based on a view that man is 'by nature solitary, asocial, unable to enter into relationships with other human beings',[122] not concerned with understanding social reality or with acting on it. Texts of this kind portray individuals ' "thrown-into-the-world": meaning-lessly, unfathomably',[123] without any development of personality and hence statically and ahistorically. They concentrate on the abstract potentialities of the individual's life – his rich imaginings – which are preferred to social realities. It is thus intensely subjective literature which colludes in the distortion of reality instead of fighting it by its obsession with styles to convey such subjective experience. Lukács calls such writing 'decadent' and judges that it heralds the end of literature.[124]

Kafka's work is, for Lukács, the prototype of modernist art. Its techniques betray a view of man terrified in the presence of 'utterly strange and hostile reality',[125] and reduced to 'total impotence, [and] paralysis in the face of the unintelligible power of circumstance'.[126] This essentially subjective vision is identified with reality itself. Kafka's description of the world serves the end of presenting 'an allegory of transcendent Nothingness'.[127] He used a wealth of naturalistic detail to convey a fragmented world and personal horror (*Angst*) and impotence, but his details are not, as in realism, the nodal points of individual or social life; they are cryptic symbols of an unfathomable transcendence. The stronger their evocative power, the deeper is the abyss, the more evident the allegorical gap between meaning and existence.[128]

According to Lukács, Thomas Mann deals with distortion in society in a different way. The settings of his novels are 'free from transcendental reference',[129] and his characterisation of individuals is based on his desire to probe 'into the complexity of present-day reality'.[130] These individuals represent different aspects of the whole. Mann made the insight that the artist is one of the main mediators of people's experience of the 'underworld of the human mind' and of social reality into the object of many of his books, from *Tonio Kröger* (1903) to *Doctor Faustus* (1947), not by stylistic experimentation, but by 'increasingly rigorous studies of the problem in its social context'.[131] *Doctor Faustus* is the apogee of such treatment. Within the novel two perspectives are contained, that of Faust, Adrian Leverkühn, the musician who inhabits the small world of the isolated artist,[132] and that of the narrator, Serenus Zeitblom, who is located in strictly observed social and historical time. A 'rounded', realist novel is created on the theme of examining 'the tragedy of modern art'.[133] The tragedy is that while the artist knows that his stylistic problems are determined by the real historical situation of his culture, he is determined to concede nothing to them, and to work independently of them, thereby creating a highly formal art which is at the same time subjective, 'the concentrated expression of intellectual and moral decadence'.[134] Mann questions the work of art itself by examining its social and historical genesis and shows 'how the purely subjective, that which is estranged from and despises all community [because it is not conducive to art] is rooted in the modern bourgeois individualism of the imperialist epoch',[135] and how

> the same situation creates a longing for synthesis, for control, for order and organization, though such a longing has no real foundation in popular life, in the social world, but is the product of the same subjectivity which creates the disintegration . . . hence it destroys itself.[136]

Adorno disagreed with Lukács on every count: with his ideas of form and style, with his notions of realism and of modernism, and with his interpretation of the contemporary plight of literature. Lukács, he argues, is unable to understand the stylistic and technical features of the novel because he subordinates such features to the underlying perspective or 'view of the world', understood as the content of a work, in marked contrast to his (Lukács') own earlier book on the novel, *The Theory of the Novel*,[137] in which he himself established the primacy of form.[138] This leads him to interpret style, whether modernist or realist, as the simple reflection of reality, and to describe modernist style in invariant, biological terms, such as 'decadent', 'sick', instead of examining the apparently invariant, atemporal quality of such style.[139] Lukács rebukes modernist novels for their ontological themes of loneliness, isolation and terror, but he had made such themes into ontological ones by not investigating the specific historical and social determination of them.[140] It is Lukács' notion of realism in literature which is fundamentally at fault. For a work of art is not 'real' in the same way that society is 'real'. Lukács has in effect taken the ground away from any aesthetics by his naïve realist account of the relation between art and reality, which ignores the importance of illusion in the portrayal of reality.[141] He concentrates on narration and not on techniques, thereby overlooking the subjective nature of his idolised realism, not seeing that a 'faithful' rendering of reality may involve fuller representation of it, or caricature of it, in a way which cuts across his distinction between 'abstract potentiality' and 'concrete possibility'.[142]

According to Adorno, all portrayal of subjectivity in the novel, whether solipsistic or not and however achieved stylistically, is based on illusion which is partly true and partly false, depending on the state of society which it both re-presents and implicitly criticises. This illusion or appearance is true in the sense that the structure of society does give rise to forms of individual isolation, but it is false in the sense that such isolation is not absolute or a primary reality.[143] The prevalence of parody in modern art which Lukács indicts as a major feature of modernist decadence is due to the recognition of the illusory nature of subjectivity on the part of modern art, which is, according to Adorno, 'the historical *a priori* of all new art'.[144] Lukács' position also prevents him from distinguishing between the different kinds of subjectivity which may be portrayed: 'objectless' subjectivity, or subjectivity reconciled with the world by having absorbed the world imaginatively into its own confines.[145] In every case the work takes a critical posture towards social reality by means of its style which forms a mode of subjectivity, not by its 'content' or view of the world.

In his examination of the works of individual authors, Adorno adheres to this idea of style as forming particular modes of subjectivity. Subjectivity is 'the correlate of reification',[146] and Adorno interprets different forms of subjectivity in a way which has affinities with his criticism of philosophy and sociology, that is, in terms of the relationship presented between the subject and the social object which structures it. He uses the same criteria which he uses to criticise philosophy and sociology to judge whether the work in question is critical of social reality or not, and to judge how successful it is as a work of art. The criteria on which this judgement is made are whether a philosophy, sociology or work of art denies subjectivity and, implicitly or explicitly, presents objective reality as absolute, or conversely, whether it presents subjectivity as absolute, and implicitly or explicitly denies objective reality.

For Adorno, therefore, there is no need to choose between Franz Kafka and Thomas Mann. He scorns the interpretation of Kafka which sees in the writing a vision of 'nothingness' and impotence, accomplished by means of 'realistic symbolism'.[147] Instead he pays close attention to various features of Kafka's style, emphasising how the texts are structured in ways which undermine conventional habits of reading and modes of communicating meaning. For example, he points out, with close reference to, and quotation from, Kafka's texts, how the latter frequently pits gestures against dialogue so as to undermine the intention of the words spoken,[148] how he uses narrative form but eschews traditional progression in the narrative by substituting various forms of repetition of events, places and so on.[149] He thus produces 'tortuous epics' in which the 'boundary between what is human and the world of things becomes blurred'.[150] This style yields the contours of Kafka's subjectivity. It is an extreme and absolute subjectivity, which does not connect with the external world – 'objectless inwardness' – and therefore cannot distinguish itself from the world. Thus, first, to withdraw into absolute subjectivity is, strictly speaking, impossible because words and sentences break any illusion of absolute immediacy, and Kafka's style is designed to avoid this paradox, but, secondly, such withdrawal succumbs to the very estrangement which it is attempting to escape: 'The subject seeks to break the spell of reification by reifying itself'.[151] Adorno therefore, like Lukács, sees the subjectivity in Kafka's texts and sees a sense in which the texts collude in the distortion to which they bear witness. However, by focusing on the process of Kafka's style and on the complex antinomies evinced in the attempt to express extreme subjectivity, Adorno is able to explain 'terror' and 'isolation' as effects, instead of resorting to them as the ultimate themes of the texts.

It is the same lack of attention to style which vitiates Lukács' interpretation of Thomas Mann's novels. Adorno points out how Lukács tries to explain away Mann's experiments with different perspectives of time in *The Magic Mountain* and in *Doctor Faustus*, and how he fails to appreciate Mann's use of irony as a medium for creating aesthetic distance in his texts, as a way of using and undermining realist illusions in the novel.[152] Mann had worked closely with Adorno on *Doctor Faustus* and had been particularly impressed by Adorno's book, *Philosophy of New Music* and by his book on Wagner.[153] In letters to Adorno, Mann affirmed his use of 'the principle of montage' in *Doctor Faustus*, by which he meant the use of precise detail drawn from a range of sources to enhance fictional

illusions, so that 'palpable reality was for ever indistinguishably merging
into painted perspectives and illusions'.[154] He described this as a
'playful'[155] approach and endorsed Adorno's criticism of the formal
principle of Wagner's work, whereby 'the production [of the work] is
hidden by the appearance of the product'.[156] Mann was also opposed to
this principle, and declared to Adorno that

> The illusionary character of the work of art as something real is
> completely alien to me and has never aroused my ambitions. My
> relationship to the 'work' was too honourably ironic, and I have always
> liked humorously compromising the [process of] production.[157]

In light of this, Lukács has mistakenly taken Mann's novels literally.[158]
For Mann was not 'in search of bourgeois man',[159] but in search of a style
appropriate to 'modern' art as he understood it.

Lukács' interpretation of *Doctor Faustus* is particularly ill-conceived.
Adorno objects to Lukács' reference to his (Adorno's) essay on 'The
Ageing [*sic*] of New Music' in support of the argument that modern art is
decadent.[160] Adorno's point in that essay and in *Philosophy of New Music*
was that new music is not the 'pure expression [of] terror',[161] as Lukács
interpreted him, but a certain stylistic principle which should submit
itself to 'insistent self-criticism'.[162] Mann based *Doctor Faustus* on
Adorno's *Philosophy of New Music*.[163] Adrian Leverkühn speaks large
chunks taken from Adorno's text to explain his style of composition, and
the music theory expounded by another character in the book, Kret-
schmar, is also based on Adorno's ideas.[164] However, it is not just music
theory but Adorno's sociological interpretation of new art which is
contained in the book, and these ideas are not merely quoted in a way
which is restricted to the isolated Leverkühn whose problems are
'studied' by Mann within the framework of a 'realist' novel, as Lukács
said. But, as Mann explicitly stated, the whole novel is composed on the
basis of the same principles and antinomies which structure the possibility
of style in new music: '. . . to portray the whole cultural crisis in addition
to the crisis of music was the fundamental motif of my book . . . I felt
clearly that my book itself would have to become the thing it dealt with:
namely, . . . constructivist music.'[165] Hence Lukács' exposition of 'the
tragedy of modern art' in relation to *Doctor Faustus* is as wrong as his ideas
about modernism differ from Adorno's ideas about new music. More
fundamentally, Lukács was wrong to read social comment from what he
considered to be the 'content' of the book, since he thereby ignored the
real social significance to be read off from the style of the book, a book,
moreover, which explicitly states its own stylistic strictures.

The same criteria regarding the relation between subject and object as
it is structured by style guided Adorno's criticism of Brecht's operas,
dramas and theory of the epic theatre. Brecht's impatience with the
Frankfurt School is revealed in the diary which he wrote when they were

all living in exile in California.[166] He considered that the Institute had defused Marxism, and thus contributed to the evils of society which it sought merely to diagnose.[167] Yet Brecht, Benjamin and Adorno, whatever their differences, all wrote sociological analyses of literature as authors or composers, unlike Lukács, and were interested both in the sociological problems which were involved in composing and also in the social effect or reception of works.

Brecht also rejected Lukács' notions of critical and socialist realism in all forms of literature. Socialist realism, according to Lukács, also portrays 'rounded' and 'harmonious' characters 'from the inside . . . whose energies are devoted to the building of a different future, and whose psychological and moral make-up is determined by this'.[168] Brecht thought that this was aesthetically and politically undesirable, but also that it was a hidebound and restricted notion of realism. In the theatre, he believed that characterisation should not be based on the creation of harmonious individuals who invite the audience to participate vicariously in their overcoming of social contradictions, but that dramatisation should dissolve such habits in the spectator by presenting social reality in a way which accentuates 'the contradiction between every-day appearance and what is historically possible and realizable',[169] primarily through revealing the 'strangeness' of what passes for normality. Benjamin, who wrote as Brecht's spokesman on the latter's theory of epic theatre, stressed the use of montage techniques to achieve this effect.[170] By montage, he meant various ways of juxtaposing reality and fiction in order to expose both the illusions of fiction and the illusions of social reality, such as interrupting action, and pitting verbal against gestural action, as ways of challenging the norms of discursive meaning. Brecht understood this as 'a realism for his time', for the truth about social reality can be conveyed in many different forms and styles, and he denied that he was advocating a formalist or constructivist view as Lukács charged him:

> Realistic means: discovering the causal complexes of society/ unmasking the prevailing view of things as the view of those who rule it/writing from the standpoint of the class which offers the broadest solutions for the pressing difficulties in which human society is caught/ emphasizing the element of development/making possible the concrete, and making possible abstractions from it.[171]

Adorno sympathised with Brecht's intentions. He reviewed *The Threepenny Opera* with enthusiasm in 1928 and in 1929, although he described the music of the early Brecht operas as achieving their effect by means of pastiche and parody, rather than by exploiting new techniques to create a wholly changed dramatic form.[172] Later, Adorno wrote an essay *Schwierigkeiten Beim Komponieren* (The Difficulties of Composing), which was based on Brecht's essay, *Funf Schwierigkeiten beim Schreiben der Wahrheit* (Five Difficulties in Writing the Truth), and in which he acknowledged the same difficulties as Brecht in finding a way to challenge the prevailing norms of exchange and reception of art.[173] Adorno had, however, come to be critical of Brecht's solution, of the very idea that there is a 'solution' to the antinomical relation of art to society, although Adorno had not perceived Brecht's earlier work as the presentation of a dogmatic solution.[174]

Adorno's argument concerns Brecht's actual plays, as opposed to his *theory* of the epic theatre. When Brecht translates the re-education of the audience into dramatic terms by eliminating the traditional concept of character, his style establishes another set of unintended and equally undesirable illusions in place of the ones destroyed.[175] This criticism is similar to Adorno's criticism of new epistemologies in philosophy and sociology, in that any aesthetic which seeks completely to deny the illusory power of the subject will tend indirectly to reinstate that illusion even more than one which overstates the power of the subject. Adorno points to the prevalence of traditional cathartic efforts in Brecht's plays, to the theatricality of their plain-spokenness, and to the frequently pantomime effect produced by their explicit political commitment.[176] In fact, Brecht was not able to practice *Verfremdung* in his plays as he preached it. He does not make social reality look strange, he makes it appear straightforward and thus creates another fiction which he ratifies by stating it in a coercive and dictatorial fashion.[177] Brecht tries to reject established meaning and modes of communication in the theatre instead of undermining them on their own ground. His commandeering of dramaturgy in the cause of anti-illusionist theatre only affects the old meanings and hence new meaning in a very external and formal way.[178] Thus Brecht does not destroy 'autonomous' art and put a new functional art in its place. On the contrary, he makes art even more autonomous, because, by using it didactically, emphasising the 'primacy of lesson over . . . form', he makes it even more formal instead of more effective.[179]

> . . . the artistic principle of simplification not only purged real politics of the illusory distinctions projected by subjective reflection into social objectivity, as Brecht intended, but it also falsified the very objectivity which didactic drama laboured to distil.[180]

For manipulation of style cannot guarantee specific social effects. Such an ambition is based on a overly simple theory of social reality. Instead of dissolving 'reified consciousness', the art work may itself be 'reified a second time' by that consciousness,[181] that is, it may well be experienced in the established ways. The social significance, or 'praxis' of a work, is not 'encysted' by its social effect, but by its 'truth content'.[182] The 'truth content' is the relation between subject and object structured by style, and that relation can only be reformulated by works which change the relation to illusion, not by attempting a direct escape from it: 'The organizing, unifying principle of each and every work of art is borrowed from that very rationality, whose claim to totality it seeks to defy'.[183]

Adorno thus seeks to demonstrate that Brecht's attempt in drama to avoid representation of subjectivity is as self-contradictory as Kafka's attempt to withdraw into absolute subjectivity. He criticises Sartre's dramaturgy on the same grounds as he criticises Brecht's: for demanding a changed attitude instead of compelling it, although Sartre's demand is, of course, quite different from Brecht's.[184] Adorno is opposed to artistic and literary thematics, that is, to composing or criticising works of art according to interpretations of their ostensible 'themes'. He is therefore equally critical of Lukács' reading of modernist style according to existential themes as he is of Brecht's composing of plays in the cause of political themes, and as he is of Sartre's composing of plays according to explicit existential themes. These explicit commitments tend to restructure meaning (style) in a way which reinstates precisely what the theme intends to eliminate, usually some form of subjectivity. For example, the theme of Sartre's plays is the 'absurdity' and 'meaninglessness' of existence, but, by making this theme into the clear message of his plays, he confers on it a positive meaning and thereby contradicts his own intention.[185] The mistake common to Sartre and Brecht is that they try to destroy the 'autonomy' of artistic meaning, that is, they try to avoid the fact that meaning in literature is based on the illusion that a literal, ordinary word once used in a fictional text retains its literal meaning entirely. They seek to renounce the change in meaning which occurs once words are, as it were, transcribed into a work of art.[186] But, because they do not concede the necessity of illusion, they 'assimilate themselves to mere existence',[187] instead of arming themselves against whatever power gives verisimilitude to illusion. They thus contribute to 'the abdication of the subject'[188] which they abhor. Sartre seeks to enthrone the existential subject; Brecht, the proletariat.

A work of art which would not fall into these paradoxes would have to present the crisis in meaning and the restructuring of meaning as a problem of its form, as part of the objective conditions which constitute the *a priori* possibility of the work, not merely as a deviation on the part of an aberrant subject. Adorno believed that Samuel Beckett achieved this in some of his plays.[189] Beckett avoided the aporia of expressionism, as for example, in Kafka's writing, of using language (meaning) to present absolute subjectivity and thereby transcending pure subjectivity, and the aporia of existentialism, as, for example, in Sartre's writing, of using language (meaning) to establish that there is no meaning and therefore reinstating the meaning discounted. Instead, Beckett elicits the support of the illusions of fictional meaning in order to restructure such meaning.[190] In a close analysis of Beckett's play *Endgame*, Adorno traces the way in which Beckett does this.[191] Adorno distinguishes three levels of 'meaning' in drama, which, conventionally, create unity between the overall intention of a play and its action: the metaphysical meaning, the overall intention or meaning of the play, and the meaning of words and sentences at the level of dialogue. Once the first of these, metaphysical meaning, is abandoned, the other two levels are fundamentally changed.[192] Beckett's achievement is to have restructured meaning at the level of dialogue in a way which strains towards overall meaning but which is continually stymied, and thus does not reconstruct a positive metaphysical meaning even one of 'absurdity' or 'nothingness'.[193] In this way, Beckett is consistent (Adorno compares him to Mann in *The Magic Mountain* and in *Doctor Faustus*), for the relation of art to society is presented as the incessant problem of the form of the work and is not simply stated or the work given a new 'function'.[194] Adorno examines the dialogue of the play which is largely duologue, emphasising Beckett's use of parody, inversion of meaning, use of gesture, although he does not suggest that Beckett relies on highly formal or constructivist techniques.[195] He draws, in the course of this analysis, the outline of a master/slave dialectic, imprisoned in the midst of dead nature, in which the slave can no longer control the master, although the master is in no way reconciled with himself.[196] The metaphysical meaning eschewed by the play would be the reconciliation of master, slave and nature, the overall meaning which it strains toward is conveyed by an impending catastrophe which never occurs, and these meanings are structured by the dialogue, which is quite open-ended.

In these analyses of works of literature, Adorno pursues the view that social critique is – and can only be – imbedded in the form of a work, not in a discrete 'content'. This is not to emphasise form as such, but meaning or significance as a relation between subjectivity and social objectivity. As in his critique of philosophy and his critique of sociology Adorno demonstrates and prescribes in his critique of literature the importance of understanding and working from necessary illusion, on pain of otherwise falling into contradictions. The illusions of literature, like the illusions of philosophy and of sociology, are determined by the reified structure of society.

New Music and Social Illusion

In his various writings on music, Adorno examined the 'contradiction between the forces and the relations of production'. His analyses of every kind of music was based on the premise that commodity fetishism (reification) in music had increased, that the commodity character of music was deeply affected by the new modes of mechanical reproduction and the new possibilities of exchange and distribution. As a result, first, classical and romantic music were exchanged and distributed, for example, on the radio and in live performances, in ways which emphasised those features of their form (internal structure of meaning) most amenable to such modes of distribution and reception at the expense of the original integrity of their form. Secondly, new kinds of music were developed in conjunction with the new modes of reproduction and exchange, for example, music for films and popular music. Thirdly, new music was composed on the basis of new techniques, and designed to avoid the new modes of distribution, for example, the music of the first Vienna School.[197] Yet such music, owing to its esoteric nature, was fated to display 'the same disastrous pattern'[198] which it sought to combat. The 'contradiction' occurs between those kinds of music which adapt to the prevalent modes of exchange and reception and music which resists them, and also within the latter kind of music. Under the relations of production Adorno looks at music which adapts, and under forces of production he looks at music which resists adaptation.

The business of the sociology of music is to investigate the relation between music and the person who listens to music, considered as a socialised individual.[199] This does not involve simply ascertaining consumer responses to music by empirical means. For such responses will convey nothing about the form in which the music is being received, and thus nothing about its social meaning, or anything about how the reception of music affects people. For example, enthusiasm expressed by people for classical music heard on the radio tells us nothing about how that music is being broadcast, how its meaning and reception are altered by the medium.[200] When Adorno examines the musical relations of production he therefore always examines the relation between the formal structure of the music and its reception.

'Music life' is one of the arenas which Adorno discusses under the relations of production. The phrase refers to the live performance of music, and 'official music life' to the great centres of musical performance, especially Vienna and Paris, as the former arbiters of general public taste.[201] Adorno explains what he means by 'contradiction' in this realm too. He argues that the overall function of music in society has changed, and that this change affects every aspect of music. Music has lost its previous 'autonomy'. This 'autonomy' was determined by the emancipation of music from an immediate context of use and ritual and its acquiring value in exchange. The result was music which partly legitimised the social order which produced it and which partly criticised that order. By contrast, the breach between these functions has now become complete. Some kinds of music legitimises the social structure, they are totally 'functionalized' kinds of music, for example, music for distraction or diversion (entertainment); while music which has a critical function has become so far removed from general reception that it no longer exercises an effective critical role.[202] An illusion of immediacy and use and hence of intelligibility surrounds the reception of totally functionalised music, whereas such music is entirely determined by its value in exchange.[203] Production and reproduction have always been relatively divorced in music in the sense that music has to be performed, and the interpretation expressed by the performance may contradict the intention of the work. The likelihood of this discrepancy is one of the ways in which Adorno explains how music could both legitimise and oppose the social structure. Performance of music takes place according to the prevalent norms of capitalist society and the privileged participation in music even when the aesthetic meaning of music has universal impli-cations.[204] Since participation in music has increased, the principles which guide performance have become even more divorced from the meaning of the music. Composers try increasingly to control the way their music is performed, while in fact the interpretation of it is increasingly taken out of their hands.[205]

Adorno also offers a more technical exposition of these hypotheses, of how the meaning of music may be altered by the medium of repro-duction, whether the music is performed in the concert hall or broadcast on the radio.[206] This exposition depends on the contrast between the technical notion of intelligibility established by classical music and the different norm of intelligibility which tends to be demanded when music is received by the untrained ear. Adorno's argument is that given the current mode of exchange and distribution of music, music is adjusted at the stage of reproduction in order to attain the greatest intelligibility in the second sense, which may amount to the least intelligibility in the first.

In classical music, especially the symphonic form of the sonata, the intelligibility of the whole composition depends on the development of the theme, accomplished by details which have an independent life but which are ultimately apprehended in terms of the overall structure of the piece, ' . . . the melodic content of the basic rhythm, that is to say, the intervals which constitute it, change perpetually . . . '[207] Romantic music, by contrast, detaches the detail by increased use of chromaticism, so that the detail itself rather than its relation to the whole becomes the unit of expression, which together with exaggerated contrasts and stress on sound colour, is easier to grasp.[208] Adorno demonstrates that all music, whether classical, romantic or popular, tends to be adjusted in the process of reproduction to the most easily intelligible standard. Thus, separable themes, strong colour, spectacular sound and single melodic lines are emphasised. Adorno calls this 'standardization', 'fetishism in music', and 'the regression of listening'.[209] The loss of unity in the music and the shift of meaning from the totality to the individual moments produces an atomised mode of listening (apprehension) or 'quotation' listening, as easily memorisable elements are loosened from the whole.[210] Works become 'conglomerates of tunes of both sensual richness and structural poverty' which render 'unnecessary the process of thinking'[211] which was needed to comprehend the overall structure of classical music. In the case of the older music, an attitude is produced in the listener

> which leads him to seek color and stimulating sounds. Music, however, composed in structural rather than coloristic terms, does not satisfy these mechanized claims.[212]

Popular music, by which Adorno understood jazz and other forms of 'light' or entertainment music, is composed according to 'these mechanized claims'. Adorno describes it as 'standardized' too. Standardization' in this kind of music means that the overall theme is clearly stated at the beginning of the piece but that the details do not develop the theme, they merely repeat it, and have no special status within the whole work. Hence the emphasis on 'beat', repeatable rhythm. This 'standardization' is hidden by devices which Adorno names 'pseudo-individualization' because they are designed to give the appearance that detail really has an autonomous role in composition, and thus endow the piece 'with the halo of free choice or open market on the basis of standardization itself'.[213] In fact the stated form of the music determines the way it must be listened to, 'The composition hears for the listener'.[214] Understanding such music means accepting these commands for listening.[215]

Adorno suggests that the desire for these forms of easily intelligible music is determined by the mode of production and the work-process. People are themselves 'products of the same mechanisms which determine the production of popular music'.[216] They treat their spare time as a means to reproduce their working activity and

> They want standardized goods and pseudo-individualization, because leisure is an escape from work and at the same time is molded after those psychological attitudes to which their workaday world exclusively habituates them.[217]

Yet, Adorno never examines the work process nor does he differentiate between different kinds of work experience, that is, between class and music. He does emphasise that popular music acts as a 'social cement', by which he means that it produces a kind of social cohesion which depends on the individual relinquishing autonomy,[218] but he adds that this is not an entirely passive process since it requires active transference of libidinal energy on the part of the individual.[219]

In the book which Adorno wrote with Hanns Eisler, *Composing for the*

Films,[220] criticism of the current abuse of music in films is more than balanced by suggestions as to how music might be used differently in this medium. The contrast is drawn between the stereotyped depiction of social reality enhanced by standardised music, and the possibility of radically changing people's perception of social reality with the aid of advanced musical effects, using both the new techniques and the new technology.[221] Adorno was also interested in altering the use of radio in the broadcasting of music. He recommended, for example, that re-hearsals of music should be broadcast and music made as accessible as possible by exposing and explaining the processes of composition and performance not by the process of standardisation.[222]

On the other hand, Adorno was not able to accept that, given the current mode of production, any art form with a popular basis could be politically invigorating, and hence he analysed jazz and popular music as corrupt styles of the traditional forms of music, not as entirely new forms of music. He was so insistent on looking at the form of music and not merely at reactions to it that he failed to differentiate between the very different kinds of reactions aroused by different forms of jazz and popular music. However, in the typology of musical behaviour which Adorno devised in order to examine the various relations between types of music and types of listeners, the jazz composer and the jazz fan are delineated in terms of a response against official music life.[223] However, this response, like many others including new music, does not constitute a consistently critical stance. As a response to reification, it is particularly reified, that is, it displays the features which it seeks to criticise in a very evident way.[224]

'New music' was, for Adorno, a form of composing which did not, initially, adapt to the prevalent mode of exchange and reception of music. The name 'new music' was a deliberately polemical appellation adopted in Vienna in the early twenties when the 'International Society for New Music' was established, and intended to disassociate the Society from the new German, impressionist and other nineteenth-century schools of music.[225] The question of why the music of this period and the music of the second Vienna School has continued to be known as 'new music' and has not been absorbed into the mainstream, in contrast to the new painting of this period, is, for Adorno, a sociological one.[226] It is not a question which can be answered by reference to the social origins and social function of the music, an approach which would tend to dismiss it as 'bourgeois' and 'decadent'.[227] The failure of this music to be generally accepted must be related to the form of the music, for the social reception of a work can only be explained by attending to its inner tensions and their resolution. Adorno interprets the social isolation of this music as a contradiction between the social meaning of the music and the norms of musical reception; one which creates a further contradiction within the music as it succumbs to the demands of social recognition and thereby defuses its social significance:

> The guiding category of contradiction is twofold: that works formulate contradiction and thereby reveal it in the markings of their imperfections, is the measure of their success, while at the same time the force of contradiction mocks formulation and destroys works.[228]

Adorno developed a typology of music which avoids the demands of the market for the traditional idiom of intelligibility. The criteria of the typology are, first, how explicitly the composer is aware of his social isolation (alienation, *Entfremdung*), secondly, how social isolation is expressed in the work, thirdly, whether the work seeks to overcome isolation or not.[229] He distinguishes four types of music in this way: first that of Schönberg which, unaware of its social position, nevertheless presents most radically the social antinomies which structure it; secondly, the neo-classicism of Stravinsky which is explicitly aware of 'alienation', and seeks to present a reconciled community in the music; thirdly, a type of music between the first two, which is based on knowledge of alienation, but which knows, too, that any 'solution' is only an illusion. This applies to the middle work of Stravinsky and to the collaboration of Kurt Weill and Brecht. The fourth type is *Gebrauchsmusik* or *Gemeinschaftsmusik*, which tries to break alienation by creating music designed to be broadly and simply intelligible, for example, the work of Hindemith and some of the work of Eisler.[230]

Adorno devoted most attention to Schönberg's work. He saw in the evolution of Schönberg's music from free atonality to the twelve tone system a change from a music which challenged most radically the norms of intelligibility in both composing and listening, to a music which attempted to found itself on a new orthodoxy and escape the destructive estrangement of its initial challenge. By means of detailed technical analyses of Schönberg's early work, Adorno shows the ways in which Schönberg's music brings out many features of music which had been *latent* in earlier music but dissolves the apparent naturalness of those features. At the same time, the music makes revolutionary demands on the listener in view of the prevalent reception of the tradition, and in view of the complex ways in which its 'ideas' are developed.[231] Adorno calls this *Verfremdung* in music, making apparent musical normality appear strange.[232] Unlike innovation at other periods, the new music does not recreate an ultimately affirmative idiom, not even for an alternative vision of society.[233] New music, in Schönberg's first phase, was relentlessly negative in the sense that the procedure for composing remained open-ended, and thus so did the question of the relation of its form to its material – of its meaning in relation to society. On the other hand, such a position is inherently unstable. Composition tends to settle in a determinate way. It was Schönberg's attempt to codify this tendency which Adorno interpreted as a return to a rigid system, as a way of granting a 'method' of composing priority over its critical relation to its material, and thus fixing its relation to society by creating the appearance of synthesis between the work of art (the aesthetic subject) and social objectivity.[234] Adorno demonstrates the effect which this had on Schönberg's later work by analysing it in great technical detail.[235] He seeks to show that Schönberg's 'solution' is a false one, partly because it results in inferior work and thus does not bring the artist any nearer the public.[236]

Originally Schönberg exposed the illusions of musical normality but composed in a way which was unintelligible to his audience. He resisted the reification of musical material, that is, resisted appealing to the prevalent norms of intelligibility, at the cost of opening up a chasm between the music and the public.[237] His work was therefore reified *by* society, in the sense that it remained divorced from the possibility of changing musical consciousness. Schönberg's subsequent development of serialism amounted to a reification of his own work in the sense that he reinstated the authority of a method over the material. His work henceforth displayed the same kind of reification it had originally sought to combat.

In this part of Adorno's work reification is most clearly explicated at the level of meaning, illusion and intelligibility. He construes the theory of value, that social relations between men appear in the form of a property of a thing, so that it provides a model and criterion for saying that something may appear to be intelligible when it is not, and conversely, that something may appear to be unintelligible when it is intelligible. Commodity fetishism does not only imply that people misunderstand the social relations underlying commodities, but that social relations appear *intelligible* because value appears to be the property of the commodity, just as use values really are properties of the commodity. Thus the social relations of consumption seem immediate and transparent. Adorno connects the ways in which social relations of exchange appear intelligible with illusions of intelligibility in music. Music which is reproduced and/or produced according to prevalent norms of the most widespread intelligibility mistakenly appears intelligible both in terms of the social relations of its production and in terms of the structuring of meaning in the music itself. For example, music may seem intelligible to the listener, such as the romanticised performance of a classical symphony, but in strict musical terms it is not intelligible. Since it appears intelligible, it seems to have immediate value in use, when in fact it is being reproduced and exchanged according to value in exchange. Similarly, popular music is formed musically so as to guarantee instant intelligibility and this creates an illusion of immediate value in use. New music is a contrasting case for its idiom is intelligible in musical terms since it relies on traditional musical language but dissolves the apparent 'naturalness' of that language. It seems, however, unintelligible to its listeners because it does not conform to the prevalent norms of immediate intelligibility and thus immediate value in use. By giving reification various meanings in terms of musical technique, Adorno established a correlation between the illusion of intelligibility (or unintelligibility) within music and the illusion that the social relations of music are intelligible. This perspective is sociological because the criterion of real intelligibility or unintelligibility of a work is given by the relation of the cultural product in question to the norms of shared meaning and intelligibility both in the sphere of composition and in the sphere of reception. Yet the real or apparent intelligibility and unintelligibility is not the object of the inquiry. The object is the relation between the social formation of the work and its reception in music, and between the way the work of art forms social relations and the structuring of meaning in texts in both music and literature.

Chapter 7

The Melancholy Science

The *Dialectic of Enlightenment* reveals the paradox of the late eighteenth-century concept of reason: instead of bringing emancipation as it promised, it turned out to be a new form of domination. Adorno, however, reveals more persistently the paradoxes of new philosophical and theoretical movements of the twentieth century which promise emancipation, 'the dialectic of humanism'. Adorno and many other German writers of the inter-war period were attracted to an anti-humanist stance.[1] They rejected the humanist legacy of historicism, philosophical anthropology, 'realism' in art, and epistemology, for these were seen as bankrupt, incapable of providing any analysis of a much-changed historical reality. Adorno held that these varieties of 'anti-humanism' were enslaving rather than liberating because they recreated the very evils which they sought to define and eschew. He thus recognised a 'dialectic of humanism' and showed how the 'new' philosophy, sociology, and literary theory relapsed into the assumptions which they deplored. He attributed this partly to the resurrection of the old ambition of philosophy to establish indubitable grounds for its own endeavour, and partly to the unrealistic attempt to make no concessions at all to the power of the old illusions and their social basis. This belief, that intellectual and social transformation can only be effective if the power of traditions is conceded, was always the measure of the radicalism of Adorno and the Frankfurt School and not of their equivocation. Adorno's originality is to acknowledge that he himself is also bound to exacerbate the syndrome which he sought to analyse, and, indeed, the application of the thesis of increasing reification to his own work is a way of accepting a degree of theoretical impotence in exchange for the abandoned claims of philosophical and political omnipotence. He strove to find a way out of the paradox of 'anti-humanism' by undermining humanism on its own grounds. His response is preoccupation with style. 'Style' is not uniform or codified, not elevated over the material which it forms, but stands for continual vigilance to the mode in which theory is presented, thereby recasting the relation between theory and praxis. If Lukács has turned Marxism into method, Adorno has turned it into the search for style.[2]

Social analysis is approached as the immanent question of 'the conceptual mediation' of social reality.[3] Adorno construes Marx's theory of value so that it describes the process which structures social reality at the level of meaning, or, more accurately, at the level of illusion. This process is the production and exchange of commodities which entails 'the reduction of the products to be exchanged to their equivalents, to something abstract',[4] and, that which is abstract, in this sense, is conceptual. This 'conceptual entity' Adorno calls 'illusion'.[5] Reality is thereby presented to people in a way which 'prevents them from becoming conscious of the conditions under which they live'.[6] This perspective cuts across the distinction between naturalism and anti-naturalism, or, in other terms, between *Erklären* and *Verstehen*. For it insists on the systematic formation of social reality according to a principle which can be specified without any reference to the meaning conferred on that reality by individuals, and yet this principle produces illusions which need to be interpreted at the level of meaning. 'Meaning' refers to the ways in which the social structure seems intelligible when it is not, and unintelligible when it is. 'Meaning' is not predicated of the intentional action of individuals, nor does it refer to the negotiation of shared meanings by social actors. 'Meaning' or 'conceptuality' is a property of the social structure. In the realm of art Adorno distinguishes between the 'meaning' of a work and its communication or reception; 'meaning' corresponds here to the process of production and thus to the way in which the work represents the relation between subjectivity and social objectivity. The sphere of production is contrasted with the sphere of exchange and consumption in which commodity fetishism may intervene and obscure the meaning of a work of art. The production of meaning is thus opposed to its communication (illusion); in this case 'meaning' is contrasted with illusion. More generally, however, 'meaning' is identified with the illusory way in which the social structure appears to be intelligible or unintelligible. This is why Adorno prefers to call meaning 'conceptuality', for 'meaning' implies directness and transparency. 'Illusion' refers therefore to the misleading appearance of social reality generated by the underlying process of production. Adorno explains the imposition of illusion by analysing the underlying mode of production; but he explains the negotiation of illusion on the part of individuals by using psychoanalytic concepts to show that 'the subject has lost its substance'. *The Authoritarian Personality* is an attempt to look at this negotiation of illusion, but, in that book, the underlying process which imposes illusion is introduced in such an inhibited fashion that Adorno fails to make a convincing connection.

Adorno's construal of Marx's theory of value develops an interesting ambiguity in Marx's theory of the formation of proletarian class-consciousness. The conventional interpretation of the formation of proletarian class-consciousness in capitalist society is that as workers who sell their labour-power come together to share the same workplace, so their common interests as a class in relation to another class, the owners of the means of production, become increasingly apparent to them. In other terms, the underlying social relations which determine the social structure become visible and intelligible to them as a result of their experience in the workplace. In pre-capitalist, feudal society, by contrast, peasants, isolated in the desmesne of their lord, had no chance of coming to realise their common interests. Yet, in the earlier mode of production, the social relations of exploitation between peasant and lord were personal and direct, and thus transparent and intelligible – in all areas of social life, not only in the organisation of work. It is this duality in the way in which social relations are intelligible and the way in which they are not intelligible within the same kind of society which recurs in Marx's account of capitalist society. For, according to Marx, commodity production depends on freely alienable forces of production and thus on the development of markets which intervene increasingly in the relations between men and obscure those relations, giving them the appearance of relations between things (commodity fetishism). If this aspect of Marx's theory of value is stressed, then as markets become more complex, social relations between men become less visible and less intelligible to them, both inside and outside the workplace. Adorno takes up this aspect of Marx's analysis as a framework for the understanding of late capitalism. He is interested in the new forms by which social reality is obscured in late capitalist society, and the centrality of 'illusion' in his analyses is a way of formulating the problem of ideological domination without any reference to class-consciousness, alienation, hegemony or legitimation. As a result, however, he does not differentiate between the experiences which people have of 'illusion'; social inequality cannot be conceptualised.

Adorno revitalises static notions of 'base' and 'superstructure' by turning back to a distinction between processes and resultant social forms. Yet he concentrates on cultural forms, intellectual and artistic works, not on the analogous social forms such as the wage-form or the money-form. This approach has the advantage that intellectual and artistic works are conceived as real, as forms, rather than as epiphenomena, or as reflections of social reality, and which, in turn, give *form* to experience of social reality. This amounts to a radically social or sociological definition of artistic and intellectual form. As forms of social illusion, the divergences as well as the continuities which may arise between cultural form and social reception are defined as the province of sociological inquiry. However, the neglect of those social forms on which the analogy of cultural form depends is serious. Adorno declares that change has occurred in the organisation of production and in markets for labour and goods, with the result that in the market for labour and in the workplace, the social structure has remained unintelligible, while, in the market for cultural goods and in the sphere of leisure, it has acquired an illusory intelligibility. Although he indicts sociologists for finding society opaque, Adorno himself only investigates the opaqueness as it appears in the sphere of culture. Thus, although his investigations into the possibility of cultural experience are based on a fully-fledged theory of artistic production, exchange and consumption, they are conducted in a theoretical vacuum.

Adorno's neglect of social forms diminishes his ability to offer a compelling analysis of political organisation and of relations of power in capitalist society. Throughout his work, power in society is paramount but elusive. This is another result of the way in which Marx's theory of value is generalised as 'reification' with minimal reference to the actual productive relations between men, and without any identification of a social subject. Hence the process of production is emphasised as all-powerful, and reification becomes a synonym for the principle of power which is universal but unlocatable, and which affects everyone equally. Adorno indicts Heidegger for his alleged voluntarism, for implying that the fulfilment and realisation of man depends on an act of personal choice. Heidegger's prescription, according to Adorno, ignores the power of social and political institutions which determine men and hence which circumscribe any possibility of self-determination or autonomy. Yet Adorno is himself in a similar predicament: he too makes it impossible to reinsert the 'individual' into a socio-political context. He redefines Marx's theory of class in a way which renders domination within the class, as well as between classes, less amenable to analysis, cripples the concept of organisation, and adapts Freudian concepts in a way which promises to be radically sociological, but which stops short at the point where those concepts might be transformed into a theory of socio-political action. This inconsistency between his critique of Heidegger and his own stance arises because Adorno provides no account of those social forms which would have to be specified prior to any account of corresponding political forms. He has thus sacrificed the unique advantage of a Marxian approach: the derivation of political relations and of the state from an analysis of the productive and social relations of a specific kind of society. This is also true of the work of Habermas.[7] Although Habermas has based his theory of late capitalism on a theory of the state, he has abandoned the analysis of the commodity-form as the basic unit of social analysis. As a result, the state is a force *sui generis*, and the relation between state and society is conceived by reducing it, ultimately, to the question of the legitimacy of the state. Thus it is impossible to ask if the separation of the political sphere from the socio-economic sphere, and the relative autonomy of the state is real or merely apparent.

The idea that Adorno is an Hegelian Marxist is a misleading oversimplification. His relation to Hegel is not comparable to that of Lukács. Adorno rejects Lukács' solution to the irresolvable antinomies of traditional epistemology – to grant primacy to a new constitutive subject, the proletariat. He does not reject the question of constitution as such, or the subject/object dichotomy. Unlike some thinkers, such as Heidegger or Althusser, who devise a new terminology in order to discard the old presuppositions, Adorno regards the antinomies of philosophy and of theory as real and powerful, to be redefined, but not to be circumvented or abrogated except on pain of contradiction. Adorno interprets these antinomies as arising from the misrecognition of the relationship between thought and social reality, between subject and object. For all philosophy – and all sociology and art – is interpreted by Adorno as cognitive activity which gives form to such a relationship, as *epistemology*, even when the philosophy in question consists of a radical attempt to abjure epistemology. In this general sense of 'sublating' the tradition, not rescinding it, Adorno betrays an Hegelian inspiration, but his conceptual apparatus, such as the criticism of identity thinking, negative dialectic, reification, is never Hegelian in origin.

Adorno's notion of the 'subject' is a residual one. He presents the view that a notion of the subject, whether individual or class, must be 'construed and denied'.[8] It must be denied as the unity of the universal and the particular in any Hegelian sense, or as the class whose particular interests represent the interests of the whole society, the universal class, in any Marxian or Lukácsian sense. However, it is sociologically and logically wrong not to construe some notion of the 'subject'. It is sociologically wrong, because social formation and deformation cannot be conceived otherwise, and, as a result, it is logically wrong, because it leads to antinomies in theory. Yet Adorno mourns the 'subject' which has lost its 'substance' and his thought is haunted by this ghostly, missing agency.

Nor can this way of conceiving the 'subject' be judged 'left-Hegelian', for Adorno consistently undermines all forms of 'abstract humanism'. He uses Freudian theory to demonstrate that the human subject, or 'ego', does not constitute a self-grounding unity, because it is constituted by a society which is based on the production of commodities. He refuses the humanist implication as in Hegel, or Feuerbach, or Lukács, that the subject is or could be reconciled or reunited with its essence, however defined – 'Man is the ideology of dehumanization'.[9]

Adorno himself drew attention to another charge of left-wing Hegelianism to which he appeared more vulnerable: that he overemphasised theory, and that he related thought to society as a whole, instead of relating thought to the productive activity of men and thus to a particular class society.[10] Adorno's answer to this charge is that his analysis of the underlying processes of society is not based on any notion of society 'as a whole'. The emphasis on commodity exchange means that the 'whole' of society cannot be the object of analysis. He admits that the process of production and the resultant social forms, and not productive activity or the agency of social classes or individuals, are the objects of his analysis. His answer to the question of the status of theory was to make more explicit how the 'melancholy science' is precisely an attempt to redefine the relation between theory and praxis.

Adorno is best known for offering critical theory as an alternative to positivism in sociology, but he deserves even more attention for offering an alternative to those positions which also reject positivism, such as Husserl's phenomenology and Heidegger's hermeneutics. His criticism of phenomenology and hermeneutics has equal force in relation to their sociological offspring, phenomenological and hermeneutic sociology, and 'reflexive' sociology.[11] This so-called 'reflexive' sociology evinces an epistemological concern with the ground of its own activity arising from a critical awareness of the way in which conventional sociology 'constitutes' its object in its theorising or in its talk.[12] All these kinds of philosophical sociology make cognitive processes, not moral facts or shared values, into the object of their inquiry.[13] Adorno's argument against phenomenology or phenomenological sociology is that it repeats more-or-less explicitly what positivism does implicitly, namely, bases truth or reality on the analysis of consciousness, and thereby reduces social reality to a demonstrably constricted consciousness of it. He thus avoids the paradox of sociological reflexivity: because a reference to self is judged logically prior to a reference to society, society and history are lost in an infinite regress of self-constitution.

Reification has been employed as a critical category in this phenomenological tradition as well as in the neo-Marxist tradition, and in sociological amalgams of the two traditions, with the result that it has become highly ambiguous. There are two distinct uses of reification which are frequently confused and even conflated: a use which locates the origin of knowledge of social reality solely in our minds, and a use which locates it in a determinative social process.[14] In the first case, reification is primarily a fact or modality of consciousness, in the second case, it is primarily an objective social process which determines consciousness. The difference between these two uses of reification is the difference between the view that something abstract is wrongly thought of as real or immutably true, and the view that something concrete is wrongly thought of as abstract. These uses have been conflated in recent attempts in sociology to generalise Marx's theory of value by using the category of reification.[15] The confusion may have arisen because in English we understand 'abstract' to mean unreal, and 'real' or 'concrete' to mean tangible or thing-like, while in the German tradition 'concrete' may mean the sum of relations which characterise a thing, and 'abstract' may mean the exclusion of some of these relations. Marx's theory of commodity fetishism implies that concrete social relations between men are structured and presented in a way which excludes some of these relations, and hence the commodity seems to exist by itself. But, in English, what exists by itself tends to be interpreted as something real or concrete (tangible or thing-like), and Marx is taken to be stressing that something is wrongly believed to be real. In this way the emphasis on how one set of relations is transformed into another, each of which is real, is lost. Thus the explication of an objective and historically specific social process is turned into a universal way of thinking.

The category of reification has also found its way into sociological literature as an ostensibly critical category via Talcott Parsons' decision to translate Weber's phrase *Begriffsrealismus* (conceptual realism), as 'reification'.[16] Outside the Marxist tradition, use of the category of reification can also give rise to problems of interpretation. Weber is opposing the ascribing of reality to theoretical concepts when such concepts can only have the status of ideal-types, the sociologist's tools, which incorporate no judgement about their reality. Yet 'reification' has also been used to describe how sets of relations or properties come to be thought of 'abstractly', in the sense that their reality is obscured.[17] Weber, however, did not propose that there is another reality, knowable in an alternative way, but distorted by our scientific constructs. Much criticism of sociology is conducted on the basis of a casual charge of reification which merely implies that an 'abstract' concept, proposition or theory has attained an illegitimate status.[18] This apparently damning charge adds nothing to the particular mistakes adduced because no criteria of adequate theory formation are offered. Such appeals to 'reification' as a sophisticated critical tool are specious.

Adorno provides an antidote to these confusions and shows how they arise. He does not undermine positivist sociology by arguing that such sociology constructs its object by projecting meanings on to an ostensibly given reality, thereby obscuring the processes by which social reality is continually created and recreated in the negotiation of meaning by social actors. Nor does he argue that once it is realised that the mind is at work in the social meanings which appear to confront it, the processes by which these meanings are constituted may be reconstructed in a way which will render social reality transparent and intelligible. He rejects, therefore, both the view that social meaning can be understood to be the result of the intentional acts of individuals, even if conceived as an intersubjective intentionality, and the view that social meaning can be interpreted merely by submission to the multiple hermeneutic circles in which it is implicated. He exposes contradictions in Husserl's notion of intentional meaning and in Heideggerian hermeneutic meaning, and would have considered their sociological epigoni profoundly asociological.

Adorno's notion of 'conceptuality' as socially-produced illusion is designed to rival any theory of the constitution of meaning which suggests that 'meaning' is direct or immediately intelligible. This is why he prefers to call his object 'conceptuality' rather than to call it 'meaning'. According to Adorno the 'knowing subject' in sociology is part of the object to be apprehended, and this remains unrecognised by phenomenological sociology as much as by positivist sociology. Any sociology partially constitutes the meanings which it imputes to society, but it does not follow that those meanings are reducible to a 'knowing subject', and to reduce them to a subject is another form of misrecognition. Adorno's account of reification and of identity thinking explain how the mind works on the meaning of received concepts without implying that it devised those concepts in the first place. According to this account, society imposes concepts on us, which we then reimpose on society. The systematic misrecognition of the relation between concepts and underlying social reality (illusion) is due to a social process, the production of value in exchange. 'Meaning' is thus opaque.

Adorno's opposition to phenomenological and to hermeneutic accounts of meaning also explains his, *prima facie*, strange separation of empirical sociological research techniques from their conventional use and interpretation. Since our access to empirical reality and our conceptual apparatus are inseparable and equally restricted, the idea of testing theoretical propositions by means of independently-defined indicators is incoherent. However, Adorno does not therefore abandon empirical research as irremediably circular, but utilises a range of empirical means to explore the divergences between the ways in which social reality is understood and the ways in which this illusory intelligibility is determined. This exploitation of empirical procedures is designed to eschew not only the 'scientistic' understanding of them, but also any adaptation of them which takes account merely of an interpretive circle between theory and its designated indicators.[19]

This insistence on the conceptual mediation of reality and not on 'meaning' as such guarantees that history can never be lost.[20] History appears throughout Adorno's thought in the sense that it depends on the notion of a historically specific society based on the production of commodities. History appears in the persistent question of the historical possibility of cultural experience in relation to changes in the mode of production. History appears in the analysis of new historical forms, intellectual and artistic, which reformulate the changing relation between subject and object. Adorno is adamant that history should not appear as any kind of historicism: 'Historicism slanders its own principle, the force of history'.[21] By 'historicism' Adorno understands any philosophy of history which posits a teleology of reconcilement in historical time, and also historical relativism in the simple sense of interpreting phenomena in relation to the period in which they occur. Conventionally, Marxism has drawn its strength from its ability to unite these two perspectives. The historically new schism between processes of production and modes of distribution and consumption means, for Adorno, that it is truer to 'the force of history' to examine the contradictions and discontinuities between intellectual and artistic works and their 'time' and not the continuities. In Adorno's view this was to eschew historicism in the sense of any appeal to the development and resolution of contradictions as the principle or motor of historical change. But, characteristically, it amounts to a form of inverted historicism, for, to examine the contradictions and discontinuities between a work and its time, between the process of production and cultural formation, is still to assume a determinate, negative, relation between a work and its time. Adorno preferred an inverted historicism to Benjamin's outright rejection of historicism.[22] For Benjamin was only able to redeem the force of history by founding a new ontology.

Habermas' work is well-known for offering an alternative to the shortcomings of Adorno's thought.[23] He accuses Adorno of confusing the critique of ideology with a theory of late capitalist society; of making theory impossible by basing it on 'the whole is the false', a proposition which must preclude any determinate negation. Habermas, furthermore, denies the possibility of 'immanent critique' because late capitalist society no longer offers any norms, values or cultural forms to which an 'immanent critique' might appeal.[24] Habermas interprets Adorno's critique of identity as Hegelian, and understands his thought as based on ideas of reconciliation and 'the resurrection of nature'. He appears to have taken Adorno's proposition 'the whole is the false' too literally, overlooking the dialectical play in it. He grants no validity to Adorno's generalisation of Marx's theory of value to produce a sociology of illusion in late capitalist society. He does not see that Adorno's critique of identity is not Hegelian, and that far from defining a problem of the resurrection of nature, Adorno redefines 'nature' to mean 'the history of culture', and emphatically rejects any reconciliation in history or any apotheosis of nature.

Adorno still offers an important challenge to Habermas. Habermas' notion of 'knowledge-constitutive interests' returns to the old presuppositions of epistemology in precisely the way which Adorno sought to avoid.[25] For this notion regrounds theory in a 'knowing subject' whose own constitution cannot then be explained as a formation within an historically specific society. His theory of 'communicative competence' and of an 'ideal speech situation' recreates a form of identity thinking and depends on the possibility of reconciliation in history.[26] Adorno's notion of 'immanent critique' was precisely designed to avoid falling back into these presuppositions. To say that there is no longer any basis for 'immanent critique' in late capitalist society is to admit that the old presuppositions of philosophy cannot be avoided, and thus to undermine the possibility of theory in a far more devastating way than Adorno ever desired to do. Similarly, the debate between Adorno and Benjamin still deserves attention. Like the more recent debate between Habermas and Gadamer,[27] the earlier one amounts to the pitting of a critique of ideology against an hermeneutics. However, Benjamin's hermeneutics, unlike Gadamer's, is based on an interpretation of advanced capitalist society. The positions of Adorno and Benjamin are more incompatible and the issues at stake more substantial than in the debate between Habermas and Gadamer, which is methodological by comparison.

If 'thinking . . . teaches itself that part of its meaning is what, in turn, is not a thought [then] its prison has windows'.[28] The 'emphatic concept of thinking' which Adorno here defines is a form of praxis.[29] But even as praxis, it is inherently limited. 'Praxis', however, is even more ambiguous when predicated of thought or theory than when opposed to it. 'Praxis', when predicated of theory, may mean that theory is a form of social activity defined in terms of its goal, that it is an instrument, or it may mean that theory is a form of social intervention as opposed to an autonomous and passive contemplation. For Adorno the relation between theory and praxis must depend on the relation between subject and object. The possibility and validity of any praxis, even understood as action directed to a specific end, can only be decided on the basis of a theoretical analysis of the subject/object relation, that is, of social reality; otherwise such action is undertaken blindly and is futile. Adorno called such action 'pseudo-activity'.[30] Thus 'praxis' is a theoretical notion.[31] Theory must have priority over praxis in this sense, but cannot have priority over the object. For theory is not capable of healing the split between subject and object by its own means. There is a sense, however, in which 'praxis' as the power of the object, is stronger than and separate from theory.[32] Adorno was convinced of the necessity of redefining theory as a form of social activity without thereby conceiving that activity as instrumental. The title *Negative Dialectic* is intended to cut across the conventional theory/praxis distinction by delineating theory as a form of intervention which combats prevalent modes of identity thinking, without in turn setting up a new identity between concepts and reality. As a result, Adorno continually challenges new attempts to make theory into an instrument. Such theory necessarily misconceives the relation between

the subject and social objectivity. It is therefore inefficacious and
regressive, exacerbating the very conditions it seeks to overthrow. This
task of recasting theory as a form of praxis without overstating its claims
to be a revolutionary weapon is, for Adorno, 'the morality of thinking'.

It was for establishing new dogmas, new forms of identity, that Adorno
criticised Lukács and Benjamin. He exposed the dogma in their work by
paying close attention to the form in which they presented their thought,
to their style. While Adorno admired Lukács' early work, including
History and Class Consciousness, he was most opposed to the principles of
Lukács' later literary criticism, and particularly disparaged his inability
to understand modernism in art. Adorno traced the inadequacies of
Lukács' notion of realism to his acceptance of the official Soviet doctrine
of art as the simple reflection of social reality, and to his acceptance of
socialist realism, which, as applied to Russia, implies that the Soviet
political system is a free society.[33] Lukács dubbed Adorno along with the
literary avant-garde as 'anti-humanist' and 'decadent', unable to
understand the reasons for Adorno's attention to style.[34] Adorno
demonstrates that this insensitivity on Lukács' part is matched by the
latter's own indifference to style which follows from his crude idea of the
relation between art and social reality.[35] Lukács succumbs to the ills
which he deplores far more than does the work of those against whom he
inveighs, by allowing his work to serve a dogmatic and regressive praxis.

Adorno believed that the excitement of Brecht and Benjamin over the
new possibilities of art, which 'instead of being based on ritual . . . begins
to be based on another practice – politics',[36] was another way of seeing art
and theory as an instrument. Their view was based on an under-
estimation of the power of the object and as such was hopelessly naïve. In
his discussions of their work, Adorno displayed the paradoxes and
ultimate impotence which must arise from such a 'functionalized' view of
art and theory. Adorno himself, however, was never able to distinguish
between the political effects of different forms of popular art.

The melancholy science is not resigned, quiescent or pessimistic. It
reasons that theory, just like the philosophy it was designed to replace,
tends to overreach itself, with dubious political consequences. The social
reality of advanced capitalist society is more intractable than such theory
is willing to concede, and Adorno had a fine dialectical sense for its
paradoxes. Adorno was planning a work of moral philosophy when he
died.[37] His 'morality' is a praxis of thought not a recipe for social and
political action.

Glossary

A glossary which lists concepts and dichotomies separately from considerations of style and argument necessarily glosses over those concepts and dichotomies as much as it provides glosses on them. Adorno's holophrastic, elliptical and inconsistent use of terms is central to his thought, and the body of this book is devoted to a discussion of his use of terms. The following glossary is therefore intended to offer preliminary and provisional orientations and to introduce the reader to difficulties of translation and interpretation.

Three criteria have guided the choice of terms for inclusion. First, terms which are always difficult to translate adequately into English, for example, *Geist, Vernunft*; secondly, terms which Adorno uses frequently and in a special way, for example, 'antinomy'; thirdly, terms which occur frequently in Adorno's texts and which present no special difficulties of translation but which, nevertheless, are conceptually complex, for example, consciousness, mediation. No attempt has been made to adumbrate the origin and history of these terms in the tradition of German philosophy and social thought; this occurs in the main text where necessary.

Abstract/Concrete (*Abstrakt/Konkret*) Loosely, a concrete individual is one considered in its relations to a totality, and as related to itself. This is the Marxian or Hegelian concrete as the 'sum of determinations'. Even more loosely, a concrete experience may mean the wholeness of a moment of experience. Hence 'concrete' does not carry the usual English connotations of discrete, tangible, individuality or thingness. Adorno uses the dichotomy in a further sense. The degree of abstractness/concreteness of a concept (q.v.) is not determined by the level of its generality, which would mean, for example, that the concept 'animal' as genus or class is more abstract than the concept 'man' as species or sub-class. It is not determined by the relation between the universal and the particular, which would mean, for example, that the concept 'rationality' is more abstract than particular instances of 'rationality'. It is determined by the relation between a concept as formally defined and any individual which is posited as a particular instance of the concept. When the individual does not instantiate the concept, the concept is abstract. *See* Concept.

Appearance (*Schein, Erscheinung*) The German verb *scheinen* means both to 'seem' and to 'shine'. Mere appearance, appearance which is not as it seems to be, or which hides something more essential, and appearance which is what it seems to be, or the shining (forth) of what is essential, are equally conveyed by the German. *Schein* and *Erscheinung* encompass the same ambiguities. *Schein* is sometimes translated as 'illusion'; *Erscheinung* as 'appearance'. *See* Essence.

Antinomy (*Antinomie*) An antinomy exists when two equally valid arguments lead to contradictory conclusions. Adorno frequently refers to 'antinomies' in reality or society, meaning, loosely, contradictions in social reality. It sometimes means, more specifically, that a concept is not 'fulfilled' by the individual which it is used to cover, although the concept is not invalid, and the individual not unreal. Adorno also calls this an immanent (q.v.) contradiction, or an aporia. *See* G.S. 12 PNM p. 27, tr. p. 18.

Becoming (*Gewordenheit, Gewordenes, Gewordensein*) These noun forms of the past participle of *werden*, to become, convey that a process of formation has occurred. A natural English translation using 'formation' and its derivatives would obscure the contrast within the words themselves between process and formation. *See* G.S. 1 IN p. 357, G.S. 7 pp. 12 – 13.

Concept (*Begriff*) The concept is not only the universal, that is, what we possess when we grasp the sense of a word, but the properties which the object (q.v.) or individual referred to ideally possesses. Concepts are thus real, substantively conceived, and not mere ideas or ideal-types. Where Adorno refers more loosely to the 'concept' of an artistic or intellectual work, he means the guiding or central idea.

Consciousness (*Bewusstsein*) Adorno uses this term without predicating it of any class or individual, and without making its intentionality clear. It refers both to consciousness of society and to consciousness on the part of society. This consciousness may be manifest by a particular discipline or by an art work, or it may be the consciousness which is diffuse and prevalent in a society at a given time.

Critical Theory (*Kritische Theorie*) Adorno uses the phrases 'critical theory' and 'dialectical theory' interchangeably. Sometimes he uses them interchangeably with philosophy and with sociology as well – all become names for the enterprise in which he is engaged. At other times, 'critical theory' is distinguished from philosophy and sociology. In those cases 'philosophy' and 'sociology' refer to non-dialectical philosophies and sociologies. Critical theory is not a theory in the standard sense of a set of interrelated propositions designed to explain observed or observable facts.

Determinate Negation (*bestimmte Negation*) Loosely, negation is criticism of society which is positive (determinate) in that it aims to attain and present knowledge of society insofar as that is possible, but not positive in the sense that it confirms or sanctions what it criticises. Similarly, the word 'negative' in 'Negative Dialectic' (*Negative Dialektik*) stresses that criticism does not reproduce what is criticised.

Derivation/Deduction (*Ableitung*) Adorno uses this term in a more general sense than in standard logic. In standard logic an argument is deductively valid if, when its premises are true, its conclusion is unfailingly true as well. For Adorno, a deduction proceeds from a contradiction in a work to the underlying processes which give rise to it. The criteria of the deduction are generated in each case by the contradiction in question.

Experience (*Erfahrung*) Attaining knowledge, for Adorno, depends on a concept of experience, but not in the way in which it does for the empiricist theory of knowledge. The empiricist axioms are that claims to knowledge are only justified by experience which involves controlled observation, and that whatever is known by experience could have been otherwise. For Adorno, knowledge is a process, coming to know (*erkennen*), not a body of received findings, or a set of theories with methods for testing them. This process of acquiring knowledge, which is self-reflective, and occurs in stages, is called 'experience'. Contrary to standard English usage, this notion of experience does not imply directness or immediateness. Knowledge depends on the realisation that experience is mediated (q.v.). *See* G.S. 8 GuEF p. 545, eSoz pp. 55 – 6.

Essence (*Wesen*) Adorno uses the distinction between essence and appearance (q.v.) to correspond, roughly, to the distinction between mode of production and social relations of production, and to designate the object (q.v.) of his inquiry. 'Essence' refers to the way in which capitalist society produces and reproduces itself, to the determining processes of formation (the 'base' or 'superstructure' in standard Marxian terms), not to multiple, discrete essences. The forms in which these processes appear are called a 'façade' or 'appearance' by Adorno, corresponding to the 'superstructure' in standard Marxian terms. This 'façade' comprises commodities, social institutions, intellectual and artistic works.

Form (*Form, Gestalt*) Form is contrasted not with content but with process and with 'essence' (q.v.). Form is the mode (or modes) of appearance of a social relation or of an idea. A social form (or formation) is contrasted with the social relations between men (the social process) which determine it. The 'form' of an intellectual or artistic work is the mode of expression appropriate to its essential or basic idea.

Identity Thinking/Negative Dialectic (*identifizierendes Denken/Negative Dialektik*) Identity thinking consists in the use of a concept (q.v.) as if the individual which it denotes instantiates it when it does not. For example, the concept 'free' is not fulfilled when the individual to which it is applied does not possess the attribute of freedom. Such a veiling use of a concept is called 'identity thinking'. The criteria which specify when a concept is not fulfilled are given by a theory of society. This theory is called 'non-identity thinking', or 'negative dialectic'.

Immanent/transcendent (*immanent/transzendent*) 'Immanent criticism' accepts the presuppositions and terms of a society or work. Such criticism judges a work by its own standards and ideals and confronts it with its own consequences. 'Transcendent criticism' brings alternative and external concepts and criteria to bear, approaching a society or work from a particular standpoint. Marxist sociology is often considered to employ 'transcendent' theory, but Adorno seeks to show that materialist and dialectical criticism must be immanent. *See* Prisms pp. 25–31, tr. pp. 31–4.

Immediate/mediate (*unvermittelt/vermittelt*) 'Immediate' does not have a temporal referent as in English. It means 'without intermediary', or, 'not a result'. Anything which appears to be immediate is always mediated. 'Mediated' means 'brought about by an agent', or, 'the result of a process'. Mediation is not an external relation, but a relation of constitution. *See* OL KS pp. 102–3, tr. p. 128.

Logic (*Logik*) This term is used more generally in German than it is in English. The English equivalent of the German phrase *Logik der Sozialwissenschaften* is 'the epistemology and methodology of the social sciences'. Within a particular discipline, Adorno calls this 'material' logic. 'Logic' therefore does not only refer to the formal structure of the laws of thought. *See* PTI pp. 72–3, PTII pp. 95–6.

Moment (*Das Moment*) A moment is one of the elements of a complex unity. It is not temporal. (*Der Moment* is a moment of time.) The English word 'element' does not stress the intrinsic connection with the totality as the German does.

Mind (*Geist*) The English translation of *Geist* is usually 'mind', or, less often, 'spirit', or 'intellect'. 'Mind', however, has too many connotations of psychological and empiricist epistemology. *Geistig*, the adjective, is translated as 'mental', 'spiritual', or, more frequently, 'intellectual'. The last of these three causes further confusion, because the English 'intellect' is nearer the German *Verstand*; the latter is usually translated as 'understanding', although *Verständnis* is more correctly translated as 'understanding'. 'Understanding' and 'intellect' are poor renderings of *Geist* or its derivatives due to their connotations of a limited faculty. Moreover, *geistig* often means simply 'of, or, pertaining to the mind' rather than 'intellectual'.

Adorno uses *Geist* and 'consciousness' almost interchangeably, although *Geist* has a higher status than consciousness (q.v.). *Geist* implies the possibility of self-determination, or freedom. Consciousness which has attained self-determination or freedom would be *Geist*. 'Mind', for Adorno, is both formed by society and has a partial autonomy. Adorno is opposed to philosophies and sociologies which make 'mind' completely autonomous, but he is equally opposed to philosophies and sociologies which eliminate any notion of 'mind'.

Natural History/History of Nature (*Naturgeschichte*)   The phrase 'natural history' is used by Adorno to stress that the underlying processes of a mode of production cannot be understood as the result of the intentions of individuals. These processes, however, are not 'natural laws', in the sense of invariant, deterministic regularities, but pertain to a historically-specific society.

The phrase 'history of nature' is used by Adorno to draw attention to the concepts of nature held by an historically-specific society. These concepts of nature, whether of human nature, or of the physical world, or of the 'naturalness' of social institutions are cultural forms which appear immutable and ahistorical, but are historically determined.

Negative Dialectic (*Negative Dialektik*)   *See* Determinate Negation and Identity Thinking.

Object/Subject (*Objekt/Subjekt*)   *Objekt, Gegenstand, Sache,* may all be translated as 'object'. *Sache* may be translated as 'object'; 'subject' in the sense of a discipline; 'thing' or 'matter'. The convention of calling a discipline a 'subject' prevents an emphasis being placed on the object of study, or a contrast being made between the object of study and the subject as the consciousness to which the epistemology of any discipline may be attributed. *Die Sache selbst* is usually translated as 'the object itself'. However, this translation has a too-material ring about it. 'Object' in English usually means a thing existing in time and space, a natural object which would be *Gegenstand* in German. *Die Sache selbst* or *Objekt* is that condition where an individual has the properties ascribed to it by its concept (q.v.). The object also refers to the underlying processes of production. Adorno tries to dissolve our perception of the apparent object, the *status quo*, to reveal its formation and its possibilities. 'Objectivity', in this sense, refers to the structure of social reality, not to the logic of validation.

Adorno criticises the criteria of 'subjectivity' and 'objectivity' in philosophies and in sociologies and in works of art. Any discipline which denies its objective elements or which bases its claim to objectivity on a constitutive subjectivity, although possibly unaware of so doing, is subjective. 'Objectivity' can only be attained by recognising that the object is mediated by subjective factors. Adorno therefore inverts the subjective/objective dichotomy, or, rather, claims that the terms of the dichotomy have, in effect, been inverted. A so-called 'objective' method which seeks to eliminate all traces of subjectivity is subjective, whereas an idiosyncratic method may attain greater 'objectivity'. *See* MM p. 84, tr. p. 69.

Philosophy, Sociology, Science (*Philosophie, Soziologie, Wissenschaft*)   Philosophy/Science. Adorno contrasts philosophy with individual disciplines (*die Wissenschaften*). Philosophy is the enterprise which transcends the prevailing intellectual division of labour and is accorded the status of genuine knowledge (*die Wissenschaft*).

Philosophy/Sociology. One of Adorno's books is entitled 'The *Philosophy* of New Music', another 'The *Sociology* of Music', another '*Aesthetic* Theory'. In each case Adorno is referring to his own enterprise which is always the same. He is usually guided by the predominance of the discipline which he is criticising: he calls his own work 'philosophy' when he is criticising philosophy, and 'sociology' when he is criticising sociology. He, nevertheless, rejects these titles as names of discrete disciplines and uses each comprehensively as genuine knowledge (*die Wissenschaft*).

Reason (*Vernunft, Verstand, Rationalität, Grund*)   These four German words are all frequently translated by the one English word 'reason', which does not translate any one of them accurately, or convey the important distinctions between them. *Grund* is better translated as 'ground' in the sense of 'foundation'. *Vernunft* is contrasted with *Verstand*, a distinction inherited from Kant and Hegel. The latter is often translated as 'understanding' meaning a faculty of classification and the sciences which proceed by classification. Hence the English 'reason' is nearer *Verstand* than *Vernunft*, given the latter's substantive connotations. Furthermore, Weber's *Verstehen* which is translated as 'understanding' too, implies quite the opposite of *Verstand*. 'Interpretive understanding' is contrasted by Weber with sciences which employ merely functional or causal explanations; the latter are thus nearer to the meaning of *Verstand*. *Vernunft* is nearer Weber's notion of *Wertrationalität*, value rationality, although they are substantive in different ways. *Verstand* has been assimilated to Weber's *Zweckrationalität*, goal rationality, as instrumental rationality, in the Frankfurt School literature. This last conflation is particularly dubious and pervasive. Hence two different English words, 'intellect' and 'understanding', are needed to translate *Verstand* and *Verstehen*; and two, 'freedom' and 'reason', to translate *Vernunft* and *(Wert) Rationalität*.

List of Abbreviations of Titles

Adorno's Works

Published by Suhrkamp, Frankfurt am Main (FaM), unless otherwise specified.

G.S. *Gesammelte Schriften*, 1971 – *Collected Works*, nine volumes of the planned twenty-two volumes have already been published (1976). References are to the *Collected Works* where available, edited by Rolf Tiedemann. The contents of each volume are listed here in German and in English, the original date of publication is given and details of any English translation. Where the volume or the books republished in it consist of articles, some of these are separately listed and abbreviated. A date in brackets indicates that a work was not previously published or that a work was written a considerable time before it was published.

G.S.1 Volume 1 *Philosophishe Frühschriften* (Early Philosophical Writings). Not previously published.
T *Die Transzendenz des Dinglichen und Noematishen in Husserls Phänomenologie* (The Transcendence of the thing-like and the noematic in Husserl's phenomenology) (1924).
BU *Der Begriff des Unbewussten in der transzendentalen Seelenlehre* (The concept of the unconscious in the transcendental theory of the soul) (1927).
AP *Die Aktualität der Philosophie* 1931 Trans. 'The Actuality of Philosophy', *Telos*, 31, 1977.
IN *Die Idee der Naturgeschichte* (The idea of the history of nature) (1932).
SP *Thesen über die Sprache des Philosophen* (Theses on the language of the philosopher) (1930).

G.S.5 Volume 5.
Husserl *Zur Metakritik der Erkenntnistheorie Studien über Husserl und die phänomenologishen Antinomien* The Metacriticism of epistemology Studies of Husserl and the antinomies of phenomenology) 1956.
Hegel *Drei Studien zu Hegel* (Three Studies on Hegel) 1963.

G.S.6 Volume 6.
ND *Negative Dialektik* 1966 Trans. E. B. Ashton, *Negative Dialectics* (London: Routledge & Kegan Paul, 1973).
JE *Jargon der Eigentlichkeit: Zur deutschen Ideologie* 1964 Trans. Knut Tarnowski and Frederic Will, *Jargon of Authenticity* (London: Routledge & Kegan Paul, 1973).

G.S.7 Volume 7 *Ästhetische Theorie* (Aesthetic Theory) 1970.

G.S.8 Volume 8 *Soziologische Schriften I* (Sociological Writings I).

Gesellschaft *Gesellschaft* 1966 Trans. F. Jameson, 'Society', in *Salmagundi*, 10 – 11, 1969 – 70.

Psychoanalyse *Die revidierte Psychoanalyse* (Revisionist psychoanalysis) (1946) 1962.

SuP *Zum Verhältnis von Soziologie und Psychologie* 1955 Trans. Irving N. Wohlfarth, 'Sociology and Psychology', *New Left Review*, 46, 1967, and 47, 1968.

SuP-PS *Postcriptum* 1966.

Halb *Theorie der Halbbildung* (Theory of Semi-education) 1959.

Kultur *Kultur und Verwaltung* (Culture and Control) 1960.

Aberglaube *Aberglaube aus zweiter Hand* (Superstition at second-hand) (1959).

Konflikt *Anmerkungen zum sozialen Konflikt heute* (Remarks on social conflict today) 1968.

SuEF *Soziologie und empirische Forschung* 1957 Trans. Glyn Adey and David Frisby, 'Sociology and Empirical Research', in *The Positivist Dispute in German Sociology* (London: Heinemann, 1976).

SuD *Über Statik und Dynamik als soziologische Kategorien* (Static and Dynamic as sociological categories) 1956.

Objektivität *Notiz über sozialwissenschaftliche Objektivität* (Notes on objectivity in social science) 1965.

Durkheim *Einleitung zu Émile Durkheim, 'Soziologie und Philosophie'* (Introduction to Emile Durkheim 'Sociology and Philosophy') 1967.

Posstreit *Einleitung zum 'Positivismusstreit in der deutschen Soziologie'* 1969 Trans. 'Introduction' in *The Positivist Dispute in German Sociology*.

SoI *Spätkapitalismus oder Industriegesellschaft?* (Late capitalist or industrial society?)1968.

Klassen *Reflexionen zur Klassentheorie* (Reflections on the theory of classes) (1942).

Bedürfnis *Thesen über Bedürfnis* (Theses on need) (1942).

Fascist I *Anti-semitism and Fascist Propaganda* 1946.

Fascist II *Freudian Theory and the Pattern of Fascist Propaganda* 1951.

PuN *Bemerkungen über Politik und Neurose* (Remarks on Politics and Neurosis) 1954.

IuO *Individuum und Organization* (The individual and organisation) 1953.

Ideologie *Beitrag zur Ideologienlehre* 1954 Trans. John Viertal, *Aspects of Sociology* (London: Heinemann, 1973) ch. xii 'Ideology'.

eS *Zur gegenwärtigen Stellung der empirischen Sozialforschung in Deutschland* (The current situation of empirical social research in Germany) 1952.

Teamwork *Teamwork in der Sozialforschung* (Teamwork in social research) 1957.

dS *Zum gegenwärtigen Stand der deutschen Soziologie* 1959 Trans. Norman Birnbaum, 'Contemporary German Sociology', in *Transactions of the Fourth World Congress of Sociology* (London, 1959).

MuO *Meinungsforschung und Öffentlichkeit* (Interviews and Public Opinion) 1964.

GuEF *Gesellschaftstheorie und empirische Forschung* (Sociological Theory and empirical research) 1969.

LS *Zur Logik der Sozialwissenschaften* 1961 Trans. 'On the Logic of the Social Sciences', in *The Positivist Dispute in German Sociology*.

G.S.9 I Volume 9 I *Soziologische Schriften II Erste Hälfte* (Sociological Writings II First half).

Thomas *The Psychological Technique of Martin Luther Thomas' Radio Addresses* (1943).

AP *Studies in the Authoritarian Personality* 1950 Chs I, VII, XVI, XVII, XVIII, XIX, from *The Authoritarian Personality*, T. W. Adorno, Else Frenkel-Brunswick, Daniel J. Levinson, R. Nevitt Stanford (New York: Norton, 1950).

G.S.9 II Volume 9 II *Soziologische Schriften II Zweite Hälfte* (Sociological Writings II Second half).

Stars   *The Stars Down to Earth* 1957.

SuA   *Schuld und Abwehr* 1955 (Guilt and Defence) Ch. 5 from *Gruppenexperiment. Ein Studienbericht* Bearbeitet von Friedrich Pollock.

ES   *Empirische Sozialforschung* (Empirical Social Research) 1954 co-authored.

G.S.11   Volume 11 *Noten zur Literatur* (Notes on Literature) Trans. forthcoming.

NzL I   *Noten zur Literatur* I 1958.

NzL II   *Noten zur Literatur* II 1961.

NzL III   *Noten zur Literatur* III 1965.

NzL IV   *Noten zur Literatur* IV 1974.

The individual essays in each volume and the other essays in G.S.11 and any translations are detailed where necessary.

G.S.12 PNM   Volume 12 *Philosophie der neuen Musik* 1949 Trans. Anne G. Mitchell and Wesley V. Bloomster, *Philosophy of Modern Music* (London: Sheed and Ward, 1973).

G.S.13   Volume 13 *Die Musikalischen Monographien* (The monographs on music).

Wagner   *Versuch über Wagner* (A study of Wagner) 1952 Trans. forthcoming.

Mahler   *Mahler Eine musikalische Physiognomik* (Mahler A musical physiognomy) 1960 Trans. forthcoming.

Berg   *Berg Der Meister des Kleinsten Übergangs* (Berg Master of the smallest modulation) (1965).

G.S.14   Volume 14.

Diss   *Dissonanzen Musik in der verwalteten Welt* (Dissonances Music in the controlled world) 1956.

FuR   *Über den Fetischcharakter in der Musik und die Regression des Hörers* (Fetishism in music and the regression of the listner) 1938.

eMS   *Einleitung in die Musiksoziologie* 1962 Trans. E. B. Ashton, *Introduction to the Sociology of Music* (New York: Seabury, forthcoming).

G.S.15   Volume 15.

KF   with Hans Eisler, *Komposition für den Film* first published 1947 under Eisler's name only, *Composing for the Films* (New York: Oxford University Press).

GK   *Der getreue Korrepetitor Lehrschriften zur musikalischen Praxis* (The faithful Repetiteur Handbook for musical practice) 1963.

Further Works by Adorno

German editions published by Suhrkamp, FaM, unless otherwise specified. Where the date of original publication differs from the date of copyright, the former is given. The English translations tend to give the latter only. Abbreviations are in alphabetical order.

DofE   *Dialektik der Aufklärung* by Max Horkheimer and Adorno (1947) 1971, S. Fischer. Trans. John Cummings, *Dialectic of Enlightenment* (New York: Herder and Herder, 1972).

Eingriffe   *Eingriffe Neun Kritische Modelle* 1963 (Interventions Nine Critical Models).

eSoz   *Vorlesung zur Einleitung in die Soziologie* 1973 (Junius) (Introductory lectures on sociology).

Kierkegaard   *Kierkegaard Konstruktion des Ästhetischen* 1933 3rd ed. 1966 (Kierkegaard Construction of the Aesthetic, Trans. forthcoming).

Krenek   Adorno and Ernst Krenek, *Briefwechsel* 1974 (Correspondence).

Kritik   *Kritik. Kleine Schriften zur Gesellschaft* (1971) 1973 Rolf Tiedemann (ed.)

(Criticism. Small Writings on Society).

KS Ibid. 'Thesen zur Kunstsoziologie' 1967 Trans. Brian Trench, 'Theses on the Sociology of Art', in *Birmingham Cultural Studies*, 2 (1972).

MM *Minima Moralia* 1951 Trans. E. F. N. Jephcott, *Minima Moralia* (London: New Left Books, 1974).

OL *Ohne Leitbild Parva Aesthetica* 1967 (Without Image Small Aesthetics).

Prisms *Prismen Kulturkritik und Gesellschaft* 1955 Trans. Samuel and Shierry Weber, *Prisms* (London: Neville Spearman, 1967).

PTI *Philosophische Terminologie* I 1973 (Philosophical Terminology I).

PTII *Philosophische Terminologie* II 1974 (Philosophical Terminology II).

Stichworte *Stichworte Kritische Modelle 2* 1969 (Catchwords Critical Models 2).

WB *Über Walter Benjamin* 1970 (On Walter Benjamin) Rolf Tiedemann (ed.).

WE 'Wissenschaftliche Erfahrung in Amerika' 1969 in Stichworte, Trans. Donald Fleming, 'Scientific Experiences of a European Scholar in America', Donald Fleming and Bernard Bailyn (eds.), *The Intellectual Migration Europe and America 1930–1960* (Cambridge, Mass.: Harvard University Press, 1969), pp. 338–70.

Further Abbreviation

ZfS *Zeitschrift für Sozialforschung* (Journal for Social Research) Vols. I–II 1 1932–3 Leipzig, vols II 2–VIII 2 1933–9 Paris, vols VIII 3–IX 1940–1 continued as *Studies in Philosophy and Social Science*, New York.

Notes and References

References to Adorno's works are to the German edition in the *Gesammelte Schriften*, where already available, as in the list of abbreviations of titles, and to the English translation where available. Further works by Adorno appear in the list of abbreviations of titles in alphabetical order. Where there is no English translation I have translated the titles of books and articles in order to assist the reader with no German. Where the date of first publication is significantly different from the publication date of the edition which I have used, I give the date of the first publication in brackets. Since I frequently paraphrase, I have given references to the sources of paraphrases so that they may be located. Where retranslation has been necessary, this is indicated by (G.R.). References to the German edition of works by other authors are given where the argument depends on a point which may be obscured in the English translation. Otherwise references are to the standard translation.

Chapter 1

1. Since the membership of the Institute changed so much from 1923 to 1969, I use the phrase 'the School' to refer to the Institute and its members at any given time. Max Horkheimer, Friedrich Pollock and Adorno were the longest standing members during this period. For an internal account of the School to 1950, see Martin Jay, *The Dialectical Imagination: A History of the Frankfurt School and the Institute of Social Research 1923–1950* (Boston: Little, Brown & Co., 1973).

2. See Fritz Ringer, *The Decline of the German Mandarins: The German Academic Community, 1890–1933* (Cambridge, Mass.: Harvard University Press, 1969) and see Fritz Stern, *The Politics of Cultural Despair* (University of California Press, 1963) for a discussion of a strain in German intellectual life which presents cultural diagnoses as political prognoses.

3. Ringer, op.cit.

4. See Susanne Petra Schad, *Empirical Social Research in Weimar Germany* (Paris: Mouton, 1972) pp. 76–96.

5. Compare Carl Grünberg's inaugural speech, 1924, with Horkheimer's, 1931. Carl Grünberg, 'Festrede, gehalten zur Einweihung des Instituts für Sozialforschung an der Universität Frankfurt am Main am 22 Juni 1924', in *Frankurter Universitätsreden*, xx (FaM: Werner und Winter, 1924) and Horkheimer, 'Die gegenwärtige Lage der Sozialphilosophie und die Aufgaben eines Instituts für Sozialforschung', in *Sozialphilosophische Studien* (FaM: S. Fischer, 1972) pp. 33–46. See Peter Gay, *Weimar*

Culture. The Outsider as Insider (New York: Harper and Row, 1972) pp. 30–1, 40–3. See *International Institute of Social Research. A Short Description of its History and Aims* (New York: n.d. 1935?).

6. Horkheimer, 'Die Schwäche der deutsche Arbeiterklasse' (The Weakness of the German Working Class) 1934, in *Notizen 1950–1959 und Dämmerung* (1934) (FaM: S. Fischer, 1974).

7. *Studien über Autorität und Familie* (Paris: Alcan, 1936) a joint publication. There was also an uncompleted study of workers, see Jay, *The Dialectical Imagination*, pp. 116–17; Schad, *Empirical Social Research in Weimar Germany*, pp. 82–91.

8. Alfred Schmidt (ed.), Horkheimer, *Kritische Theorie* (FaM: S. Fischer, 1968) I and II. This is a reprint of articles first published, with one exception in ZfS, although in some cases substantially altered. A selection from this edition has been published in English: trans. Matthew J. O'Connell and others, *Critical Theory* (New York: Herder and Herder, 1972).

9. Ringer, *The Decline of the German Mandarins*, pp. 384–404.

10. Karl Marx, 'Economic and Philosophical Manuscripts of 1844', in Karl Marx and Frederick Engels, *Collected Works* (London: Lawrence and Wishart, 1975) vol. 3, p. 327 (G.R.).

11. Horkheimer, 'Die gegenwärtige Lage . . .', in *Sozialphilosophische Studien*, pp. 40–5.

12. Ibid. pp. 42–3.

13. Ringer, *The Decline of the German Mandarins*, pp. 227–41; Schad, op.cit., pp. 10–55.

14. *Studien über Autorität und Familie.*

15. See István Mészáros, *Lukács' Concept of Dialectic* (London: Merlin, 1972) Bibliography, pp. 153–60.

16. Horkheimer, 'Traditionelle und Kritische Theorie', in ZfS, VI (1937) reprinted in *Kritische Theorie* II, 137–200, tr. pp. 188–243.

17. See Martin Jay, 'The Frankfurt School's Critique of Marxist Humanism', *Social Research*, XXXIX (1972) 285–305.

18. See George Lichtheim, 'From Marx to Hegel', in *From Marx to Hegel and Other Essays* (London: Orbach and Chambers, 1971) pp. 1–49.

19. See Adorno *et al.*, *Der Positivismusstreit in der deutschen Soziologie* (Neuwied: Luchterhand, 1972 (1969)), and trans. Glyn Adey and David Frisby, *The Positivist Dispute in German Sociology* (London: Heinemann, 1976).

20. Ibid., see the contributions by Hans Albert and the piece included in the tr., Karl R. Popper, 'Reason or Revolution?', pp. 288–300.

21. See *Grünbergs Archiv* and the ZfS.

22. See Jay, *The Dialectical Imagination*, ch. 5.

23. ZfS, IX (1941) 200–25. See Giacomo Marramao, 'Political Economy and Critical Theory', in *Telos*, 24 (1975) 56–80.

24. Pollock, ZfS, IX (1941) 200 n.

25. DofE, 1947, tr., 1972.

26. Adorno, G.S.6 ND, p. 186, tr., p. 185.

27. Cf. William Leiss, *The Domination of Nature* (New York: George Braziller, 1972) Part Two, Ch. 7, pp. 145–65.

28. See Horkheimer, 'Verwort', ZfS, VI (1937) 1–3.

29. ZfS, VIII (1939–40) 321.

30. Paul Lazarsfeld, an Austrian *émigré*, helped the Institute with its empirical work. See ZfS, IX (1941) 1–16.

31. See Adorno, WE and '*Auf die Frage*: was ist deutsch', in *Stichworte*, pp. 102–12.

32. Adorno, WE, pp. 129–30, 132, tr. p. 353, but the relevant sentence is omitted in

the English translation: 'Then again *The Philosophy of New Music*, actually completed in America, was essential for everything which I wrote on music after that . . . ', pp. 355–6.

33. They had written DofE together. Adorno acknowledged the influence of Horkheimer's article 'Egoismus und Freiheitsbewegung: zur Anthropologie des burger-lichen Zeitalters' ZfS, v (1936) 161–234 on his work on Wagner which he began in 1937–8, G. S. 13 Wagner p. 9. He said that PNM, written in 1941 and 1948, 'should be regarded as an extended appendix to *Dialectic of Enlightenment*', PNM p. 7, tr. pp. xvii–xviii (G.R.) and see MM pp. 11–12, tr. p. 18.

34. In 1961 Bloch left East Germany and went to live in West Germany.

35. Published simultaneously in Hungary and Germany (Berlin, Aufbau) in 1954. Trans. forthcoming.

36. Commissioned by the Institute and published as a series *Frankfurter Beiträge zur Soziologie* (Frankfurt Contributions to Sociology) (FaM, Europäische Verlaganstalt). See vol. 3, *Betriebsklima* (1955) vol. 1, *Gruppenexperiment*, (1955), a joint work, and vol. 5, Friedrich Pollock, *Automation* (1956); vol. 13, Ludwig von Friedeburg, *Soziologie des Betriebsklimas*, (1963). See too Adorno's essays on education, *Erziehung zur Mündigkeit* (FaM: Suhrkamp, 1972).

37. G.S.8 SuEF, tr. eS, dS, GuEF.

38. Personal interviews conducted in West Berlin, 1972, with Sebastian Herkommer and Lothar Hack, both sociologists. Some of Adorno's lecture series on philosophy, sociology, and aesthetics have been published: *Vorlesung zur Einleitung in die Erkenntnistheorie* (FaM: Junius, 1957–8), *Vorlesungen zur Ästhetik 1967–8* (Zürich: H. Mayer Nachfdger, 1973) PTI, PTII; eSoz.

39. See *Sociologica* 1 (1954) and Horkheimer's (ed.), *Zeugnisse*, 1963 (FaM: Euro-päische Verlaganstalt) dedicated to Horkheimer's and to Adorno's sixtieth birthdays respectively; and *Sociologica* 11 (1962) reprinted articles by each of them.

40. *Soziologische Exkurse*, vol. 4 of the *Frankfurter Beiträge*, (1956) trans. John Viertal, *Aspects of Sociology* (London: Heinemann, 1973).

41. See Werner Post, *Kritische Theorie und metaphysicher Pessismus. Zum Spätwerk Max Horkheimers* (München, Kösel, 1971).

42. Published posthumously as G.S. 7, the first of the collected works to be published.

43. M. Clemenz, 'Theorie als Praxis?', in *neue politische literatur*, 2 (1968) 178–194; W. F. S. Schoeller (ed.), *Die neue Linke nach Adorno* (München: Kindler, 1969) Günter Rohrmoser, *Das Elend der Kritischen Theorie* (Frieburg: Rombach, 1970).

44. For discussions of the School's work in this period, see Clauss Grossner, 'Anfang und Ende der Frankfurter Schule' and 'Keine Ende der "Frankfurter Schule"?' In *Verfall der Philosophie Politik deutscher Philosophen* (Hamburg: Wegner, 1971) pp. 106–12, 255–61; Arnold Künzli, *Aufklärung und Dialektik. Politische Philosophie von Hobbes bis Adorno* (Frieburg: Rombach, 1971) *Die Linke antwortet Jurgen Habermas* (FaM: Europäische Verlaganstalt, 1969) Bernhard Schäfers (ed.), *Thesen zur Kritik der Soziologie* FaM: Suhrkamp, 1969).

45. *Inter alia*, G.S.6 ND. pp. 31–3, 35–6, tr. pp. 20–2, 24–6.

46. See Jay, *The Dialectical Imagination*, pp. 22–4, for more details of Adorno's early life.

47. G.S.11 NzL III, 'Der wunderliche Realist', on Siegfried Kracauer pp. 388–9.

48. Rolf Tiedemann, 'Editorische Nachbemerkung', in G.S. 1, p. 382.

49. Krenek, 12. Adorno to Krenek, 7 Oct 1934, p. 44.

50. Ibid., 3. Adorno to Krenek, 8 Oct 1930, p. 20.

51. Ibid., 12. Adorno to Krenek, 7 Oct 1934, pp. 43–4.

52. Ibid.

53. WE p. 116, tr. p. 341. The rest of this paragraph depends on the rest of this source.

54. For accounts of Adorno's personality, see Habermas, 'Urgeschichte der

Subjektivität und verwilderte Selbstbehauptung' in *Philosophish-politische Profile* (FaM: Suhrkamp, 1971 (1969)) pp. 188 – 9; and Paul Lazarsfeld, 'An Episode in the History of Social Research: A Memoir', in Fleming and Bailyn, *The Intellectual Migration*, pp. 300 – 1 and 332 – 5; and Thomas Mann, *The Genesis of a Novel* (London: Secker and Warburg, 1961 (1949)) trans. Richard and Clara Winston, *passim*; and Mann, *Briefe*, Erika Mann (ed.) (FaM: S. Fischer, 1963, 1965), vols. II and III, letters to Adorno, *passim*, some of which appear in Mann, *Letters*, trans. R. and C. Winston (Harmondsworth: Penguin, 1975).

55. See Krenek, *passim*.

56. *inter alia*, see Krenek; and G.S.13 Berg. Errinnerung (Memoir), pp. 335 – 67; and 'Schwierigkeiten I Beim Komponieren II In der Auffassung neuer Musik' (Difficulties I In composing II In understanding New Music), in *Impromptus* (FaM: Suhrkamp, 1973 (1964, 1966) and G.S.15 GK.

57. For example, G.S. 12, PNM.

58. G.S.8 and G.S. 9 I and II.

59. Susan Buck-Morss und Rolf Tiedemann (eds.), 'Editorische Nachbemerkung', in G.S.9 II pp. 401 – 2.

Chapter 2

1. G.S.11 NzLI, pp. 9 – 33, first published 1958.

2. MM 1951, tr. 1974.

3. G.S.6 ND p. 52, tr. p. 41.

4. Ibid., p. 10, tr. p. xx.

5. G.S.5 Hegel p. 351.

6. See G.S.9 II 'Editorische Nachbemerkung', pp. 404 – 14, and G.S.11 'Editorische Nachbemerkung', pp. 697 – 701 and pp. 706 – 7.

7. For example, 'Notes on Literature'; 'Prisms'; 'Interventions'; 'Nine Critical Models'; DofE is subtitled in German 'Philosophische Fragmente' (Philosophical Fragments), but this subtitle is omitted, quite arbitrarily, from the English translation. See List of Abbreviations for details of these works.

8. G.S.11 NzL III 'Titel', pp. 325 – 34.

9. NzL I 'Satzzeichen', pp. 106 – 13.

10. Ibid., NzL II 'Wörter aus der Fremde', pp. 216 – 32.

11. Ibid., NzL III 'Bibliographische Grillen', pp. 345 – 57.

12. Ibid., NzL I 'Der Essay als Form', pp. 9 – 33.

13. MM *passim*; '*Auf die Frage*: was ist deutsch' in Stichworte, pp. 102 – 12.

14. See G.S.11

15. For example, G.S.6 ND; G.S.12 PNM; G.S.5 Husserl.

16. G.S.6 ND p. 369, tr. p. 376.

17. In the English translation of *Negative Dialectic* all the impersonal constructions are turned into personal ones.

18. G.S.11 NzL II p. 224.

19. MM p. 100, tr. p. 80; G.S.8 Posstreit p. 319, tr. p. 35.

20. Ibid., p. 336, tr. p. 51.

21. Cf. ibid., pp. 292 – 3, tr. p. 12.

22. G.S.6 ND pp. 164 – 8, tr. pp. 162 – 6.

23. G.S.7 'Editorische Nachbemerkung', p. 541.

24. MM p. 108, tr. p. 87.

25. Ibid.

26. G.S.11 NzLI p. 21.

27. G.S.7 'Editorische Nachbemerkung', p. 541.

28. Ibid.

29. Ibid.

30. G.S.11 NzLI 'Der Essay als Form', *passim*; G.S.5 Hegel pp. 326–75; G.S.8 Posstreit pp. 280–353 *passim*, tr. pp. 1–67.

31. Cf. Friedrich Schiller, *On the Aesthetic Education of Man*, trans. Elizabeth M. Wilkinson and L. A. Willoughby (Oxford: Clarendon Press, 1967) pp. lxviii–lxxii.

32. G.S.8 SuD pp. 217–37.

33. For example, ibid., SuP p. 45ff., tr. pp. 69–70; and ibid., Posstreit p. 315f., tr. p. 32f.

34. G.S.11 NzLI 'Der Essay als Form', pp. 9–33.

35. G.S.5 'Editorische Nachbemerkung', p. 386.

36. See G.S.1 especially SP p. 366.

37. Trans. Anna Bostock (London: Merlin, 1974) 'On the Nature and Form of the Essay', pp. 1–18, and see Mészáros, *Lukács' Concept of Dialectic*, pp. 120, 155.

38. *Soul and Form*, tr. pp. 9–10.

39. See, for example, Georg Simmel, 'Der Begriff und die Tragödie der Kultur', in *Philosophie der Kultur: Gesammelte Essais* (Leipzig: Werner Klindhardt, 1911) pp. 245–77, trans. K. Peter Elzkorn, 'On the Concept and the Tragedy of Culture', in Georg Simmel, *Conflict in Culture and Other Essays* (New York: Columbia Teachers College, 1968), pp. 27–46. See, too, Georg Simmel, *Brücke und Tür* (Stuttgart: Koehler, 1957 (1896–1921)) especially *Geschichte und Kultur*, pp. 43–104.

40. G.S.11 NzLI p. 16f., p. 20.

41. Ibid., *passim*.

42. Ibid., p. 9.

43. Ibid., pp. 16–17, pp. 18–19f.

44. Ibid.

45. Ibid., p. 28.

46. G.S.11 NzLI p. 27, quoted with approval from Max Bense, 'Über den Essay und seine Prosa', in *Merkur* 1 (1947) 418.

47. Ibid., p. 22. See *The Philosophical Works of Descartes*, trans. Elizabeth S. Haldane and G. T. Ross (Cambridge University Press, 1967) 1, p. 92.

48. G.S.11 NzLI p. 22.

49. Ibid.

50. Ibid.

51. Ibid., p. 23.

52. Ibid., pp. 23–4.

53. Ibid., p. 25.

54. Ibid., p. 13ff.

55. Ibid., p. 18.

56. Ibid., p. 27.

57. Ibid., pp. 12–13; cf. MM pp. 105–9, tr. pp. 85–7.

58. G.S.11 NzLI pp. 20–1.

59. For example, see G.S.8 Posstreit p. 301 note 21, tr. p. 20 note 21.

60. G.S.11 NzLI pp. 19–20.

61. See G.S.6 JE pp. 441–2, tr. p. 42.

62. G.S.11 NzLI pp. 19–20; and Krenek 11, Adorno to Krenek, 30 Sept 1932, p. 39.

63. G.S.6 JE pp. 416–523 and tr., the subtitle 'Zur deutschen Ideologie' (On German Ideology) is omitted, quite arbitrarily, from the English translation and thus the reference to Marx's *German Ideology* is lost.

64. Ibid., p. 12, tr. p. 18.

65. G.S.6 ND pp. 9–11, tr. pp. ixx–xx.

66. See Dieter Schnebel, 'Komposition von Sprache–sprachliche Gestaltung von Musik in Adorno's Werk', in Hermann Schweppenhäuser (ed.), *Theodor W. Adorno zum Gedächtnis* (FaM: Suhrkamp, 1971) pp. 129–45, in which he analyses, *inter alia*, MM§78, p. 158, tr. pp. 121–3, as a poetic and musical composition and demonstrates how subtle the process of the style is, especially the reversal of themes. Even a translation as good as Jephcott's must detract from these features of composition.

67. G.S.8 Posstreit pp. 317–18, tr. pp. 34–5.

68. 'Auxesis' is a form of hyperbole which intensifies as it proceeds.

69. MM p. 68, tr. p. 58.

70. Søren Kierkegaard, *The Sickness unto Death* (1843) trans. Walter Lowrie, 1941 (New York: Anchor, 1954).

71. MM pp. 68–71, tr. pp. 58–60.

72. Ibid., p. 71, tr. p. 60.

73. Sigmund Freud, *Beyond the Pleasure Principle* (1920) trans. James Strachey, (London: Hogarth, 1953–73) Standard Edition, xviii 7.

74. Nietzsche, *Beyond Good and Evil* (1886) trans. Walter Kaufmann (New York: Vintage, 1966).

75. MM p. 57, tr. p. 50.

76. G.F.W. Hegel, *Phenomenology of Mind* (1807) trans. James Baillie (London: Allen and Unwin, 1931) p. 81.

77. MM p. 7, tr. p. 15.

78. 1887, trans. Kaufmann, *The Gay Science* (New York: Vintage, 1974).

79. For example, MM§5 and §6, pp. 21–4, tr. pp. 25–8.

80. Ibid., pp. 330–33, tr. pp. 244–7.

81. Ibid., pp. 105–9, tr. pp. 85–7.

82. Ibid., p. 107, tr. p. 86 (G.R.).

83. Ibid., p. 282, tr. p. 211.

84. Ibid., p. 280, tr. p. 210.

85. Ibid., p. 282, tr. p. 211.

86. Ibid. (G.R.).

87. *Prisms* p. 25, tr. p. 31.

88. Ibid., p. 27, tr. p. 32.

89. Ibid.

90. Ibid.

91. The quotations from *Prisms* apply equally well to ND and other works.

92. PT 1 p. 56; Nietzsche, *Beyond Good and Evil*, pp. 50–1. On the question of a dialectic in Nietzsche's work, see Alfred Schmidt, 'Zur Frage der Dialektik in Nietzsches Erkenntnistheorie', in Max Horkheimer (ed.), *Zeugnisse*, pp. 115–32, and Jürgen Habermas, 'Nietzsche: Erkenntnistheoretische Schriften', in *Arbeit, Erkenntnis, Fortschritt* (Amsterdam: de Munter, 1970) pp. 356–75. On the relation between Nietzsche and the Frankfurt School, see Peter Pütz, 'Nietzsche im Licht der Kritischen Theorie', in *Nietzsche Studium* 3 (Berlin: de Gruyter, 1974) pp. 175–91, and Jay, *The Dialectic Imagination*, *passim*.

93. Quotation from Ferdinand Kürnberger, MM p. 13, tr. p. 19.

94. See Nietzsche, *Ecce Homo* (1888) trans. Kaufmann (New York: Vintage, 1969).

95. *Prisms* p. 70, tr. p. 65.

96. MM *passim*, DofE *passim*.

97. Nietzsche, *Beyond Good and Evil*, p. 48.

98. MM p. 89, tr. p. 73.

99. Ibid., p. 128, tr. p. 101.

100. DofE p. 74, tr. p. 81.

101. Ibid., p. 107, tr. p. 119. Adorno does not concentrate elsewhere on 'reason' and

the domination of nature.

102. Ibid., p. 76, tr. pp. 83–4.

103. Horkheimer and Adorno admit, at the beginning of the paragraph from which the quotation comes, that there are 'difficulties in the concept of reason [*Vernunft*]'. They exploit the interconnections of *Verstand, Vernunft, Rationalität*, in a way which is obvious in the German but lost in the translation.

104. Ibid., pp. 42–3, tr. p. 44.

105. Ibid. (G.R.).

106. Ibid.

107. MM p. 89, tr. p. 73.

108. Ibid., p. 122, tr. p. 97.

109. Ibid., p. 119, tr. p. 95.

110. G.S.8 Klassen pp. 386–7.

111. Cf. J. Habermas, 'Wozu noch Philosophie?', in *Philosophisch-politische Profile*, pp. 11–36, trans. E. B. Ashton, 'Why more Philosophy?', in *Social Research*, 38 (1971), 633–55, where Habermas makes this point. It could be argued that Hegel too was avoiding 'first' principles.

112. For discussion of issues raised in this paragraph, see Chapter Four below.

113. See *Prisms*, 'Das Bewusstsein der Wissensoziologie', pp. 32–50, tr. pp. 37–49.

114. G.S.6 ND p. 34, tr. p. 23.

115. G.S.5 Hegel p. 314.

116. G.S.6 ND p. 33, tr. pp. 22–3.

117. Ibid., p. 151, tr. p. 148.

118. Ibid., pp. 149–51, tr. pp. 146–8, and see Chapter Three below.

119. Ibid., p. 34, tr. p. 23.

120. Ibid.

121. Nietzsche, *The Will to Power* (Notebooks 1883–8) trans. W. Kaufmann and R. J. Hollingdale (New York: Vintage, 1968) p. 267, and see pp. 277, 278.

122. G.S.6 ND p. 153, tr. p. 150.

123. G.S.8 SuEF p. 209, tr. p. 80 (G.R., my emphasis).

124. DofE p. 23, tr. p. 21.

125. G.S.8 SuD p. 236.

126. G.S.7 p. 12, my round brackets.

127. Nietzsche, *Twilight of the Idols* (1888) trans. R. J. Hollingdale (Harmondsworth: Penguin, 1968) p. 35 (G.R.). Adorno quotes a very similar passage from p. 37 (G.R.) in G.S.5 Husserl p. 26.

128. G.S.11 NzLI pp. 32–3.

129. See *Beyond Good and Evil*, tr. pp. 28–30; *Twilight of the Idols*, pp. 120–2 and *passim*.

130. G.S.8 p. 301; and cf. *Soziologische Exkurse*, p. 22, tr. p. 16 (G.R.); Nietzsche, *On the Genealogy of Morals*, trans. Kaufmann (New York: Vintage, 1969) p. 80 (G.R.). 'Semiology' meant the branch of medicine concerned with symptoms.

131. G.S.6 ND p. 193, tr. p. 192; G.S.5 Husserl p. 26.

132. G.S.11 NzLI p. 33, from Nietzsche, *The Will to Power*, tr. pp. 532–3.

133. Nietzsche, *Twilight of the Idols*, p. 110.

134. Ibid., p. 110 (G.R.).

135. Ibid., p. 109.

136. G.S.11 NzLI p. 33.

137. See MM pp. 123–4, tr. p. 98.

138. Ibid., p. 123, tr. p. 98.

139. See ibid., pp. 122–4, tr. pp. 97–8.

140. Ibid., p. 122, tr. p. 97.

141. G.S.6 ND p. 91, tr. p. 84.

142. See 'Musik und Technik', in *Klangfiguren*, 1959, p. 350.

143. However, the relation between the work of Nietzsche and the work of Weber has not been explored sufficiently, in spite of Eugène Fleischmann, 'De Weber a Nietzsche', in *European Journal of Sociology*, v (1964); and in spite of Mitzman's remarks in *Sociology and Estrangement*, pp. 6–7, note, and p. 34: Mitzman's, *The Iron Cage An Historical Interpretation of Max Weber* (New York: Knopf, 1970), contains much of interest on this point, pp. 181–306, *passim*.

144. Cf. Max Scheler's attempt to ground Nietzsche's notion of 'ressentiment' sociologically, *Ressentiment* (1912) trans. William W. Holdheim (New York: Schocken, 1972).

145. *Pace*, W. Leiss, *The Domination of Nature*, p. 107.

Chapter 3

1. See *Grundrisse der Kritik der politischen Ökonomie* (Frankfurt: Europäische Verlaganstalt, n.d. 1953?) pp. 23–5, and tr. Terrell Carver, *Karl Marx: Texts on Method* (Oxford: Blackwell, 1975) 'Introduction' to the 'Grundrisse', pp. 75–8.

2. 'Notes on Adolf Wagner', tr. Carver, op. cit., p. 198.

3. *Capital A Critique of Political Economy*, 1867, trans. Samuel Moore and Edward Aveling (London: Lawrence and Wishart, 1970) i, 38, my emphasis, and cf. the new trans. Ben Fowkes (Harmondsworth: Penguin, 1976) p. 128.

4. 'Notes on Wagner', op. cit., p. 202.

5. But see Lee Baxandell and Stefan Morawski (eds.), *Marx and Engels on Literature and Art* (New York: International General, 1974).

6. Cf. Steven Lukes, 'Alienation and Anomie', in P. Laslett and W. G. Runciman (eds), *Philosophy, Politics and Society* (Oxford University Press, 1967) Series III, 134–56.

7. Mitzman, *The Iron Cage*, p. 4, note.

8. Ibid.

9. See Heinrich Popitz, *Der Entfremdete Mensch, Zeitkritik und Geschichtsphilosophie des jungen Marx* (Basel: Verlag für Recht und Gesellschaft, 1953) and see Hans Freyer, *Die Bewertung der Wirtschaft im philosophischen Denken des neunzehnten Jahrhunderts* (Leipzig: Wilhelm Engelmann, 1921).

10. 'Economic and Philosophical Manuscripts of 1844', in *Collected Works*, vol. 3, 270–82. The four aspects are helpfully summarised by Lukes, 'Alienation and Anomie', p. 137.

11. See Iring Fetscher, *Karl Marx und der Marxismus Von der Philosophie des Proletariats zur proletarischen Weltanschauung* ch. II (München: Piper, 1973) (1967); and Bertrell Ollman, *Alienation* (Cambridge University Press, 1971) pp. 198–228 *passim*; Jay, *The Dialectical Imagination*, p. 181.

12. See Mészáros, *Marx's Theory of Alienation* (London: Merlin, 1970) pp. 140–6; Paul Walton and Andrew Gamble, *From Alienation to Surplus Value* (London: Sheed and Ward, 1971) pp. 19–21, Alfred Sohn-Rethel, *Geistige und körperliche Arbeit* (FaM: Suhrkamp, 1972), p. 53. Trans. forthcoming.

13. Mitzman, *Sociology and Estrangement*, p. 6, p. 13.

14. Ibid., p. 10, p. 13.

15. Ibid., p. 6, p. 10.

16. Ibid., pp. 8–9.

17. Ibid., p. 13.

18. Mitzman, *The Iron Cage*, p. 176, p. 209 and note.

19. Mitzman, *Sociology and Estrangement*, p. 34.

20. See Zygmunt Bauman, *Towards a Critical Sociology* (London: Routledge & Kegan Paul, 1976) p. 55; Jean Duvignaud notes that 'There are two kinds of Marxist concepts—those that belong to the 'canon' of the doctrine (such as class, ideology, revolution,

surplus-value, etc.), and those that come out of the 'vulgate', having been brought to light or invented by the Marxists of the end of the last century or the beginning of the present one (such as alienation, mystification, reification, etc).'—'France: The Neo-Marxists', in Leo Labedz (ed.), *Revisionism* (New York: Praeger, 1962) p. 320. Mészáros suggests that *sich verdingen* as used by Kant means 'to make into a thing, to reify', *Marx's Theory of Alienation*, pp. 33 – 6. But although in German as in English, 'to alienate' may mean 'to sell or transfer property', there is no etymological basis for translating *Verdingung* as 'reification', and no philosophical basis for considering *sich verdingen* to be the origin of *Verdinglichung*. The only place, to my knowledge, where Marx uses the actual word *Verdinglichung* is *Kapital, III, Marx-Engels Werke*, p. 838, tr. *Capital, III* (London: Lawrence and Wishart, 1971) p. 830. However, it does not appear in the English translation as 'reification', but as 'conversion . . . into things'.

21. Published in *History and Class Consciousness*, 1923, trans. Rodney Livingstone (London: Merlin, 1967) pp. 86, 93, 209, n. 16. Marx did use the verb *versachlichen* in *Grundrisse*, p. 12, p. 866, tr. p. 59. It means 'to materialise', and is nearer *vergegenständlichen* than to *Verdinglichung*.

22. *Reason and Revolution. Hegel and the Rise of Social Theory*, 1941 (London: Routledge & Kegan Paul, 1969) p. 112. Marcuse concedes, although mistakenly, that he is borrowing the word from Marx in order to explicate Hegel's philosophy. Lukács, *The Young Hegel Studies in the Relations between Dialectics and Economics*, 1948, trans. Rodney Livingstone (London: Merlin, 1975) and Günter Rohrmoser in his reply to Lukács, *Subjekturtät und Verdinglichung Theologie und Gesellschaft im Denken des jungen Hegel* (Gütersloh: G. Mohn, 1961), are responsible for the persistence of this mistake.

23. Peter Berger, 'Response' (to Ben Brewster's 'Comment' on Berger and Stanley Pullberg, 'Reification and the Sociological Critique of Consciousness'), in *New Left Review* 35 (1966) 75–7. Cf. the debate about whether Hegel equated objectification and alienation: Marx, 'Critique of the Hegelian Dialectic' in 'Economic and Philosophical Manuscripts of 1844', *Collected Works*, vol. 3, 326–46 and endorsed by Lukács in his 1967 'Preface' to *History and Class Consciousness*, tr. p. xxiii. Marcuse refuted this interpretation of Hegel, 'The Foundation of Historical Materialism', 1932, in trans. Jons de Bres, *Studies in Critical Philosophy* (London: New Left Books, 1972), pp. 1–48; and see too John O'Neill's 'Introduction' to his trans. of Jean Hyppolite, *Studies on Marx and Hegel* (London: Heinemann, 1969 (1955)), pp. xi–xix.

24. For an account of Marx's theory of value, see Hans-Georg Backhaus, 'Zur Dialektik der Wertform' in Alfred Schmidt (ed.), *Beiträge zur marxistischen Erkenntnistheorie* (FaM: Suhrkamp, 1971), pp. 128–52; and parts III–V of Carver, 'Marx's Commodity Fetishism', in *Inquiry* (1975) 18, 42–54.

25. Lucien Goldmann, 'La Reification', in *Recherches Dialectiques* (Paris: Gallimard, 1959), pp. 64–106, is an interesting exception. Andrew Arato, 'Lukács' Theory of Reification', in *Telos*, 2 (1972), 27, and Lucio Colletti, *From Rousseau to Lenin*, trans. John Merrington and Judith White (London: New Left Books, 1972 (1969)), pp. 131–5, construe 'reification' in a very general way, as a fusion of Hegel's phenomenology of mind and Marx's theory of commodity fetishism. See too the Lukácsian discussion by Pier Aldo Rovatti, 'Fetishism and Economic Categories', in *Telos*, 14 (1972), 87–105.

26. Vol. 1, Ch. 1.

27. 1862–3 (London, Lawrence and Wishart. 1963–71), Part I, Part II, Part III.

28. The *Grundrisse* was not available until 1939 and 1941.

29. *Capital*, vol. 1, 72ff, tr. 1976, 164ff.

30. *Grundrisse*, pp. 452–3, trans. Martin Nicolaus (Harmondsworth: Penguin, 1973), p. 356.

31. For example, *Capital*, vol. 1, 72, tr. 1976, 164–5.

32. For example, *Grundrisse*, p. 909.

33. For example, *Theories of Surplus Value*, Part III, pp. 295–6; *Grundrisse*, p. 356, tr. p. 452.

34. Ibid., p. 75, tr. p. 157.

35. *Capital*, vol. I, p. 72 tr. 1976 165.

36. *Das Kapital, Marx-Engels Werke* (Berlin: Dietz, 1956 et seq.), vol. 23, p. 86.

37. Ibid., tr. p. 72.

38. For example, Lukács, *History and Class Consciousness*, tr. p. 86; Frederic Jameson, *Marxism and Form* (Princeton University Press, 1971) p. 296. Even the new translation of *Capital*, i, repeats this mistake, p. 165.

39. First complete edition 1932.

40. Simmel, *Hauptprobleme der Philosophie*, 1910 (Berlin: Göschen, 1969); and see Siegfried Kracauer, 'Georg Simmel', *Logos*, IX (1920), 309–38; and Rudolph H. Weingartner, *Experience and Culture: The Philosophy of Georg Simmel* (Connecticut: Wesleyan University Press, 1960).

41. For a chronological list of Simmel's works, see Bibliography below. See Friedrich H. Tenbruck, 'Georg Simmel (1858–1918)', *Kölner Zeitschrift für Soziologie*, 10 (1958), 587–614; and Nicholas J. Spykman, *The Social Theory of Georg Simmel* (University of Chicago Press, 1925).

42. Simmel, 'On the Concept and Tragedy of Culture', 1911, tr. *Conflict in Culture and Other Essays*, p. 27; and 'Wandel der Kulturformen', in *Brücke und Tür*, pp. 86–94.

43. Simmel, 'On the Concept and Tragedy of Culture', p. 39.

44. Ibid., p. 29.

45. Ibid.

46. Ibid.

47. Ibid., p. 30.

48. Donald N. Levine makes a similar point in his 'Introduction' to Georg Simmel, *On Individuality and Social Forms* (Chicago and London: University of Chicago Press, 1971) pp. ix–lxv; see too the essays by Levine and by Weingartner in Kurt H. Wolff (ed.), *Georg Simmel Essays on Sociology, Philosophy and Aesthetics* (New York: Harper and Row, 1965 (1959)).

49. Simmel, op.cit., p. 42, and *Philosophie des Geldes*, Ch. I, Part II, pp. 30–61.

50. 'Wandel der Kulturformen', p. 98.

51. 'On the Concept and Tragedy of Culture', tr. pp. 41–2.

52. Ibid., pp. 40–1.

53. Ibid., p. 42.

54. *Philosophie des Geldes*, p. 457ff.

55. Ibid., pp. 30–40.

56. Ibid., p. 336 and pp. 357–86.

57. Ibid., pp. 322–54, 438–55.

58. Ibid., p. 511ff.

59. Ibid., p. 502ff.

60. Ibid., pp. 511–21, and 'On the Concept and Tragedy of Culture', pp. 40–1, 45–6.

61. Ibid., p. 531.

62. Ibid.

63. Ibid., p. 532.

64. Ibid.

65. Lukács, *History and Class Consciousness*, tr. pp. 156–7.

66. Ibid., p. 157.

67. See Lukács, 'Erinnerungen an Simmel', in Kurt Gassen und Michael Landmann (eds), *Buch des Dankes an Georg Simmel. Briefe, Errinnerungen, Bibliographie* (Berlin: Duncker und Humblot, 1958) pp. 171–6; and Silvie Rücker, 'Totalität als ethisches und ästhetisches Problem', in Heinz Ludwig Arnold (ed.), *Georg Lukács. Text + Kritik*

(München: Richard Boorberg, 1973) pp. 52–64.

68. *Soul and Form*, for example, 'Richness, Chaos and Form', tr. pp. 124–51.

69. Translated into German by Denes Zalan, 'Zur Theorie der Literaturgeschichte', *Text + Kritik*, pp. 24–51.

70. Ibid., p. 29.

71. Ibid., p. 31.

72. First published 1920. Subtitled 'A historico-philosophical essay on the forms of great epic literature', trans. Anna Bostock (London: Merlin, 1971).

73. 'Zur Theorie der Literaturgeschichte', p. 32.

74. Trans. *Telos*, 5 (1970), 21–30, reprinted in *Marxism and Human Liberation Essays on History, Culture and Revolution*, E. San Juan Jr. (ed.) (New York: Delta, 1973).

75. Ibid., p. 23.

76. For Adorno and Benjamin's personal relationship, see Adorno, WB, a collection of his writings on Benjamin (originally published elsewhere in most cases), pp. 67–74; and Hannah Arendt, 'Introduction' to Benjamin, *Illuminations*, trans. Harry Zohn (London: Fontana, 1970), especially pp. 2, 10–11; and Gershom Scholem, *Walter Benjamin – die Geschichte einer Freundschaft* (FaM: Suhrkamp, 1975) *passim*. See, too, Susan Buck-Morss, 'The Dialectic of Theodor W. Adorno', *Telos*, 14 (1972), 137–44.

77. Especially Benjamin, *Schriften* (FaM: Suhrkamp, 1955), vols. I and II. Adorno (ed.). The complete works of Benjamin are now appearing in six volumes, Rolf Tiedemann and Hermann Schweppenhäuser (eds), *Schriften* (FaM: Suhrkamp, 1974–), vols, I, III and IV have already been published.

78. WB p. 9.

79. Ibid., p. 33 and cf. pp. 33–55 with 103–61 and with 11–29. Adorno was accused of suppressing Benjamin's involvement with communism, see pp. 91–5.

80. Ibid., *passim*.

81. *Ursprung der deutschen Trauerspiel*, 1928, *Schriften* I. 1, trans. John Osborne (London: New Left Books, 1977).

82. There is a unity in Benjamin's work, albeit not of the kind which Adorno sought. Cf. Burkhardt Lindner, '"Naturgeschichte" – Geschichtsphilosophie und Welterfahrung in Benjamins Schriften', in *Text + Kritik. Walter Benjamin*, Burkhardt Lindner (ed.) (Munich: Richard Boorberg, 1971) pp. 41–58.

83. Rolf Tiedemann, *Studien zur Philosophie Walter Benjamins* (FaM: Suhrkamp, 1973 (1964)), p. 30n.

84. *Schriften*, I 1 (1920), pp. 71–122.

85. Ibid., pp. 18–61.

86. *Origin* . . ., pp. 215–18, tr. pp. 35–8; Tiedemann, *Studien zur Philosophie Walter Benjamins*, pp. 23–42.

87. 'Über die Wahrnehmung 1 Erfahrung und Erkenntnis', unpublished, quoted by Tiedemann, ibid., pp. 15–68, *passim*.

88. Unpublished postscript to *Ursprung der deutschen Trauerspiel*, quoted in ibid., p. 79.

89. Benjamin, *Origin* . . ., p. 227, tr. 47 (G.R.).

90. *Origin* . . ., pp. 228–32, 299ff., tr. pp. 48–51, 120ff; Tiedemann, op.cit., pp. 94–8.

91. *Origin* . . ., pp. 343–4, tr. pp. 166–7.

92. *Origin* . . ., pp. 299, 353, tr. pp. 120, 177; and see Lindner, 'Natur-Geschichte . . .' in *Walter Benjamin Text + Kritik*, p. 43.

93. *Origin* . . ., pp. 242–5, 255–7, 253, tr. pp. 62–4, 76–8.

94. Ibid., p. 343, tr. p. 166 (G.R.).

95. G.S.1 IN pp. 345–65.

96. Ibid., p. 346.

97. Ibid.

98. Ibid., pp. 353–4.

99. Ibid., pp. 354–5.

100. Ibid., p. 365.

101. Ibid., p. 355; Lukács, loc. cit., tr. p. 62.

102. G.S.1 IN pp. 356–7, Lukács, p. 64.

103. G.S.1 IN p. 357.

104. Ibid.; Benjamin, *Origin* . . ., p. 355, tr. p. 179.

105. G.S.1 IN p. 360.

106. Ibid., p. 346, p. 350.

107. Ibid., pp. 361–3. See also Benjamin, 'Theses on the Philosophy of History', 1940, in *Illuminations*, pp. 255–66.

108. Adorno, ibid., p. 364.

109. Ibid., p. 365.

110. G.S.6 ND pp. 192–3, tr. pp. 191–2; and, for example, Lukács, *History and Class Consciousness*, tr. p. 88.

111. G.S.6 ND pp. 367–8, tr. pp. 374–5; and, for example, Lukács, op. cit., p. 157.

112. G.S.6 ND p. 15, p. 50, tr. p. 3, p. 40.

113. Ibid., p. 192, tr. p. 191.

114. Loc. cit., tr. p. xxiv.

115. For example, G.S.6 ND p. 191, tr. p. 190.

116. Ibid., p. 191, tr. pp. 190–1.

117. Benjamin, *Briefe*, Gershom Scholem and Adorno (eds) (FaM: Suhrkamp, 1966), vol. 2, *passim*. Some of Adorno's letters to Benjamin are included in WB pp. 103–61. A few are translated by Harry Zohn in *New Left Review*, 81 (1973), 55–80.

118. WB (1950) p. 17, and in *Prisms* p. 289, tr. p. 233.

119. Quoted in Peter Krumme, 'Zur Konzeption der dialektischen Bilder', in *Text + Kritik*, p. 74.

120. Quoted in Tiedemann, *Studien zur Philosophie Walter Benjamins*, p. 131.

121. 1935 *Exposé*, some of which was published in the 1955 edition of Benjamin's work, *Schriften*, 2 vols., Adorno (ed.), (FaM), and trans. in *Charles Baudelaire*. The manuscripts have yet to appear in the *Schriften*, vol. 5, *Das Passagen-Werk*; and see Adorno to Benjamin, 2 Aug 1935 in WB pp. 111–25, tr. pp. 55–63.

122. Adorno to Benjamin 10 Nov 1938, ibid., pp. 138–42, tr. pp. 70–2.

123. Ibid., p. 142, tr. p. 72.

124. Ibid., p. 141, tr. p. 72.

125. 'Über einige Motive bei Baudelaire' (1939), *Schriften*, I. 2, pp. 605–53, tr. 'Some Motifs in Baudelaire' in *Charles Baudelaire*, pp. 107–54.

126. *Briefe*, vol. 2, Benjamin to Adorno, 23 Feb 1939, pp. 805–6.

127. Adorno to Benjamin, 2 Aug 1935, in WB, p. 116, tr. p. 58; and WB, p. 17, tr. Prisms p. 233.

128. Ibid.

129. Ibid., Adorno to Benjamin, 10 Nov 1938, p. 137, tr. pp. 69–70.

130. Ibid., Adorno to Benjamin, 2 Aug 1935, p. 112, tr. p. 56.

131. Ibid., Adorno to Benjamin, 17 Dec 1934, p. 106 and 2 Aug 1935, p. 116, tr. p. 58.

132. WB p. 56, Tiedemann, *Studien zur Philosophie Walter Benjamins*, p. 148.

133. WE p. 117, tr. pp. 341–2. The article was first published in ZfS VIII (1938). See G.S.14 Diss pp. 14–50.

134. First published in ZfS VI (1936). See *Illuminations*, pp. 219–53.

135. 'The Arcades work', the name by which Benjamin's uncompleted work 1928–40 on nineteenth-century Paris is known. See *Charles Baudelaire — A Lyric Poet in the Era of High Capitalism*, trans. Harry Zohn (London: New Left Books, 1973), p. 7.

136. 'Das Dreigroschenprozess', (1931), in Siegfried Unseld (ed.), *Bertolt Brecht, Das Dreigroschenbuch* (FaM: Suhrkamp, 1968) p. 93.

137. Karl Wittfogel, *Oriental Despotism*, 1928 (New Haven: Yale University Press, 1957), p. 381.

138. Henryk Grossmann, 'Die gesellschaftlichen Grundlagen der mechanistischen Philosophie und die Manufaktur', in ZfS IV (1935), 162.

139. Martin Heidegger, *Sein und Zeit*, 1927 (Tübingen: Max Niemeyer, 1972) pp. 46, 420, 437, trans. John Macquarrie and Edward Robinson (Oxford: Basil Blackwell, 1967) pp. 72, 472, 487; and see Youssef Ishaghpour (ed.), Lucien Goldmann, *Lukács et Heidegger* (Paris: Denoël, 1973) pp. 91–105.

140. But see Eugene Lunn, 'Marxism and Art in the Era of Stalin and Hitler: A Comparison of Brecht and Lukács', in *New German Critique*, 3 (1974), 12–44, who construes and contrasts the ideas of Lukács and Brecht around the concept.

141. He also used it in his withdrawn *Habilitation*, 1927, G.S.1 BU p. 228, p. 240, in the sense of 'hypostatize', which he accredits (p. 82) to Horkheimer's *Habilitation, Über Kants Kritik der Urteilskraft als Bindeglied zwischen theoretischer und praktischer Philosophie* (Stuttgart: W. Kohlhammer, 1925). Jay fails to see the importance of 'reification' in Adorno's work, 'The Concept of Totality in Lukács and Adorno', *Telos*, 32, 1977.

142. Krenek, especially Adorno to Krenek, 30 Sept 1932, p. 36; and Adorno to Krenek, 7 Aug 1934, p. 45, p. 47; and Adorno to Krenek, 26 May 1935, p. 85.

143. PT I, PT II, eSoz, *passim*.

144. *Prisms* p. 25, tr. p. 31.

145. G.S.6 ND p. 191, tr. p. 190 (G.R.).

146. *Prisms* p. 126, tr. p. 106.

147. G.S.5 Hegel p. 312.

148. G.S.8 SuEF p. 197, tr. p. 69 (G.R.).

149. Ibid., p. 209, tr. p. 80 (G.R.).

150. G.S.6 ND pp. 152–4, tr. pp. 148–51.

151. 'paradigmatically', that is, 'typically and generally', not a paradigm case nor a scientific paradigm.

152. Ibid., p. 148, tr. p. 147.

153. Ibid., p. 152, tr. p. 149 (G.R.).

154. Ibid., p. 153, tr. p. 150 (G.R.).

155. Ibid., pp. 153–4, tr. p. 150 (G.R.).

156. G.S.8 SuEF p. 197, tr. p. 69 (G.R.).

157. Ibid., p. 208, tr. p. 79 (G.R.).

158. G.S.8 Posstreit p. 347 and p. 302, tr. p. 62 and p. 21. See G.S.14 Diss FuR pp. 24–5 for the earliest development of this theme.

159. 'On the Jewish Question', 1843, in *Collected Works*, vol. 3, 151–2.

160. G.S.6 ND pp. 149–51, tr. pp. 146–8.

161. Ibid., p. 149, tr. p. 146 (G.R.).

162. *Capital*, vol. 1, 38, tr. 1976, 128.

163. Ibid., 69, tr. 1976, 162.

164. *Theories of Surplus Value*, Part 3, 129.

165. *Capital*, vol. 1, 72, tr. 1976 165 (G.R.).

166. Ibid., 38, tr. 1976 128, my emphasis.

167. *Theories of Surplus Value*, Part 3, 129.

168. G.S.8 MuO pp. 533–4.

169. *Capital*, vol. 1, 38, tr. 1976 129.

170. PT II p. 233, pp. 281–2.

171. G.S.6 ND p. 66, tr. p. 56 (G.R.).

172. *Prisms* p. 17, tr. p. 25.

173. G.S.8 SoI p. 361.

174. G.S.14 Diss FuR p. 25.

175. G.S.8 SoI p. 359.
176. Ibid., p. 359.
177. Ibid., p. 369.
178. G.S.6 ND p. 302, tr. p. 307.
179. Cf. C. B. Macpherson, *The Political Theory of Possessive Individualism* (Oxford University Press, 1962) p. 49.
180. Cf. Ernest Gellner, 'Concepts and Society', in Dorothy Emmet and Alasdair Macintyre (eds.), *Sociological Theory and Philosophical Analysis* (New York: Macmillan, 1970), pp. 119-20 and p. 147.
181. G.S.8 LS p. 549, tr. p. 107 (G.R.).
182. The work of Jürgen Habermas moves explicitly in this direction. See for example, 'Technik und Wissenschaft als "Ideologie" ', in book of the same title, pp. 48-103 (FaM: Suhrkamp, 1970 (1968)) trans. Jeremy J. Shapiro, *Towards a Rational Society Student Protest, Science and Politics* (London: Heinemann, 1971), pp. 81-122 (not all the same articles as in the German).
183. G.S.6 ND p. 314, tr. p. 320.

Chapter 4

1. Stichworte, *Marginalien zu Theorie und Praxis*, 1969, pp. 169-91.
2. G.S.1 AP p. 331 tr. p. 124.
3. G.S.6 ND p. 10, tr. p. xx.
4. *Prisms* p. 27, tr. p. 32.
5. On 7 May 1931. Not published before its appearance in the collected works, but a publication was planned at the time, with a dedication to Walter Benjamin. See G.S.1 'Editorische Nachbemerkung', p. 383. This has been translated as 'The Actuality of Philosophy', *Telos*, 31, 1977.
6. *Kritik*, pp. 10-19.
7. 1962, Eingriffe, pp. 11-28.
8. G.S.6 Hegel p. 250, two of the studies were originally lectures delivered in 1956 and 1958. All three were published together in 1963.
9. See Mészáros, *Lukács' Concept of Dialectic*, p. 134.
10. See Ibid., p. 133; and Benjamin to Gershom Scholem, 13 June 1924, *Briefe* 1, p. 350, and Benjamin's brief review of the book, in *Schriften* III, p. 171, 1929.
11. See Ringer, *The Decline of the German Mandarins*, pp. 310, 371-2.
12. G.S.6 ND p. 57, tr. p. 47 (G.R.).
13. Ibid., p. 75, tr. p. 67.
14. Ibid., p. 20, tr. p. 8, and cf. G.S.11 Anhang 'Henkel, Krug und frühe Erfahrung' (1965), pp. 558, 562.
15. 'Husserl and the Problem of Idealism', *The Journal of Philosophy*, XXXCII, 1 (1940), 5.
16. G.S.6 JE p. 475, tr. p. 92. Adorno initially intended the text to be part of *Negative Dialectic*. See p. 524, tr. p. xix.
17. G.S.6 ND p. 97, tr. p. 90 (G.R.).
18. Ibid., p. 91, tr. p. 84.
19. *Prisms* p. 27, tr. p. 32.
20. G.S.5, Husserl p. 9.
21. PT II p. 265.
22. G.S.6 ND p. 178, tr. pp. 176-7.
23. Ibid., p. 184, tr. p. 183 (G.R.).
24. G.S.1 AP p. 338, tr. p. 129.
25. G.S.6 ND p. 347f., tr. p. 354f.
26. Eingriffe p. 7.

27. G.S.5 Hegel pp. 326–75.
28. Ibid., pp. 295–325.
29. Ibid., p. 304.
30. Ibid., p. 359.
31. Ibid., p. 358.
32. Ibid., p. 255.
33. Ibid., p. 295.
34. Ibid., pp. 256–60.
35. Friedrich Engels, *Ludwig Feuerbach and the Outcome of Classical German Philosophy* 1888, (C. P. Dutt (ed.), New York: International Publishers, 1970 (1941)), p. 13, my emphasis.
36. For example, G.S.5 Hegel pp. 257–60, 265f, 273f.
37. For example, ibid., pp. 253–7 and 259–61.
38. For example, ibid., pp. 275–7 and 274.
39. For example, G.S.6 ND pp. 31–3, tr. pp. 20–2, and p. 36, tr. p. 27.
40. For example, ibid., pp. 23–4, tr. pp. 11–12, and p. 38, tr. p. 28.
41. MM p. 9, tr. p. 16, my emphasis.
42. G.S.5 Hegel p. 14 and see Joseph O'Malley (ed.), *Karl Marx, Critique of Hegel's Philosophy of Right* (Oxford University Press, 1967) pp. 16–17.
43. G.S.5 Hegel pp. 252–3.
44. For example, G.S.5 Hegel pp. 288–92.
45. Ibid., p. 356, and trans. T. M. Knox, *Hegel's Philosophy of Right* (Oxford University Press, 1967) pp. 16–17.
46. G.S.5 Hegel pp. 355–6.
47. Ibid., p. 256.
48. G.S.6 ND p. 37, tr. p. 26.
49. Ibid., pp. 198–9, tr. p. 198 (G.R.).
50. G.S.5 Hegel p. 265.
51. Ibid., pp. 265–6.
52. Ibid., pp. 266–7. *Arbeit* can be translated both as 'work' and as 'labour'.
53. Ibid., pp. 267–8.
54. Ibid., p. 270.
55. Ibid., pp. 270–1.
56. Ibid., p. 272.
57. Ibid.
58. Ibid., pp. 272–3.
59. G.S.6 ND pp. 161–3, tr. pp. 158–61, 'Critique of Positive Negation'..
60. For an example of the absurdities which result if it is so interpreted, see Raymond Geuss, 'Review of *Negative Dialectic*', *The Journal of Philosophy*, LXXII, 6 (1975), 167–75.
61. G.S.6 ND for example, p. 20, tr. p. 8.
62. Ibid., pp. 23–4, tr. pp. 11–12.
63. Marx, ' "Introduction" to the "Grundrisse" ', in *Karl Marx: Texts on Method*, p. 72.
64. For example, PT1 p. 144.
65. WB pp. 9, 40, 69–70. See too, Tiedemann, *Studien zur Philosophie Walter Benjamins*, p. 36. Benjamin is opposing the Husserlian position that consciousness is intentional and that its analysis will produce knowledge of essences.
66. Benjamin, *Origin . . .* , p. 214, tr. p. 34.
67. Ibid., p. 217, tr. p. 37.
68. WB p. 62.
69. It is impossible to follow the career of *Vermittlung* (mediation) and its cognates in Ashton's translation of *Negative Dialectic*, because he translates them in so many unrelated ways, as 'transmission' and 'indirectness' as well as 'mediation'.

70. G.S.6 ND p. 184, tr. p. 183.

71. Ibid., p. 172, tr. p. 170 (G.R.).

72. 'Kierkegaard noch Einmal', 1963, in Kierkegaard (pp. 295–318) p. 299.

73. First published in 1933. Second and third editions, 1962, 1966; each with the addition of one article.

74. First published in English in ZfS, 8 (1939), 413–29. Published later in German as an appendix to the 1962 edition of Kierkegaard, pp. 267–91. It is shorter and somewhat altered in the German.

75. Ibid., 423, cf. the German rendition, pp. 281–2.

76. Ibid.

77. Kierkegaard p. 305.

78. Ibid., p. 13.

79. Ibid., p. 27.

80. Ibid., p. 29.

81. Ibid., p. 28.

82. Ibid., pp. 44–5.

83. Ibid., p. 59.

84. Ibid., p. 49.

85. Ibid., p. 46.

86. Ibid., p. 56.

87. Ibid., p. 55.

88. Ibid., pp. 126–7.

89. Ibid., pp. 310–11, and 55.

90. Ibid., p. 60.

91. Ibid., p. 61.

92. Ibid., pp. 62–3.

93. Ibid., pp. 61–2, and 64–5.

94. Ibid., p. 65.

95. Ibid.

96. Ibid., p. 53.

97. Ibid., pp. 302, 306, 308.

98. Ibid., p. 302.

99. ZfS, 8, 417, (Kierkegaard pp. 272–3).

100. Ibid., 415 (Kierkegaard p. 270).

101. Ibid., 415 (Kierkegaard p. 275).

102. Ibid., 420 (cf. Kierkegaard pp. 277–8).

103. Ibid., 421 (Kierkegaard p. 278).

104. See *Vorlesung zur Einleitung in die Erkenntnistheorie* (FaM: Junius-Drucke, 1957–8) p. 8. This argument has been put in various ways by Husserl's critics. For an early statement of it, see J. P. Sartre, *The Transcendence of the Ego*, 1936–7, trans. Forrest Williams and Robert Kirkpatrick (New York: Farrar, Strauss and Giroux, 1957); and for a recent, pellucid one, see Leszek Kolakowski, *Husserl and the Search for Certitude* (New Haven and London: Yale University Press, 1975). Chs. I, II, and IV of Adorno's book on Husserl were written in 1937, the Introduction and Ch. III in 1956.

105. Cf. G.S.5 Husserl pp. 30–3.

106. Ibid., pp. 34–5.

107. Ibid., pp. 22–5.

108. Ibid., p. 37.

109. Ibid.

110. Ibid., pp. 37–8.

111. Immanuel Kant, *Critique of Pure Reason*, trans. Norman Kemp-Smith (New York: St. Martin's Press, 1965), p. 386.

112. G.S.5 Husserl p. 13.

113. Ibid., p. 14.

114. Ibid., p. 32.

115. Ibid., pp. 31–2.

116. 'Husserl and the Problem of Idealism', p. 8.

117. Ibid., p. 6.

118. G.S.5 Husserl p. 16. See Chapter Two above, for Adorno's debt to Nietzsche on these issues.

119. Ibid.

120. Ibid., pp. 24–7.

121. G.S.5 Husserl pp. 25–6; Nietzsche, *Twilight of the Idols*, p. 37 (G.R.).

122. G.S.5 Husserl p. 20.

123. Ibid., p. 23.

124. Ibid., p. 193.

125. Ibid., pp. 15, 31, 194.

126. 'Husserl and the Problem of Idealism', p. 6.

127. G.S.5 Husserl pp. 40, 45–7, discussed further below.

128. The first volume of the three German volumes of the *Logical Investigations*, trans. J. N. Findlay (London: Routledge & Kegan Paul, 1970, 2 vols.) I, 53–266.

129. Investigation II 'The Ideal Unity of the Species and Modern Theories of Abstraction', Vol. I, pp. 337–432.

130. G.S.5 Husserl pp. 131–3.

131. Ibid., pp. 170–1.

132. Ibid., pp. 134–5.

133. Ibid., p. 172.

134. Ibid., p. 145.

135. Ibid., pp. 159, 165.

136. Ibid., p. 140.

137. Ibid., p. 181.

138. Ibid., pp. 160–1.

139. Ibid., p. 161.

140. *Sein und Zeit*, first published 1927. I have used the 12th (unchanged) German edition (Tübingen: Max Niemeyer, 1972), trans. John Macquarrie and Edward Robinson (Oxford: Basil Blackwell, 1967).

141. Cf. J. P. Stern, *Hitler, The Führer and the People* (London: Fontana, 1975), pp. 23–7.

142. I 'The Ontological Need', II 'Being and Existence'.

143. G.S.11 NzL III 'Parataxis' pp. 447–91.

144. G.S.5 Husserl pp. 40–6.

145. Heidegger, *Sein und Zeit*, p. 7, tr. p. 27.

146. G.S.5 Husserl p. 234.

147. Ibid., pp. 43–7.

148. G.S.1 IN pp. 349–50.

149. G.S.5 Husserl p. 192.

150. Ibid., pp. 191–2 and G.S.1 IN pp. 350–5.

151. G.S.6 ND p. 76, tr. p. 69.

152. Ibid., p. 75, tr. p. 67 (G.R.).

153. Eingriffe, 'Wozu noch Philosophie', p. 17.

154. G.S.6 ND pp. 97–8, tr. p. 90; cf. Heidegger, *Vom Wesen des Grundes* (FaM: Klostermann, 1955 (1929)), trans. Terrence Malik, *The Essence of Reasons* [Ground] (Evanston: Northwestern University Press, 1969) contains the German text, p. 10, 11ff.

155. G.S.6 ND p. 112, tr. p. 106 (G.R.).

·156. Ibid., p. 90, tr. p. 83 and cf. note p. 113, tr. pp. 106–7, 'Being, as the basic theme of philosophy, is no class or genus of entities; yet it pertains to every entity. Its 'universality' is to be sought higher up. Being and the structure of Being lie beyond every entity and every possible character which an entity may possess. *Being is the transcendens pure and simple*'. Heidegger, *Sein und Zeit*, p. 38, tr. p. 62, and cf. the note on *Dasein*, p. 114, tr. pp. 107–8.

157. Ibid., p. 11, tr. p. 104.

158. Ibid., p. 105, tr. p. 98.

159. Ibid., p. 94, tr. p. 87.

160. Ibid., p. 91, tr. p. 84.

161. Ibid., p. 122, tr. p. 116.

162. Ibid., p. 123, tr. p. 117, Heidegger, *Sein und Zeit*, p. 42, tr. p. 67.

163. G.S.6 ND p. 111, tr. p. 104 (G.R.).

164. Ibid., pp. 110 and 109–10 note, tr. pp. 103–4 and 103 note.

165. G.S.6 JE p. 489, tr. p. 114 (Heidegger, *Sein und Zeit*, pp. 42–3, tr. p. 68).

166. Ibid.

167. Ibid., p. 462, tr. p. 73. This criticism of Heidegger applies with even greater force to Sartre's appropriation of Heidegger.

168. Ibid., p. 490, tr. p. 115.

169. Ibid., p. 462, tr. p. 73.

170. Ibid., p. 490, tr. p. 115.

171. Ibid., p. 491, tr. p. 117, the second clause is quoted from Heidegger, *Sein und Zeit*, p. 13, tr. p. 34.

172. Ibid., pp. 491–2, tr. pp. 116–17.

173. Ibid., pp. 454–5, tr. p. 62 (G.R.).

174. Ibid., pp. 484–5, tr. p. 107.

175. For example, ibid., p. 508, tr. p. 142.

176. Ibid., p. 496, tr. p. 85.

177. Ibid., p. 421, tr. p. 12.

178. Ibid.

179. G.S.6 ND p. 117, tr. p. 111.

180. *Geborgenheit* may be translated as 'security' or 'safety'. It is unnecessary to use the awkward 'shelteredness' as in the English translation.

181. G.S.6 JE p. 430, tr. p. 26 (G.R.).

182. Ibid., p. 456, tr. p. 65 (G.R.).

183. Ibid., p. 452, tr. p. 59.

184. Ibid., p. 448, tr. p. 52.

185. Ibid., G.S. Hegel, p. 250.

186. G.S.6 ND p. 368, tr. p. 375.

Chapter 5

1. G.S.8 SeF p. 197, tr. p. 68 (G.R.).

2. Ibid., Posstreit p. 316, tr. p. 33 (G.R.).

3. Ibid., dS p. 503, tr. p. 35 (G.R.).

4. Ibid.

5. Ibid., p. 502, tr. p. 34.

6. Ibid., Posstreit p. 292, tr. p. 12 (G.R.).

7. Ibid., p. 289, tr. pp. 9–10.

8. Ibid., p. 289, tr. p. 9 (G.R.).

9. Ibid., p. 321, tr. p. 38 (G.R.).

10. Ibid., pp. 320 – 1, tr. p. 37 (G.R.).

11. Ibid., p. 292, tr. p. 12.

12. Cf. Herbert Marcuse, *One Dimensional Man* (London: Sphere Books, 1968 (1964)).

13. See Michael Theunissen, *Gesellschaft und Geschichte, Zur Kritik der kritishen Theorie* (Berlin: Walter de Gruyter & Co., 1969) for an excellent discussion of Horkheimer and of Habermas on this issue.

14. G.S.8 dS p. 504, tr. p. 36.

15. Ibid.

16. G.S.6 ND p. 348, tr. p. 355.

17. See G.S.6 ND pp. 347 – 51, tr. pp. 354 – 8.

18. G.S.8 SuEF p. 202, tr. pp. 73 – 4 (G.R.). (The reference* is to 'Sociology and Empirical Research', in *Soziologische Exkurse*, p. 112, tr. p. 124 (G.R.).)

19. Ibid., tr. p. 73 (G.R.).

20. See WE *passim*.

21. See List of Abbreviations of Titles, pp. 155 – 8, for a list of essays in G.S.8 plus English translations of the titles.

22. G.S.7, 'Editorisches Nachwort', p. 540; and see G.S.9 II 'Editorische Nachbemerkung', pp. 401 – 3.

23. Heinz Maus and Friedrich Fürstenberg (eds.), *Der Positivismusstreit in der deutschen Soziologie* (Neuwied und Berlin: Luchterhand, 1969) tr. 1976.

24. See David Frisby, 'Introduction to the English Translation', ibid., tr. pp. ix – xiv. Frisby says least about Adorno's contributions; but see too Frisby, 'The Popper – Adorno Controversy: the Methodological Dispute in German Sociology', *Philosophy of the Social Sciences*, 2, 2(1972), 105 – 19; and 'The Frankfurt School: critical theory and positivism', in John Rex (ed.), *Approaches to Sociology* (London and Boston: Routledge and Kegan Paul, 1974) pp. 205 – 29. See also Anthony Giddens, 'Introduction' to Giddens (ed.) *Positivism and Sociology* (London: Heinemann, 1974), pp. 17 – 21; and John O'Neill, 'Scientism Historicism and the Problem of Rationality', in O'Neill (ed.) *Modes of Individualism and Collectivism* (London: Heinemann, 1973), p. 3f.

25. Adorno's discussion of Durkheim and Weber occurs in several places, among them, eSoz pp. 38 – 40; 125 – 33.

26. See Max Horkheimer, *The Eclipse of Reason* (New York: Seabury, 1974 (1947)); and Herbert Marcuse, 'Industrialization and Capitalism', in Otto Stammer (ed.), *Max Weber and Sociology Today* (Oxford: Basil Blackwell, 1971 (1965)) pp. 133 – 51.

27. G.S.8 dS p. 503, tr. p. 35. The point is confusing because Adorno uses 'to understand' with connotations of reason (*Vernunft*), although *verstehen* (to understand) does not carry such implications normally. See Glossary, Reason (s.v.). Debate about how formally or substantively to interpret Weber's methodology has occurred outside the Marxist tradition. For a famous interpretation which emphasises Weber's concern with autonomy, see, trans. Salvator Attanasio, Karl Löwith, 'Weber's Interpretation of the Bourgeois-Capitalistic World in Terms of the Guiding Principle of "Rationalization"', in Dennis Wrong (ed.) *Max Weber Makers of Modern Social Science* (New Jersey: Englewood Cliffs, 1970), pp. 101 – 22.

28. See G.S.8 Gesellschaft pp. 13 – 19, tr. pp. 148 – 53.

29. Ibid., Durkheim p. 250.

30. Ibid., Gesellschaft p. 12, tr. p. 147 (G.R.).

31. Ibid.

32. Ibid., tr. (G.R.).

33. Ibid.

34. Ibid., Durkheim p. 258.

35. Ibid., p. 259.

36. Ibid.

37. Ibid., p. 258. The question of whether 'value-relatedness' in Weber's methodology is limited to the selection of problems or extends into theory formation and validation has been widely discussed. See, for example, the essay by Talcott Parsons and the discussion on 'Value-freedom and objectivity', in *Max Weber and Sociology Today*, op.cit., pp. 27–82.

38. Emile Durkheim, *Sociology and Philosophy* trans. David Peacock (New York: The Free Press, 1974 (1953)) p. 95.

39. G.S.8 Durkheim p. 258.

40. 'Value Judgements and Judgements of Reality', the third essay in *Sociology and Philosophy*, pp. 96–7.

41. Ibid., p. 92.

42. Ibid., p. 95.

43. G.S.8 Durkheim pp. 258–9.

44. G.S.8 Durkheim. This essay is Adorno's introduction to the German translation of Durkheim's *Sociology and Philosophy*, 1967 (first published as a book in 1924). Adorno concentrates on Durkheim's notion of 'collective consciousness', although after the latter had written *The Division of Labour in Society*, he used the notion of 'collective representations', see Lukes, *Émile Durkheim*, pp. 4–8. However, Durkheim continued to use phrases such as 'the collectivity', 'collective feelings'.

45. G.S.8 Durkheim p. 276. Adorno quotes Durkheim's statement that ' . . . there is a further reason why objective and average evaluation should not be confused: namely, because the reactions of the individual remain individual reactions . . . There exists no essential difference between the propositions *I want that* and *A definite number of us want that'* (English tr. p. 83 (G.R.)).

46. Ibid., p. 247.

47. Quoted by Adorno, ibid., p. 263 (tr. p. 61 (G.R.)).

48. Quoted by Adorno, ibid., pp. 275–6 (tr. p. 65 (G.R.)).

49. Quoted by Adorno, ibid., p. 253 (tr. p. 66 (G.R.)).

50. Ibid.

51. Ibid., p. 255.

52. Ibid., p. 253.

53. Ibid., p. 253 (tr. p. 36).

54. Ibid., p. 254.

55. G.S.8 Durkheim p. 251.

56. Ibid., p. 250.

57. G.S.8 LS p. 549, tr. p. 107 (G.R.).

58. Cf. Lukács, 'Reification and the Consciousness of the Proletariat', in *History and Class Consciousness*, pp. 98–100, 102–3.

59. Cf. G.S.8 Konflikt, in which Adorno discusses, *inter alia*, Ralf Dahrendorf, *Class and Class Conflict in Industrial Society* (London: Routledge & Kegan Paul, 1967 (1957)).

60. G.S.8 SoI pp. 367–70.

61. Ibid.

62. Marcuse, *One Dimensional Man*, pp. 19–31.

63. Jürgen Habermas, 'Technology and Science as "Ideology" ', in *Towards a Rational Society*, especially pp. 113–22.

64. G.S.8 Klassen, ('Reflections on the Theory of Classes'). The editors do not offer any reason why this essay remained unpublished.

65. Ibid., pp. 377, 379.

66. Ibid., p. 378.

67. Ibid., pp. 378–9.

68. Ibid., p. 379.

69. Ibid., p. 379.

70. Ibid., p. 380.

71. Ibid., p. 384.
72. Adorno seems to have no more specific concept of liberalism.
73. Ibid., p. 386.
74. Ibid., p. 388.
75. Ibid., p. 389.
76. Ibid., p. 390.
77. G.S.8 Konflikt 1968 ('Remarks on Social Conflict Today').
78. Ibid., p. 183.
79. Ibid.
80. Ibid.
81. Ibid.
82. Ibid., p. 184.
83. Ibid., pp. 184–5.
84. Ibid., p. 188.
85. Ibid.
86. G.S.8 IuO 1953 ('The Individual and Organization').
87. Ibid., p. 441.
88. Ibid., p. 446.
89. Ibid., pp. 443–4; 447–8.
90. Ibid., p. 451.
91. Ibid., p. 455.
92. Ibid.
93. G.S.6 ND pp. 164–6, tr. pp. 162–3.
94. Ibid., p. 168, tr. pp. 165–6.
95. Ibid., p. 168, tr. p. 166.
96. G.S.1 BU ('The Concept of the Unconscious in the Transcendental Theory of the Soul'). First published in the collected works, 1973.
97. Ibid., p. 225.
98. It is surprising that Adorno did not extend this argument to his criticism of Husserl's philosophy, since it could equally well be applied to Husserl's distinction between empirical and transcendental psychology.
99. G.S.8 Fascist 1 p. 401; G.S.9 11 'Vorurteil und Charakter' p. 361.
100. G.S.8 Fascist 1 p. 397.
101. Ibid., PuN pp. 437–8.
102. G.S.8 Psychoanalyse. Written in English in 1946, first published in German, 1962 ('Revisionist Psychoanalysis').
103. London, Routledge and Kegan Paul, 1939. Translated into German, 1951.
104. G.S.8 Psychoanalyse p. 27.
105. Ibid.
106. Ibid., p. 28.
107. Ibid., p. 31.
108. Ibid., p. 32. Cf. Marx, 'Competition generally, this essential locomotive force of the bourgeois economy, does not establish its laws, but is rather their executor. Unlimited competition is therefore not the presupposition for the truth of the economic laws, but rather the consequence – the form of appearance in which their necessity realizes itself'. *Grundrisse*, p. 450, tr. p. 552.
109. G.S.8 SuP p. 46, tr. p. 70, with reference to Parsons, 'Psychoanalysis and the Social Structure', in *The Psychoanalytic Quarterly*, XIX, 3 (1950), 373.
110. Ibid.
111. Ibid., p. 44, tr. p. 69.
112. Ibid., p. 50, tr. p. 73.
113. Ibid., p. 51, tr. p. 74.

114. Ibid., p. 44, tr. p. 69.
115. Ibid.
116. Ibid., p. 45, tr. p. 70.
117. Ibid., pp. 53-4, tr. p. 76.
118. Cf. Max Horkheimer, 'Sociological Background of the Psychoanalytic Approach', in Ernst Simmel, (ed.), *Anti-Semitism. A Social Disease* (New York: International Universities Press, 1946) pp. 8-9.
119. G.S.8 SuP p. 70, tr. p. 86.
120. Ibid.
121. Ibid., pp. 70-1, tr. pp. 86-7.
122. Ibid., p. 70, tr. p. 86.
123. Ibid., p. 71, tr. p. 87.
124. Ibid., pp. 70-1, tr. p. 87.
125. Ibid., p. 71, tr. p. 87.
126. Ibid.
127. Ibid.
128. Ibid.
129. Ibid., p. 72, tr. p. 88.
130. Ibid., pp. 72-3, tr. p. 88.
131. G.S.8 Posstreit p. 323, tr. p. 40 (G.R.).
132. G.S.8 Durkheim pp. 246-7 n.
133. Ibid., Posstreit p. 282, tr. p. 3. This notion was defined further by subsequent contributors to the debate. See the articles by Habermas and Hans Albert, which do not, however, clarify Adorno's position.
134. See the list of them in the List of Abbreviations of Titles (pp. 155-8), under G.S.8. I include parts of WE in this category.
135. Schad, *Empirical Social Research in Weimar Germany*, pp. 17-24⊦.₁
136. eSoz pp. 10-11.
137. G.S.9 II ES p. 327. This article was written jointly by Adorno and six others. See p. 327 n.
138. Horkheimer, 'Vorwort', ZfS 1 (1932), I-IV.
139. Ibid., II.
140. Ibid., III.
141. Ibid.
142. G.S.9 II ES p. 331.
143. Ibid., pp. 331-2.
144. Ibid., p. 332.
145. Ibid., p. 356.
146. See, for example, G.S.8 eS, MuO, GuEF.
147. See especially ibid., dS.
148. Begun in 1936-7. Adorno worked with the Project 1938-9.
149. Lazarsfeld, 'A Memoir', in *The Intellectual Migration*, quoting from a letter written by Hadley Cantril, in which the latter expounded the purpose of the project, p. 305.
150. WE p. 117, tr. p. 343.
151. Ibid., p. 118, tr. p. 343.
152. Ibid.
153. Ibid., p. 119, tr. 343.
154. Ibid., p. 119, tr. pp. 343-4.
155. Ibid., p. 120, tr. p. 345, (G.R.).
156. Ibid.
157. Ibid., p. 121, tr. p. 245.
158. Ibid.

159. Ibid., p. 123, tr. p. 348; and Lazarsfeld, op.cit., pp. 323–4. It is not clear to what extent Adorno concurred in this effort.

160. 'Administrative and Critical Communications Research', ZfS ix (1941), 2–16.

161. Ibid., 16.

162. Ibid., 16 and 10.

163. Ibid., 12–13.

164. WE p. 121, tr. p. 346.

165. Cf. SuEF§ 7.

166. G.S.8 dS.

167. Ibid., p. 506, tr. p. 37.

168. Ibid., p. 507, tr. p. 38.

169. Ibid., p. 513, tr. pp. 42–3.

170. Ibid., p. 515, tr. p. 43.

171. Ibid., p. 512, tr. p. 42.

172. Ibid., p. 515, tr. p. 44 (G.R.).

173. Ibid., p. 517, tr. p. 45.

174. Ibid.

175. Ibid., p. 523, tr. p. 50.

176. Ibid.

177. Ibid.

178. G.S.14 Diss FuR p. 25.

179. G.S.14 Diss FuR 25.

180. G.S.8 dS p. 531, tr. p. 55.

181. Ibid., p. 529, tr. p. 54.

182. Ibid., SuEF p. 201, tr. p. 73 (G.R.).

183. Ibid.

184. G.S.8 Posstreit pp. 342–4, tr. pp. 57–9.

185. eSoz p. 26. Adorno's stipulation that concepts cannot be defined independently of experience, is open to the charge that it is *a priori* too. His response might be (roughly) that the stipulation arises from examining the antinomies which occur if one tries to proceed otherwise.

186. G.S.8 Konflikt p. 186.

187. Ibid.

188. eSoz p. 27.

189. For example, G.S.8 Posstreit p. 291, tr. p. 11; SuEF p. 209, tr. p. 80.

190. For example, G.E.9 ii p. 356.

191. G.S.8 Posstreit p. 291, tr. p. 11 (G.R.).

192. Cf. ibid., p. 326, tr. p. 42.

193. Ibid., p. 291, tr. p. 11.

194. Ibid., SuEF § 2.

195. Ibid., p. 215, tr. p. 85; and Hegel, *Philosophy of Right*, pp. 318, 205.

196. G.S.8 SuEF pp. 202–3, tr. p. 74.

197. Ibid., Posstreit p. 315, tr. p. 32.

198. Ibid., p. 320, tr. p. 38.

199. Ibid., SuEF p. 214, tr. p. 85.

200. Ibid., Posstreit p. 315, tr. p. 32.

201. WE p. 123, tr. p. 374.

202. Ibid.

203. Ibid.

204. Ibid., pp. 115–17, tr. pp. 340–2.

205. 'The Radio Symphony', in Lazarsfeld and Frank Stanton (eds.) *Radio Research* (New York: Duell, Sloan and Pearce, 1941), pp. 110–39.

206. 'On popular Music', ZfS ix (1941), 17–48; further developed in eMS pp. 12–30.

207. WE p. 127, tr. p. 351.

208. G.S.9 ii Ch. 5 pp. 121–329 (1955).

209. G.S.9 i 'The Psychological Technique of Martin Luther Thomas' Radio Addresses', 1942, previously unpublished, pp. 7–141.

210. G.S.9 ii 'The Stars down to Earth', 1952–3, first published 1957, pp. 7–120.

211. 'Fernsehen als Ideologie', *Frankfurter Hefte*, 10, 1 (1955) 25–33; reprinted slightly altered in Eingriffe, pp. 81–98.

212. WE p. 143, tr. p. 366.

213. Ibid., p. 132, tr. pp. 355–6; and G.S.9 ii 'Starrheit und Integration', p. 376.

214. Amsterdam, Querido Verlag, 1947.

215. See Richard Christie and Marie Jahoda (eds.) *Studies in the Scope and Method of 'The Authoritarian Personality'* (Glencoe: The Free Press, 1954); and see too Rupert Wilkinson, *The Broken Rebel. A Study in Culture, Politics and Authoritarian Character* (New York: Harper and Row, 1972), especially pp. 1–6.

216. ZfS ix (1941), 124–43.

217. DofE p. 155, tr. p. 173.

218. Ibid., pp. 155–6, tr. p. 173; and cf. Marx, *Theories of Surplus Value*, Part iii, Addenda p. 453ff.

219. DofE p. 156, tr. p. 174.

220. Cf. 'Research Project on Anti-Semitism', ZfS ix, 137–8.

221. DofE p. 156, tr. p. 174.

222. Ibid.

223. ZfS ix, art.cit. 137.

224. DofE p. 156, tr. p. 174 (G.R.).

225. Cf. Horkheimer, 'Sociological Background to the Psychoanalytical Approach', p. 8.

226. DofE p. 178, tr. p. 199.

227. Cf. G.S.8 Fascism ii p. 417ff.

228. Ibid., p. 414.

229. Ibid., p. 431.

230. G.S.8 GuEF pp. 542–3; G.S.9 ii 'Vorurteil und Charakter' pp. 370–3; and see Russell Jacoby, 'Negative Psychoanalysis and Marxism', *Telos*, 14 (1972), 1–22.

231. References to *The Authoritarian Personality* (AP) are to the New York, Norton Library Edition, 1969; the chapters which Adorno wrote himself and Chs. i, vii written jointly are reprinted in G.S.9 i pp. 143–508.

232. G.S.9 ii 'Vorurteil und Charakter' pp. 371–2.

233. WE p. 140, tr. p. 363.

234. AP p. 224.

235. WE pp. 138–9/40, tr. pp. 361–3.

236. AP Ch. xix 'Types and Syndromes'.

237. Ibid., p. 749.

238. Ibid., p. 747.

239. Ibid., p. 749.

240. Ibid., p. 749n.

241. Ibid., pp. 665–6.

242. Ibid., p. 665.

Chapter 6

1. See Krenek, Adorno to Krenek, 9 April 1929, p. 12; 7 Oct 1934, p. 46; 26 May 1935, pp. 85–7; and Adorno, 'Zur gesellschaftlichen Lage der Musik', 1, ZfS, 1 (1932) p. 105.

Adorno insists that art is a cognitive activity *sui generis* and that it is commensurable with sociological theory.

2. Adorno to Krenek, 30 Sept 1932 in Krenek, 11, pp. 35 – 6. These propositions apply to literature as well as to music.

3. Stichworte; Eingriffe.

4. For example, *Dissonanzen* (Diss); *Klangfiguren* [Figures of Sound] *Musikalische Schriften* 1 (FaM: Suhrkamp, 1959); two books on/music published under titles of compositions by Franz Schubert: *Moments Musicaux*, op.94 (FaM: Suhrkamp, 1964, containing essays first published from 1928 onwards); *Impromptus,*\op.90 and op.142 (FaM: Suhrkamp, 1968, containing essays first published from 1922 onwards).

5. For example, on Aldous Huxley, and on Thorstein, Veblen, in *Prisms*.

6. For example, 'Cultural Criticism and Society', in ibid.

7. Written 1937 – 8, first published complete 1952.

8. First published 1960.

9. Written in 1948.

10. Written in 1941.

11. First published 1968. Vols 21 and 22 will consist of miscellaneous writings on Beethoven.

12. Published in 1949. The title of the English translation is wrong: *Philosophy of Modern Music*.

13. *Ohne Leitbild Parva Aesthetica*, 1967, containing essays first published from 1958 onwards.

14. Volume 7 of the collected works, but the first of the works to be published, 1970.

15. The lectures on music were delivered at the University of Frankfurt, 1961 – 2; the lectures on aesthetics were delivered 1967 – 8.

16. See Rene Leibowitz, 'Der Komponist Theodor W. Adorno' in *Zeugnisse*, pp. 355 – 59.

17. Krenek *passim*.

18. This is based on conversations and correspondence with the late Gilbert Ryle, and with A. J. Ayer, Isaiah Berlin and Stuart Hampshire in Oxford, 1972 – 4.

19. Thomas Mann (1949) *The Genesis of a Novel*, trans. Richard and Clara Winston (London: Secker and Warburg, 1961) p. 39.

20. 'Schwierigkeiten I Beim Komponieren', in *Impromptus*, pp. 93 – 111.

21. For a complete list see Klaus Schultz, 'Vorläufige Bibliographie der Schriften Theodor W. Adornos' in *Theodor W. Adorno zum Gedächtnis*, pp. 177 – 239.

22. See Mosco Carner, *Alban Berg: The Man and The Work* (London: Duckworth, 1975) pp. 36, 48.

23. G.S.14 eMS.

24. In *Klangfiguren*, 1958, pp. 9 – 31.

25. In *Quasi una Fantasia Musikalische Schriften II* (FaM: Suhrkamp, 1963) written 1934 – 40, first published 1955.

26. I use these terms in the conventional sense: 'classical' music refers to music of c.1750 to c.1820; 'romantic' music to music of c.1820 to c.1910.

27. *Sonata quasi una Fantasia is* the name of Beethoven's Sonatas, op.27/1 and 2; the second of these in C Sharp Minor has come to be known as the 'Moonlight Sonata'.

28. Frederic Jameson, in spite of the title of his book, does not bring out the contrasts between the writers whom he discusses on the problem of form, and he does least justice to Adorno's many writings on the issue, *Marxism and Form: Twentieth Century Dialectical Theories of Literature* (New Jersey: Princeton University Press, 1971).

29. Cf. Steven Lukes, *Emile Durkheim His Life and Work* (London: Allen Lane, 1973) pp. 462 – 77.

30. See Weber, *The Rational and Social Foundations of Music*, trans. Don Martindale *et.al.* (Carbondale: Southern Illinois University Press, 1969). Published posthumously and now included as an appendix to the German edition of *Economy and Society*, but unfortunately not included in the English translation.

31. *Aspects of Sociology*, Ch. VII, 'Sociology of Art and Music', p. 99, tr. p. 109.

32. *Aspects of Sociology*, p. 99, tr. p. 109.

33. See OL KS p. 96, tr. p. 123.

34. See ibid., p. 97, tr. p. 124.

35. See ibid., pp. 98–9, tr. p. 125.

36. See ibid., p. 94, tr. p. 121.

37. See ibid., p. 97, tr. pp. 123–4.

38. See 'Ideen zur Musiksoziologie', in *Klangfiguren* pp. 10–11.

39. Ibid.

40. See ibid., p. 14.

41. Ibid., pp. 25, 14.

42. See ibid., p. 26.

43. G.S.7 p. 16.

44. See, for example, his 'Diskussionen über Expressionismus', *Das Wort*, 6 (1938) 103–12.

45. See his 'Art and Mass Culture', in English in ZfS, IX (1941) 290–304, republished in *Critical Theory*, pp. 188–243.

46. See his 'Uber den Affirmative Charakter der Kultur', ZfS, VI (1937) 54–94, trans. Jeremy J. Shapiro, 'The Affirmative Character of Culture', *Negations* (Harmondsworth: Penguin, 1968), pp. 88–133.

47. See Ernst Bloch and Hanns Eisler, 'Die Kunst zu Erben', *Die Neue Weltbühne*, 1 (1938) 13–18.

48. See Karl Wittfogel, 'Zur frage einer marxistischen Ästhetik', *Die Linkskurve*, 1/11 (May–November 1930).

49. See Helga Gallas, *Marxistische Literaturtheorie Kontroversen im Bund proletarisch-revolutionärer Schriftsteller* (Neuwied und Berlin: Luchterhand, 1971) p. 18.

50. See Roy Pascal, *From Naturalism to Expressionism: German Literature and Society 1880–1918* (London: Weidenfield and Nicolson, 1973) pp. 59–60.

51. See ibid., pp. 62–5.

52. Ibid., p. 65.

53. See Gallas, *Marxistische Literaturtheorie*, p. 19f.

54. See ibid., p. 11, and Lukács, 'Aus der Not eine Tugend', *Die Linkskurve*, 4 (1932) 15–24.

55. See, for example, Andor Gabor, 'Zwei Bühnenereignisse', *Die Linkskurve*, 4 (1932) 27–32.

56. Listed in ibid., p. 183; and see Brecht, 'Against Georg Lukács', trans. Stuart Hood, *New Left Review*, 84 (1974) 39–53.

57. See Gallas, *Marxistische Literaturtheorie*, pp. 18–19.

58. Brecht's relation to expressionism is complex: he both disparaged expressionist drama and acknowledged a debt to it. See the anonymous 'Introduction' to Brecht, op.cit., 33–8; and Brecht's text, ibid., 44; see too Hans Mayer, 'Mann and Brecht: Anatomy of an Antagonism', *New German Critique*, 6 (1975) 112.

59. Lukács' work in this field culminated in his *Ästhetik*, of which he only completed the first of three projected parts, *Die Eigenart des Ästhetischen*, (Neuwied und Darmstadt: Luchterhand, Werkausgabe, 1963).

60. See also his essay on Bloch, 'Blochs Spuren', 1960, G.S.11 NzL II and on Siegfried Kracauer, 'Der Wunderliche Realist', 1964, ibid., NzL III.

61. 'The Old Culture and the New', *Telos*, 5 (1970) 21.

62. Ibid., 23.
63. Ibid.
64. Ibid., 25.
65. Ibid., 26.
66. Ibid.
67. Ibid.
68. G.S.8 Kultur p. 122.
69. Ibid., p. 128.
70. Ibid.
71. Ibid., p. 127.
72. Ibid., p. 128.
73. Ibid., p. 131.
74. 'The Work of Art in the Age of Mechanical Reproduction', 1936, trans. Harry Zohn, in *Illuminations* (London: Fontana, 1973).
75. WE p. 117, tr. p. 342.
76. 'The Work of Art in the Age of Mechanical Reproduction', p. 223.
77. Ibid., p. 227.
78. Ibid., p. 223.
79. Ibid., p. 225.
80. Ibid., p. 226.
81. Ibid., p. 241.
82. Ibid., p. 226.
83. Ibid., p. 233.
84. Ibid., p. 226.
85. Ibid., pp. 243 -4.
86. 'Eduard Fuchs: Collector and Historian', ZfS vi (1937) 348 and see n.1, trans. Knut Tarnowski, *New German Critique*, 5 (1975) 29 (G.R.) and n.3.
87. See the essays on Kafka in *Illuminations* and on Brecht in *Understanding Brecht*, trans. Anna Bostock (London: New Left Books, 1973).
88. This paragraph is based on Adorno's letter to Benjamin, 18 March 1936, in WB pp 126–34, tr. *New Left Review*, 81 (1973) 63 -8.
89. See ibid., pp. 130; 1, tr. 66.
90. See ibid., p. 128, tr. 65.
91. Ibid., pp. 131–2, tr. 67. By 'alienating', I mean *Verfremdung*, Brecht's idea. It means 'making strange or alien' and should not be confused with *Entfremdung* which is usually translated as 'alienation'.
92. Ibid., p. 132, tr. 67.
93. Ibid., p. 131, tr. 67.
94. Ibid., pp. 129–30, tr. 166.
95. Ibid.
96. Ibid., p. 129, tr. 166. The phrase *avant-garde* is inappropriate since Adorno's point is that this *avant* does not lead a *garde*. Habermas simplifies Adorno's position in a misleading way when he argues that, in relation to Benjamin, Adorno interpreted the mass art arising out of new techniques of reproduction as a 'degeneration of art'. See Habermas, 'Bewusstmachende oder rettende Kritik – die Aktualität Walter Benjamin', in Siegfried Unseld (ed.), *Zur Aktualität Walter Benjamin* (FaM: Suhrkamp, 1972) p. 191.
97. Adorno to Krenek, 30 Sept 1932, Krenek p. 36.
98. Krenek to Adorno, 11 Sept 1932, ibid., pp. 28–39.
99. Ibid., p. 37.
100. Cf. G.S.14 Diss FuR pp. 24–5.
101. Adorno to Krenek, 30 Sept 1932, p. 37.
102. Adorno quotes Marx, *Capital*, vol. 1, ch. 1, §4 in G.S.14 Diss FuR p. 24.

103. See 'Résumé über Kulturindustrie' in OL p. 60, trans. Anson G. Rabinbach, 'Culture Industry Reconsidered', *New German Critique* 6 (1975) 12. This essay was written to counteract misinterpretation of the chapter 'The Culture Industry: Enlightenment or Mass Deception' in DofE. Adorno effectively abandons the phrase because it refers, in an overly compressed way, to production, reproduction and distribution but not at all to industry.

104. Ibid., p. 61, tr. p. 17.

105. G.S.14 eMS p. 425 and n.

106. 'Résumé über Kulturindustrie', pp. 63–4, tr. pp. 14–15.

107. Ibid., pp. 62–3, tr. p. 14.

108. 'Zur gesellschaftlichen Lage der Musik', II, ZfS, I (1932) 356.

109. G.S.14 eMS p. 429.

110. Published 1958, trans. John and Necke Mander, with many omissions, as *Realism in Our Time* (New York: Harper and Row, 1964).

111. 'Franz Kafka or Thomas Mann?' ibid., p. 92.

112. Subtitled *Zu Georg Lukács: 'Wider der missverstandenen Realismus'*, 1958, G.S.11 NzL II.

113. 'Aufzeichnungen zu Kafka', written 1942–53, published in *Prisms*, tr. 'Notes on Kafka'.

114. 'The Ideology of Modernism', in *Realism in our Time*, p. 19.

115. Ibid.

116. Ibid.

117. Ibid., and p. 81.

118. Ibid., p. 23.

119. Ibid., p. 45.

120. Ibid., pp. 22–3.

121. Ibid., p. 23.

122. Ibid., p. 20.

123. Ibid., p. 21, *geworfen*, 'thrown-into-the-world', is an allusion to Heidegger's philosophy.

124. Ibid., pp. 37, 54–6.

125. Ibid., p. 36.

126. Ibid.

127. Ibid., p. 53.

128. Ibid., p. 78.

129. Ibid.

130. Ibid., p. 79.

131. Ibid.

132. 'The Tragedy of Modern Art', 1948, in *Essays on Thomas Mann*, trans. Stanley Mitchell (London: Merlin, 1969) pp. 61–4.

133. Ibid., pp. 68–9.

134. Ibid., p. 68.

135. Ibid., p. 69.

136. Ibid.

137. First published 1920, trans. Anna Bostock (London: Merlin, 1971) see Pt. I which contains a typology of forms of epic literature, and Pt. II 'Attempt at a typology of the novel form'.

138. G.S.11 NzL II 'Erpresste Versöhnung', p. 253.

139. Ibid., pp. 255–7.

140. Ibid., p. 259.

141. Ibid., pp. 260–1.

142. Ibid., pp. 258–9.

143. Ibid., p. 262.
144. Ibid., p. 266.
145. Ibid., p. 261.
146. G.S.6 ND p. 98, tr. p. 91 (G.R.).
147. 'Notes on Kafka', *Prisms*, pp. 302–3, tr. p. 245.
148. Ibid., pp. 308–9, tr. pp. 248–9.
149. Ibid., pp. 314–15, 332–3, tr. pp. 252–3, 265–6.
150. Ibid., p. 329, tr. p. 262.
151. Ibid., p. 327, tr. p. 261.
152. G.S.11 NzL II 'Erpresste Versöhnung', pp. 273–4.
153. See *The Genesis of a Novel*, p. 38, and Mann's letter to Adorno, 30 Oct 1952, in Thomas Mann *Briefe 1948–55*, Erika Mann (ed.) (FaM: S. Fisher, 1965) pp. 274–6. Mann wrote *The Genesis of a Novel*, 1949, to acknowledge Adorno's assistance with *Doctor Faustus*, see Mann to A. M. Frey, 19 Jan 1952, ibid., p. 240, trans. Richard and Clara Winston, *The Letters of Thomas Mann* (Harmondsworth: Penguin, 1975) (1970)) p. 448.
154. Mann to Adorno, 30 Dec 1945, *Briefe 1937–47* (1963), pp. 469–72, tr. 360–3; and see *The Genesis of a Novel*, p. 29.
155. Ibid.
156. G.S.13 Wagner p. 82, quoted by Mann to Adorno, 30 Oct 1952, *Briefe*, p. 275.
157. Ibid.
158. In this and the following paragraph, I extrapolate Adorno's position.
159. The title of Lukács' first essay on Mann (n.d.) in *Essays on Thomas Mann*.
160. G.S.11 NzL II 'Erpresste Versöhnung', pp. 269–70, and see G.S.14 Diss 'Das Altern der Neuen Musik', pp. 143–67.
161. G.S.11 ibid., p. 269.
162. Ibid.
163. See Gunilla Bergsten, *Thomas Mann's Doctor Faustus: The Sources and Structure of the Novel*, 1963, trans. Clara Winston (Chicago University Press, 1969) ch. 2, '*The Basis of the Montage Technique*', p. 99f.
164. See Mann, *The Genesis of a Novel*, p. 40, and Bergsten, op.cit., pp. 79–81.
165. Mann, *The Genesis of a Novel*, pp. 54–5 (G.R.).
166. See Iring Fetscher, 'Bertolt Brecht and America', *Salmagundi*, 10–11 (1969–70) 262–5.
167. Ibid., 264.
168. Lukács, 'Critical Realism and Socialist Realism', in *Realism in our Time*, pp. 95–6.
169. See Eugene Lunn, 'Marxism and Art in the Era of Stalin and Hitler: the Brecht-Lukács Debate', *New German Critique*, 3 (1974) 15.
170. See 'The Author as Producer', 1934, in *Understanding Brecht*, pp. 99–100 and 'What is Epic Theatre?' 1939, ibid., pp. 15–22.
171. Brecht, 'Against Georg Lukács', *New Left Review*, 84, 50.
172. Adorno, 'Zur Frankfurter Aufführung der "Dreigroschenoper"', 1928, and 'Zur Musik der Dreigroschenoper', 1929, in *Bertolt Brecht's Dreigroschenbuch* (FaM: Suhrkamp, 1960) pp. 183–7; 'Mahagonny', 1930, in *Moments Musicaux*, pp. 131–40.
173. Adorno, 1964, in *Impromptus*, pp. 93; 113, with reference to Brecht, 193/5, *Schriften zur Literatur und Kunst*, 2, 1934–41 (FaM: Suhrkamp, 1967) pp. 11–34.
174. Adorno, 'Zur gessellschaftlichen Lage der Musik', 1, ZfS, 1, (1932) 108–9.
175. Adorno, 'Engagement', 1962, G.S.11 NzL in pp. 15–16, trans. Francis McDonagh, 'Commitment', *New Left Review*, 87–8 (1974) 80.
176. Ibid., pp. 421; 2, 426, tr. 84, 86.
177. Ibid., p. 421, tr. 83.
178. Cf. G.S.7 *Asthetische Theorie* p. 367.
179. 'Engagement' p. 418, tr. 82.

180. Ibid., p. 419, tr. 82.
181. G.S.7 p. 368.
182. Ibid., p. 367.
183. 'Engagement', p. 427, tr. 87.
184. Ibid., p. 426, tr. 86–7.
185. Ibid., p. 411, tr. 77.
186. Ibid., pp. 409–10, tr. 76.
187. Ibid., p. 409, tr. 76 (G.R.).
188. Ibid., p. 425, tr. 86.
189. Adorno's *Ästhetische Theorie* was to have been dedicated to Beckett. See G.S.7 'Editorisches Nachwort', p. 544.
190. G.S.11 NzL II pp. 290–3.
191. 'Versuch, das Endspiel zu verstehen' (An Attempt to Understand Endgame), 1961, in G.S.11 NzL II.
192. Ibid., p. 282.
193. G.S.7 p. 230.
194. G.S.11 NzL III p. 283. Cf. G.S.7 p. 231.
195. Ibid., p. 232.
196. See ibid., pp. 370–1, and G.S.11 ibid., p. 312 and *passim*.
197. The expression 'the first Vienna School' refers to the work of Schönberg and his pupils, Berg and Webern, 1908–13; and 'the second Vienna School' to the work of the same men in the 1920s which was based on Schönberg's development of serialism. This school was notoriously hostile to the contemporary school of Stravinsky in Paris. See Charles Rosen's brief account, *Schoenberg* (London: Fontana, 1976).
198. Adorno, *Minima Moralia*, p. 71, tr. p. 60.
199. G.S.14 eMS p. 178.
200. Ibid., pp. 178–9.
201. Ibid., ch. VIII 'Musikleben', p. 312f.
202. Ibid., ch. III 'Funktion', p. 221.
203. Ibid., p. 221 and Diss FuR pp. 24–6.
204. Ibid., eMS pp. 308–9.
205. See Adorno 'Zur gesellschaftlichen Lage der Musik', 11 ZfS, 1 (1932) 355–78.
206. Cf. Ibid., 11 'Reproduktion, Konsum', 355–78, 'The Radio Sympony: An Experiment in Theory', in *Radio Research*, pp. 110–39.
207. Ibid., p. 121.
208. Ibid., pp. 124–7.
209. Title of Adorno's essay, 'Fetishism in Music and the Regression of the listener', 1938, but he analysed the syndrome as 'regression of listening' not of the listener, see G.S.14 Diss FuR p. 34f.
210. 'The Radio Symphony', pp. 129–33.
211. Ibid., p. 135.
212. Ibid., p. 136.
213. Adorno, with the assistance of George Simpson, 'On Popular Music', ZfS, IX (1941), 25.
214. Ibid., 22.
215. Ibid., 26.
216. Ibid., 38.
217. Ibid.
218. Ibid., 39–42.
219. Ibid., 42–8.
220. Written in 1944, first published in English under Eisler's name only (New York: Oxford University Press, 1947, and London: Dennis Dobson, 1951). The two English

editions and a German edition (München: Rogner & Bernhard, 1969) contain the same text. Eisler published a changed version under his name alone in East Germany (East Berlin: Henschel, 1949). See Adorno's account of the various texts, G.S.15 KF pp. 144–6. In its original editions the book demonstrates the *theoretical* compatibility of a Brechtian and an Adornitian position, but in practice this compatibility was precarious as the fate of the text testifies. See, too, Hartmut Lück, 'Adornos Zusammenarbeit mit Eisler', in Wilfred F. Schoeller (ed.), *Die neue Linke nach Adorno* (München: Kindler, 1969) pp. 141–57.

221. G.S.15 KF and *Composing for the Films*, chs. VI–VIII.

222. See Adorno, 'Neue Musik, Interpretation, Publikum', 1957 *Nervenpunkte der neuen Musik* (Hamburg: Rowolt, 1969, contains extracts from *Klangfiguren*) pp. 16–30, trans. 'New Music and the Public: Some Problems of Interpretation', in Rollo Myers (ed.), *Twentieth Century Music: A Symposium* (London: John Calder, 1960) pp. 40–51. Most of *Der getreue Korrepetitor* is devoted to detailed technical 'Directions for listening to new music', G.S.15 GK pp. 188–368.

223. G.S.14 eMS ch. 1 'Typen Musikalische Verhaltens', pp. 178–98.

224. Ibid., pp. 190–2.

225. Adorno remarks how the English title of the society was changed to 'International Society for Contemporary Music' (SCM), to a neutral, chronological epithet from a specific, polemical one. See 'Musik und neue Musik', 1960, in *Quasi una Fantasia*, pp. 339–40. Hence the English translation of *Philosophie der neuen Musik* as *Philosophy of Modern Music* does a double disservice to Adorno. It substitutes a general term for a polemical one, while 'modern' in much debate on literature and music is dated from the mid-nineteenth century not from *c.* 1908. See G.S.7 pp. 31–56.

226. 'Musik und neue Musik', p. 339f.

227. G.S.12 PNM p. 32, tr. p. 25.

228. Ibid., p. 34, tr. p. 27 (G.R.).

229. 'Zur gesellschaftlichen Lage der Musik', p. 108. This essay contains the least polemical statement of Adorno's position, while PNM contains the most partisan position.

230. Ibid., 108–9 and f.

231. Schönberg preferred to refer to his 'ideas' rather than to his style. See Arnold Schönberg, *Style and Idea* (London: Faber and Faber, 1975). For Adorno's analysis, see G.S.12 PNM pp. 55–101, tr. pp. 51–104.

232. 'Musik und neue Musik', p. 360.

233. Ibid., pp. 348–9.

234. See Adorno, 'Arnold Schönberg (1884–1951)', 1953, *Prisms*, pp. 202–4, tr. pp. 64–5.

235. See in addition to PNM, 'Der Dialektische Komponist', 1934, in *Impromptus* pp. 39–44; and 'Sakrales Fragment. Über Schönbergs Moses and Aron', 1963, in *Quasi una Fantasia*, pp. 306–38.

236. As Adorno was aware, Schönberg opposed the commercialisation of music and the hypostatisation of technique. See Adorno, 'Klassik, Romantik, neue Musik', 1959, in *Nervenpunkte der neuen Musik*, p. 24.

237. Cf. G.S.12 PNM p. 17, tr. p. 8.

Chapter 7

1. See, for example, Husserl, *The Crisis of European Sciences and Transcendental Phenomenology: An Introduction to Phenomenological Philosophy*, 1936, trans. David Carr (Evanston: Northwestern University Press, 1970); and Heidegger, 'Brief über den

"Humanismus" ', 1946, in *Wegmarken* (FaM: Klostermann, 1967) pp. 145–94. For discussions of Adorno and 'Humanism', see Schmidt, 'Adorno – ein Philosoph des realen Humanismus', in *Theodor W. Adorno zum Gedächtnis*, pp. 52–75, and Jay, 'The Frankfurt School's Critique of Marxist Humanism', in *Social Research*, xxxix (1972) 285–305.

2. Cf. Tom Bottomore, 'Class structure and social consciousness', in Mészáros (ed.) *Aspects of History and Class Consciousness* (London: Routledge & Kegan Paul, 1971) pp. 49–64.

3. G.S.8 SuEF p. 209, tr. p. 80.

4. Ibid.

5. Ibid.

6. Ibid., p. 210, tr. p. 81.

7. See, for example, Habermas, 'What does a crisis mean today? Legitimation problems in late capitalism', in *Social Research* xl (1973) 643–67, and *Legitimation Crisis*, 1973, trans. Thomas McCarthy (London: Heinemann, 1976). However, Claus Offe has re-established the connection between commodity analysis and the state. See *Strukturprobleme des Kapitalistischen Staates* (FaM: Suhrkamp, 1972) and Offe and Volker Ronge, 'Theses on the Theory of the State', *New German Critique*, 6, 1975.

8. I adapt Adorno's dictum, 'Universal history must be construed and denied', G.S.6 ND p. 314, tr. p. 320.

9. G.S.6 JE p. 452, tr. p. 59.

10. 'Relation to Left-Wing Hegelianism', in G.S.6 ND pp. 146–7, tr. pp. 143–4.

11. I draw here on Adorno's lectures on sociology, eSoz, and extrapolate from his criticism of sociology.

12. See, for example, Peter McHugh *et al.*, *On the Beginning of Social Inquiry* (London: Routledge & Kegan Paul, 1974) and Alan Blum, *Theorizing* (London: Heinemann, 1974).

13. Herminio Martins has called this 'the cognitive paradigm', 'Time and Theory in Sociology', in John Rex (ed.), *Approaches to Sociology An Introduction to major trends in British Sociology* (London: Routledge & Kegan Paul, 1974) pp. 251, 263. See, too, Aaron V. Cicourel, *Cognitive Sociology* (Harmondsworth: Penguin, 1973).

14. Russell Keat and John Urry, *Social Theory as Science* (London: Routledge & Kegan Paul, 1975), ch. 8, make a similar distinction, but then go on to make the mistake which I discuss, p. 180f.

15. For example, Peter L. Berger and Thomas Luckmann, *The Social Construction of Reality* (Harmondsworth: Penguin, 1971) pp. 106, 222, 225, and Berger and Stanley Pullberg, 'Reification and the Sociological Critique of Consciousness', 1965, *New Left Review*, 35 (1966) 56–71 and 36, 76–7; and see Geoff Pearson, 'Misfit Sociology and the politics of socialization', in Ian Taylor *et al.* (eds), *Critical Criminology* (London: Routledge & Kegan Paul, 1975) p. 148f.

16. Talcott Parsons (ed. and tr.), *The Theory of Social and Economic Organization* (New York: Macmillan, 1947) p. 103, and Weber, *Wissenschaftslehre* (Tübingen: Mohr, 1973) p. 554.

17. Cf. Morris Cohen, *Reason and Nature* (Glencoe: Free Press, 1952 (1931)) pp. 302, 390, to whom Parsons refers, op. cit., n. 25.

18. See Ralf Dahrendorf's discussion of this, 'Sociology and Human Nature', in *Essays in the Theory of Society* (London: Routledge & Kegan Paul, 1968) pp. 95–106; and Dean C. Tipps, 'Modernization Theory and the Comparative Study of Societies: A Critical Perspective', in *Comparative Studies in Society and History*, 15 (1973) 222.

19. For example, Aaron Cicourel, *Method and Measurement in Sociology* (Glencoe: Free Press, 1964).

20. Martins has drawn attention to the failure of post-functionalist sociology and of structuralist Marxism to conceptualise history. Such sociology evinces a concern with

'process', and the Marxism a concern with history, but at the thematic level rather than at the substantive level; see Martins, 'Time and Theory in Sociology', pp. 246 – 50.

21. G.S.14 Diss 'Tradition', 1961, p. 141.

22. Benjamin, 'Theses on the Philosophy of History', 1940, *Illuminations*, pp. 255 – 66.

23. Habermas, 'Urgeschichte der Subjektivität und verwilderte Selbstbehauptung', *Philosophisch-politische Profile*, pp. 184 – 99.

24. Habermas, 'Einleitung: Historischer Materialismus und die Entwicklung normativer Strukturen', *Zur Rekonstruktion des Historischen Materialismus* (FaM: Suhrkamp, 1976) pp. 10 – 11.

25. See, Habermas, *Knowledge and Human Interests*, 1968, trans. Jeremy J. Shapiro (London: Heinemann, 1972) esp. 'Appendix' (1965).

26. Habermas, 'Toward a Theory of Communicative Competence', *Recent Sociology no. 2 Patterns of Communicative Behaviour*, Hans Peter Dreitzel (ed.) (New York: Macmillan, 1970) pp. 114 – 48.

27. See Habermas' and Gadamer's contributions to Karl-Otto Apel *et al.*, *Hermeneutik und Ideologiekritik* (FaM: Suhrkamp, 1971).

28. G.S.8 Posstreit p. 306, tr. p. 24.

29. 'Marginalien zu Theorie und Praxis', in Stichworte, p. 171, and 'Resignation', in *Kritik*, pp. 149–50.

30. 'Marginalien . . . ', p. 181, and 'Resignation', p. 147.

31. G.S. 6 ND p. 147, tr. p. 144.

32. G.S.1 AP p. 338; *Prisms* p. 28, tr. pp. 32 – 3.

33. G.S.11 NzL ii 'Erpresste Versöhnung', p. 277 and *passim*.

34. Lukács, *Realism in our Time*, p. 37, and Adorno, op. cit., p. 257.

35. Ibid., pp. 254 – 5.

36. Benjamin, 'The Work of Art in the Age of Mechanical Reproduction', p. 226.

37. See, G.S.7 'Editorisches Nachwort', p. 537.

Bibliography

Adorno's Works

This list of Adorno's works is not complete. For a complete list see Klaus Schultz, 'Vorläufige Bibliographie der Schriften Theodor W. Adornos', in Hermann Schweppenhäuser (ed.), *Theodor W. Adorno zum Gedächtnis* (FaM: Suhrkamp). Schultz's list does not include some of the works published after Adorno's death. English translations are noted thus (tr.) and listed together.

1924   'Die Transzendenz des Dinglichen und Noematischen in Husserls Phäno-menologie', G.S. 1.
1927   'Der Begriff des Unbewussten in der Transzendentalen Seelenlehre', G.S. 1.
1930   'Thesen über die Sprache der Philosophen', G.S. 1.
1931   'Die Aktualität der Philosophie', G.S. 1.
1932a 'Die Idee der Naturgeschichte', G.S.1.
1932b 'Zur Gesellschaftlichen Lage der Musik', ZfS, 1.
1933   *Kierkegaard Konstruktion des Ästhetischen* (Tübingen: J. C. B. Möhr).
1936   'Über Jazz', ZfS, 5.
1937   Contributor to Willi Reich (ed.) *Alban Berg* (Vienna: Reichner).
1938   'Über den Fetischcharacter in der Musik und die Regression des Hörers, G.S.14.
1939   'Fragmente über Wagner', ZfS, 8.
1940a 'Husserl and the Problem of Idealism', *The Journal of Philosophy*, 37 (1).
1940b 'On Kierkegaard's Doctrine of Love', ZfS, 8.
1941a With George Simpson 'On Popular Music', ZfS, 9.
1941b 'The Radio Symphony. An Experiment in Theory', Paul F. Lazarsfeld and Frank Stanton (eds), *Radio Research* (New York: Duell, Sloan and Pearce).
1941c 'Spengler Today', ZfS, 9.
1941d 'Veblen's Attack on Culture', ZfS, 9.
1942   'Für Ernst Bloch', *Aufbau – Reconstruction*, 8.
1945a 'A Social Critique of Radio Music', *Kenyon Review*, 7.
1945b 'Theses upon Art and Religion Today', *Kenyon Review*, 7.
1946   'Anti-semitism and Fascist Propaganda', Ernst Simmel (ed.), *Anti-semitism: A Social Disease* (New York: International Universities Press) G.S. 8.
1947   With Max Horkheimer, *Dialektik der Aufklärung Philosophische Fragmente* (Amsterdam: Querido, (tr.)).
1949a *Philosophie der neuen Musik* (Tübingen: J. C. B. Mohr) G.S.12 (tr.)
1949b 'Zur Philosophie Husserls', *Archiv für Philosophie*, 3.

1950 With Else Frenkel-Brunswick, Daniel J. Levinson, R. Nevitt Sanford, *The Authoritarian Personality* (New York: Harper and Brothers) G.S. 91.

1951 *Minima Moralia Reflexionen aus dem Beschädigten Leben* (FaM: Suhrkamp, (tr.)).

1952a *Versuch über Wagner* (Berlin and FaM: Suhrkamp) G.S. 13 (tr. forthcoming).

1952b 'Zur gegenwärtigen Stellung der empirischen Sozialforschung in Deutschland', *Empirische Sozialforschung* (FaM: Wissenschaftliche Schriftenreihe des Instituts zur Förderung öffentlicher Angelegenheiten) G.S. 8.

1952c With Max Horkheimer, 'Vorurteil und Charakter', *Frankfurter Hefte* 7, G.S. 9 2.

1952d 'Zum Verhältnis von Psychoanalyse und Gesellschaftstheorie', *Psyche* 6, G.S. 8.

1953 'Fernsehen als Ideologie', *Rundfunk und Fernsehen* 9.

1954a 'Individuum und Organisation', Fritz Neumark (ed.) *Individuum und Organisation* (Darmstadt) G.S. 8.

1954b 'Television and the Patterns of Mass Culture', *Quarterly of Film, Radio and Television*, VIII.

1955a *Prismen Kulturkritik und Gesellschaft*, (Berlin und FaM: Suhrkamp).

1955b 'Zum Verhältnis von Soziologie und Psychologie', with Walter Dirks (eds.) *Sociologica Aufsätze, Max Horkheimer zum Sechzigsten Geburtstag gewidmet*, Frankfurter Beiträge zur Sociologie, vol 1 (FaM: Europäische Verlaganstalt) G.S. 8 (tr.).

1955c Friedrich Pollock, *Gruppenexperiment Ein Studienbericht*, Frankfurter Beiträge zur Soziologie, vol 2, ch 5 by Adorno, G.S. 9 2.

1956a *Dissonanzen Musik in der verwalteten Welt* (Göttingen, Vandenhoeck und Ruprecht) G.S. 14.

1956b *Zur Metakritik der Erkenntnistheorie Studien über Husserl und die phänomenologischen Antinomien* (Stuttgart: W. Kohlhammer) G.S. 5.

1956c 'Bemerkungen über Statik und Dynamik in der Gesellschaft' *Kölner Zeitschrift für Soziologie und Sozialpsychologie*, 8, G.S. 8.

1956d With Max Horkheimer (eds.) *Soziologische Exkurse Nach Vorträgen und Diskussionen*, Frankfurter Beiträge zur Soziologie, vol 4 (FaM: Europäische Verlaganstalt) (tr.) G.S. 8, ch. XII.

1957 'The Stars Down to Earth: The Los Angeles Times Astrology Column. A Study in Secondary Superstition', *Jahrbuch für Americastudien* 2, G.S. 8 and G.S. 9 2.

1958 *Noten zur Literatur I*, (Berlin und FaM) G.S. 11 (tr. forthcoming).

1959a *Klangfiguren Musikalische Schriften I* (Berlin und FaM; Suhrkamp).

1959b 'Starrheit und Integration', *Psychologische Rundschau* 10, G.S. 9 2.

1959c 'Zum gegenwärtigen Stand der deutschen Soziologie', *Kölner Zeitschrift für Soziologie und Sozialpsychologie* 11, G.S. 8 (tr.).

1960 *Mahler Eine Musikalische Physiognomik* (FaM: Suhrkamp, G.S. 13 (tr. forthcoming).

1961 *Noten zur Literatur II* (FaM: Suhrkamp) G.S. 11 (tr. forthcoming).

1962a *Einleitung in die Musiksoziologie Zwölf theoretische Vorlesungen* (FaM: Suhrkamp) G.S. 14 (tr. forthcoming).

1962b With Max Horkheimer, *Sociologica II Reden und Vorträge*, Frankfurter Beiträge zur Soziologie, vol 10 (FaM: Europäische Verlaganstalt) G.S. 8 (tr.).

1963a *Drei Studien zu Hegel* (FaM: Suhrkamp) G.S. 5.

1963b *Eingriffe Neun Kritische Modelle* (FaM: Suhrkamp).

1963c *Der getreue Korrepetitor, Lehrschriften zur musikalischen Praxis* (FaM: S. Fischer) G.S. 15.

1963d *Quasi una Fantasia Musikalische Schriften* II (FaM: Suhrkamp).

1964a *Jargon der Eigentlichkeit zur deutschen Ideologie* (FaM: Suhrkamp) G.S. 6 (tr.).

1964b *Moments Musicaux Neu gedruckte Aufsätze 1928 bis. 1962* (FaM: Suhrkamp) (tr.).

1965 *Noten zur Literatur* III (FaM: Suhrkamp) G.S.11 (tr. forthcoming).

1966 *Negative Dialektik* (FaM: Suhrkamp) G.S. 6 (tr.).

1967a *Ohne Leitbild Parva Aesthetica* (FaM: Suhrkamp) (tr.).

1967*b* 'Introduction', *Emile Durkheim, Soziologie und Philosophie* (FaM: Suhrkamp) G.S. 8.

1968*a* *Berg Der Meister des kleinsten Übergangs* (Vienna: Elisabeth Lafite) G.S. 13.

1968*b* *Impromptus Zweite Folge neu gedruckter musikalischer Aufsätze* (FaM: Suhrkamp).

1968*c* With Ursula Jaerisch, 'Anmerkungen zum sozialen Konflikt heute', Heinz Maus (ed.) *Gesellschaft, Recht und Politik* (Neuwied und Berlin) G.S. 8.

1969*a* With Hanns Eisler, *Komposition für den Film* (München: Rogner und Bernhard) G.S. 15 (English first edition).

1969*b* *Stichworte Kritische Modelle 2* (FaM: Suhrkamp) (tr.).

1969*c* Introduction and Contributions, *Der Positivismusstreit in der deutschen Soziologie* (Neuwied und Berlin: Luchterhand) G.S. 8 (tr.).

1969*d* *Nrvenpunkte der neuen Musik* (Hambourg: Rowohlt).

Posthumous Publications

1970*a* *Ästhetische Theorie*, Gretel Adorno and Rolf Tiedemann (eds.) (FaM: Suhrkamp) G.S. 7.

1970*b* *Aufsätze zur Gesellschaftstheorie und Methodologie* (FaM: Suhrkamp) G.S. 8 (tr.).

1970*c* *Erziehung zur Mundigkeit Vorträge und Gespräche mit Hellmut Becker 1959–1969*, Gerd Kadelbach (ed.) (FaM: Suhrkamp).

1970*d* *Über Walter Benjamin*, Rolf Tiedemann (ed.) (FaM: Suhrkamp).

1971 *Kritik. Kleine Schriften zur Gesellschaft*, Rolf Tiedemann (ed.) (FaM: Suhrkamp).

1972 Contribution to *Autorität – Organisation – Revolution* (The Netherlands: Van Everskijck).

1973*a* *Vorlesungen zur Ästhetik 1967–8* (Zürich: H. Mayer Nachfolger).

1973*b* *Vorlesung zur Einleitung in die Soziologie* (FaM: Junius).

1973*c* *Philosophische Terminologie Zur Einleitung*, vol 1, Rudolf zur Lippe (ed.) (FaM: Suhrkamp).

1973*d* Adorno and Ernst Bloch, *Gesprach über die Utopie* (Die Waage: Zollikerberg).

1974*a* *Philosophische Terminologie Zur Einleitung*, vol II, Rudolf zur Lippe (ed.) (FaM: Suhrkamp).

1974*b* *Theodor W. Adorno und Ernest Krenek Briefwechsel*, Wolfgang Rogge (ed.) (FaM: Suhrkamp).

1974*c* *Noten zur Literatur* IV, Rolf Tiedemann (ed.) (FaM: Suhrkamp) G.S. 11 (tr. forthcoming).

n.d. *Vorlesung zur Einleitung in die Erkenntnistheorie 1957–8* (FaM: Junius).

1975 L. Goldmann, Th. W. Adorno: 'Discussion . . . sur la sociologie de la litterature', in *Lucien Goldmann et la sociologie de la littérature* (Editions de l' Université de Bruxelles).

English Translations of Adorno's Works

The translations are listed in chronological order of the German edition as given in the list of Adorno's works above.

1931 'The Actuality of Philosophy', *Telos*, 31, 1977.

1947 *Dialectic of Enlightenment*, trans. John Cumming (New York: Herder and Herder, 1972).

1949 *Philosophy of Modern Music*, trans. Anne G. Mitchell and Wesley W. Bloomster (London: Sheed and Ward). This translation is atrocious.

1951*a* *Minima Moralia*, trans. E. F. N. Jephcott (London: New Left Books, 1974). This translation is excellent.

1955*a* *Prisms*, trans. Samuel and Shierry Weber (London: Neville Spearman, 1967).

1955*b* 'Sociology and Psychology', trans. Irving N. Wohlfarth, *New Left Review*, 46–7 (1966–7).

1956d   *Aspects of Sociology*, trans. John Viertel (London: Heinemann, 1973).

1958   'Lyric Poetry and Society', trans. Bruce Mayo, *Telos*, 20 (1974).

1959a   'New Music and the Public: Some problems of Interpretation', Rollo H. Myers (ed.), *Twentieth Century Music* (London: John Calder, 1960).

1959b   'Music and Technique', trans. Wes Bloomster, *Telos*, 32, 1977.

1959c   'Contemporary German Sociology', trans. Norman Birnbaum, *Translations of the Fourth World Congress of Sociology* (1959).

1964a   *Jargon of Authenticity*, trans. Knut Tarnowski and Frederic Will (London: Routledge & Kegan Paul, 1973).

1964b   'Alienated Masterpiece: The *Missa Solemnis* (1959)', trans. Duncan Smith, *Telos*, 28 (1976).

1965   'Commitment', trans. Francis Mcdonagh, *New Left Review*, 87–8 (1974).

1966   *Negative Dialectics*, trans. E. B. Ashton, 1973. For comments on the translation, see my 'Review of *Negative Dialectics*', *American Political Science Review*, 70 (1976) 598–9.

1967a   'Culture Industry Reconsidered', trans. Anson G. Rabinbach, *New German Critique*, 6 (1975).

1967b   'Theses on the Sociology of Art', trans. Brian Trench, *Birmingham Cultural Studies*, 2, (1972).

1969a   Hanns Eisler, *Composing for the Films* (New York: Oxford University Press, 1947) first published in English.

1969b   'Scientific Experiences of a European Scholar in America', trans. Donald Fleming, Donald Fleming and Bernard Bailyn (eds), *The Intellectual Migration. Europe and America 1930–1960* (Cambridge (Mass): Harvard University Press, 1969).

1969c   *The Positivist Dispute in German Sociology*, trans. Glyn Adey and David Frisby (London: Heinemann, 1976). Maladroit translations of Adorno's contributions.

1970b   'Society' (1966), trans. F. R. Jameson, *Salmagundi*, 10–11, (1969–70).

1970d   'Letters to Walter Benjamin', trans. Harry Zohn, *New Left Review*, 81, (1973).

1975   in Lucien Goldmann, *Cultural Creation in Modern Society*, trans. Bart Grahl (St. Louis: Telos Press, 1976).

Frederic Jameson (ed.), *Aesthetics and Politics* (London: New Left Books, 1978) contains reprints of 1965 and 1970d.

Selected Secondary Literature on Adorno

This list is highly selective, limited largely to German works on Adorno most of which consist of collections of articles. For bibliographies of works on Adorno, see *Über Theodor W. Adorno*, pp. 143–9, and Friedemann Grenz, *Adorno's Philosophie in Grundbegriffen*, pp. 315–21. Other works on Adorno are listed in the bibliography below.

Beyer, Raimund Wilhelm, 1970, *Vier Kritiken: Heidegger, Sartre, Adorno, Lukács*, Cologne, Kleine Bibliothek Politik Wissenschaft Zukunft 5.

Böckelmann, Frank (1972) *Über Marx und Adorno Schwierigkeiten der spätmarxistischen Theorie* (FaM: Makol).

Da Wydow, Juri (1971) *Die sich selbst negierende Dialektik Kritik der Musiktheorie Theodor Adornos* (Berlin: Akademie – Verlag).

(1971) *Die 'Frankfurter Schule' im Lichte des Marxismus* (Berlin: Akademie – Verlag).

Grenz, Friedemann (1974) *Adornos Philosophie in Grundbegriffen* (FaM: Suhrkamp).

Jablinski, Manfred (1976) *Theodor W. Adorno 'Kritische Theorie' als Literatur – und Kunstkritik* (Bonn: Bouvier).

Jimenez, Marc (1973) *Theodor W. Adorno: Art, Idéologie et Théorie de L'Art* (Paris: Union Générale d'Éditions).

Kaiser, Gerhard (1974) *Benjamin, Adorno Zwei Studien* (FaM: S. Fischer).

Koch, Traugott, *et al.* (1973) *Negative Dialektik und die Idee Der Versöhnung. Eine Kontroverse über Theodor W. Adorno* (Stuttgart: W. Kohlhammer).

Kritik und Interpretation der Kritischen Theorie (1975) (Giessen: Achenbach).

Künzli, Arnold (1971) *Aufklärung und Dialektik Politische Philosophie von Hobbes bis Adorno* (Freiburg: Rombach).

Massing, Otwin (1970) *Adorno und die Folgen Über das 'Hermetische Prinzip' der kritischen Theorie* (Neuwied und Berlin: Luchterhand).

Paetzold, Heinz (1974) *Neomarxistische Aesthetik*, vol I and II (Düsseldorf: Schwan).

Rohrmoser, Günter (1970) *Das Elend der kritischen Theorie* (Freiburg: Rombach).

Schmidt, Alfred, and Rusconi, Gian Enrico (1971) *La Scuola di Francoforte, Origini e Significato Attuale* (Bari: de Donato).

Schoeller, Wilfried F. (1969) *Die neue Linke nach Adorno* (München: Kindler).

Schweppenhäuser, Hermann (ed.) (1971) *Theodor W. Adorno zum Gedächtnis* (FaM: Suhrkamp).

—— *et al.* (1975) *Presences d'Adorno, Revue d'Esthétique*, 1 (Paris: Union Générale d'Editions).

(1968) *Über Theodor W. Adorno* (FaM: Suhrkamp).

Vacatello, Marzio (1972) *Th. W. Adorno: il rinvio della prassi* (Firenze: La Nuova Italia).

Vincent, Jean-Marie (1973) *Fétichisme et Societé* (Paris: Éditions Anthropos).

Other German Sources and Translations

The following list is restricted to works cited in the text and notes and to some of the other related works which I have found important in the course of my work.

Albert, Hans (1972) *Konstruktion und Kritik Aufsätze Zur Philosophie des kritischen Rationalismus* (Hamburg: Hoffmann und Campe).

—— (1971) *Plädoyer für kritischen Rationalismus* (München: R. Piper).

Apel, Karl-Otto (1972) *Hermeneutik und Ideologiekritik* (FaM: Suhrkamp).

Benjamin, Walter. For a bibliography, see Rolf Tiedemann, 'Bibliographie der Erstdrucke von Benjamins Schriften', Siegfried Unseld (ed.), *Zur Aktualität Walter Benjamins* (FaM: Suhrkamp, 1972). References here are to first, often posthumous, editions and to English translations, not to the collected works.

—— (1928) *Ursprung des deutschen Trauerspiels* (Berlin: Rowohlt), *Origin of German Tragic Drama*, trans. John Osborne (London: New Left Books, 1977).

—— (1928) *Einbahnstrasse* (Berlin: Rowohlt) (tr. forthcoming).

—— (1931) 'Left-Wing Melancholia', trans. Ben Brewster, *Screen*, 15 (1974) 2.

—— (1956) *Berliner Kindheit um Neunzehnhundert* (FaM: Suhrkamp).

—— (1966) *Briefe 1, 2*, Gershom Scholem and Adorno (eds.) (FaM: Suhrkamp).

—— (1969) *Über Literatur* (FaM: Suhrkamp).

—— (1969,) *Über Kinder, Jugend und Erziehung* (FaM: Suhrkamp) (tr. forthcoming).

—— (1973) *Charles Baudelaire: a Lyric Poet in the Era of High Capitalism*, trans. Harry Zohn (London: New Left Books).

—— (1973) *Understanding Brecht*, trans. Anna Bostock (London: New Left Books).

—— (1973) *Illuminations*, trans. Harry Zohn (London: Fontana).

—— (1975) 'Eduard Fuchs: Collector and Historian', *New German Critique*, 5.

(1968) *Über Walter Benjamin* (FaM: Suhrkamp).

Scholem, Gershom (1975) *Walter Benjamin – Die Geschichte einer Freundschaft* (FaM: Suhrkamp).

Bloch, Ernest (1970) *A Philosophy of the Future* (New York: Herder & Herder).

—— (1971) *On Karl Marx* (New York: Herder and Herder).

Brecht, Bertolt (1967) *Schriften zur Literatur und Kunst 2 1934–1941*, (FaM: Suhrkamp) tr.

'Against Georg Lukács', *New Left Review*, 84 (1974).

—— (1968) *Das Dreigroschenbuch* (FaM: Suhrkamp).

Engels, Frederick (1941) *Ludwig Feuerbach and the Outcome of Classical German Philosophy*, (ed.) Dutt C. P., (New York: International Publishers).

Gadamer, Hans-Georg (1960) *Truth and Method* (London: Sheed and Ward, 1975).

Habermas, Jürgen (1968) *Knowledge and Human Interests*, trans. Jeremy J. Shapiro (London: Heinemann, 1972).

—— (1968) *Antworten auf Herbert Marcuse* (FaM: Suhrkamp).

—— (1968) *Technik und Wissenschaft als 'Ideologie'* (FaM: Suhrkamp) *Towards a Rational Society*, trans. Jeremy J. Shapiro (London: Heinemann, 1971).

—— (1970) *Arbeit Erkenntnis Fortschritt Aufsätze 1954 – 1970* (Amsterdam: De munter).

—— (1970) *Zur Logik der Sozialwissenschaften* (FaM: Suhrkamp).

—— (1971) *Philosophisch – Politische Profile* (FaM: Suhrkamp) 'Why More Philosophy?', trans. E. B. Ashton, *Social Research*, 38.

—— (1971) *Theory and Practice*, trans. John Viertel (London: Heinemann, 1974).

—— (1973) 'What does a crisis mean today? Legitimation Problems in Late Capitalism', *Social Research*, 40.

—— (1973) *Legitimationsproblem im Spätkapitalismus* (FaM: Suhrkamp) *Legitimation Crisis*, trans. Thomas McCarthy (London: Heinemann, 1976).

—— (1976) *Zur Rekonstruktion des Historischen Materialismus* (FaM: Suhrkamp).

Hegel, G. F. W. (1807) *Phenomenology of Mind*, trans. James Baillie (London: Allen and Unwin, 1931).

—— (1821) *Hegel's Philosophy of Right*, trans T. M. Knox (Oxford: Clarendon Press, 1952).

Heidegger, Martin (1927) *Being and Time*, trans. John Macquarrie and Edward Robinson (Oxford: Basil Blackwell, 1967).

—— (1929) *The Essence of Reasons*, trans. Terrence Mazik (Evanston: Northwestern University Press, 1969).

—— (1961) *Nietzsche*, vols. I and II (Pfullingen).

Horkheimer, Max (1925) *Über Kants Kritik der Urteilskraft als Bindeglied zwischen theoretischer und praktischer Philosophie* (Stuttgart: W. Kohlhammer).

—— (1936) *Studien über Autorität und Familie* (Paris: Alcan).

—— (1947) *Eclipse of Reason* (New York: Seabury).

—— (1963) *Zeugnisse Theodor W. Adorno zum sechzigsten Geburtstag*, (FaM: Europäische Verlaganstalt).

—— (1968) *Kritische Theorie*, Alfred Schmidt (ed.) (FaM: S. Fischer) trans. Matthew J. O'Connell and others, *Critical Theory Selected Essays* (New York: Herder and Herder, 1972).

—— (1970) *Verwaltete Welt? Ein Gespräch* (Zurich: Die Arche).

—— (1970) *Vernunft und Selbsterhaltung* (FaM: S. Fischer).

—— (1971) *Anfänge der Burgerlichen Geschichtsphilosophie* (FaM: S. Fischer).

—— (1972) *Sozialphilosophische Studien*, Werner Brede (ed.) (FaM: S. Fischer).

—— (1974) *Notizen 1950 – 1969 und Dämmerung*, (FaM: S. Fischer).

Husserl, Edmund (1900) *Logical Investigations*, vol. I, II, trans. J. N. Findlay (London: Routledge & Kegan Paul).

Korsch, Karl (1970) *Marxism and Philosophy*, trans. Fred Halliday (London: New Left Books).

Kracauer, Siegfried (1947) *From Caligari to Hitler: A Psychological Study of The German Film* (Princeton University Press).

—— (1971) *Schriften I* (FaM: Suhrkamp).

Lukács, Georg. For a Bibliography, see István Mészáros, *Lukács' Concept of Dialectic* (London: Merlin, 1972) pp. 153 – 200. References here are to first editions and to

English translations, not to the collected works (*Gesamtausgabe*, vols 2 – 16, 1967 –   ) (Neuwied und Berlin: Luchterhand).

—— (1911) *Soul and Form*, trans. Anna Bostock (London: Merlin, 1974).

—— (1918) 'Die Subjekt –Objekt Beziehung in der Ästhetik', *Logos*, VII, 1 – 39.

—— (1920) *The Theory of the Novel*, trans. Anna Bostock (London: Merlin, 1971).

—— (1920) 'The old culture and the new', trans. and introduction Paul Breines, *Telos*, 5, 1970, and in *Marxism and Human Liberation Essays on History, Culture and Revolution*, E. San Juan Jr. (ed.) (New York: Delta, 1973).

—— (1923) *George Lukács History and Class Consciousness Studies in Marxist Dialectics*, trans. Rodney Livingstone (London: Merlin, 1971).

—— (1954) *Die Zerstörung der Vernunft* (Berlin: Aufbau) (tr. forthcoming).

—— (1963) *Die Eigenart des Ästhetischen* (Neuwied und Berlin: Luchterhand).

—— (1964) *Essays on Thomas Mann*, trans. Stanley Mitchell (London: Merlin).

—— (1968) *Goethe and his Age*, trans. Robert Anchor (London: Merlin).

—— (1970) *Writer and Critic, and Other Essays*, trans. Arthur D. Khan (New York: Grosset and Dunlap).

—— (1970) *Lenin: A Study on the Unity of his Thought*, trans. Nicholas Jacobs (London: New Left Books).

—— (1971) 'An Unofficial Interview', *New Left Review*, 68.

—— (1971) *Realism in Our Time Literature and the Class Struggle*, trans. John and Necke Mander (New York: Harper and Row).

—— (1972) *Studies in European Realism A Sociological Survey of the Writings of Balzac, Stendhal, Zola, Tolstoy, Gorki* (London: Merlin).

—— (1972) *Political Writings 1919 – 1929*, trans. Michael McColgan (London: New Left Books).

—— (1975) *The Young Hegel Studies in the Relations between Dialectics and Economics*, trans. Rodney Livingstone (London: Merlin).

Mann, Thomas (1949) *The Genesis of a Novel*, trans. Richard and Clara Winston (London: Secker and Warburg, 1961).

—— (1963, 1965) *Briefe* vols. II and III, Erika Mann (ed.) (FaM: S. Fischer).

—— (1975) *Letters of Thomas Mann 1889 – 1955*, trans. Richard and Clara Winston (Harmondsworth: Penguin).

Marcuse, Herbert (1941) *Reason and Revolution. Hegel and the Rise of Social Theory* (London: Routledge & Kegan Paul, 1969).

—— (1964) *One Dimensional Man* (London: Sphere, 1968).

—— (1969) *Negations*, trans. Jeremy J. Shapiro (Harmondsworth: Penguin).

Marx, Karl and Engels, Frederick, *Collected Works*, vols. 1 – 7 (London: Lawrence and Wishart).

—— (1857) *Grundrisse der Kritik der Politischen Ökonomie* (Frankfurt: Europäische Verlagsanstalt) *Grundrisse*, trans. Martin Nicolaus (Harmondsworth: Penguin, 1976).

—— (1867) *Capital*, vol. 1 (1970) trans. Samuel Moore and Edward Aveling (London: Lawrence and Wishart) *Capital*, vol. 1, trans. Ben Fowkes (Harmondsworth: Penguin, 1976).

—— (1970) *Critique of Hegel's Philosophy of Right*, Joseph O'Malley, (ed.) (Cambridge University Press).

—— (1974) *Karl Marx, Frederick Engels on Literature and Art*, Lee Baxandall, and Stefan Morawski, (eds.) (New York: International General).

—— (1975) *Karl Marx, Texts on Methods*, Terrell Carver, (ed.) (Oxford: Basil Blackwell):

Nietzsche, Friedrich (1886) *Beyond Good and Evil*, trans. Walter Kaufmann (New York: Vintage, 1966).

—— (1887) *The Gay Science*, trans. Walter Kaufmann (New York: Vintage, 1974).

——— (1887) *On the Genealogy of Morals*, trans. Walter Kaufmann (New York: Vintage, 1969).

——— (1883–8) *The Will to Power*, trans. Walter Kaufmann and R. J. Hollingdale (New York: Vintage, 1968).

——— (1888) *Twilight of the Idols*, trans. R. J. Hollingdale (Harmondsworth: Penguin, 1968).

——— (1888) *Ecce Homo*, trans. Walter Kaufmann (New York: Vintage, 1969).

Schiller, Friedrich (1795) *On the Aesthetic Education of Man*, trans. Elizabeth N. Wilkinson and L. A. Willoughby (Oxford University Press, 1967).

Schmitt, Hans-Jürgen (ed.) (1973) *Die Expressionismusdebatte Materialien zu ener Marxistischen Realismuskonzeption* (FaM: Suhrkamp).

Simmel, Georg. For a bibliography, see Michael Landmann (ed.), *Brücke und Tür* (Stuttgart: K. F. Koehler, 1957) pp. 274–9.

——— (1900) *Philosophie des Geldes* (Leipzig: Duncker und Humbolt) (tr. forthcoming).

——— (1907) *Schopenhauer und Nietzsche* (Leipzig: Duncker und Humbolt).

——— (1908) *Soziologie, Untersuchungen über die Formen der Vegesellschaftung* (Leipzig: Duncker und Humblot).

——— (1911) *Philosophische Kultur. Gesammelte Essais* (Leipzig: W. Klinkhardt).

——— (1917) *Grundfragen der Soziologie Individuum und Gesellschaft* (Berlin und Leipzig: Goschen).

——— (1918) *Der Konflikt der Modernen Kultur* (München und Leipzig: Duncker und Humbolt).

——— (1922) *Zur Philosophie der Kunst. Philosophische und Kunstphilosophische Aufsätze*, Gertrud Simmel (ed.) (Potsdam: Kiepenheuer).

——— (1957) *Brücke und Tür*, Michael Landmann (ed.) (Stuttgart: K. F. Koehler).

——— (1958) *Buch des Dankes an Georg Simmel, Briefe, Errinnerungen, Bibliographie*, Michael Landmann & Kurt Gassen, (eds.) (Berlin: Duncker und Humbolt).

——— (1964) *The Sociology of Georg Simmel*, Kurt H. Wolff (ed.) (New York: The Free Press).

——— (1964) *Conflict and the Web of Group–Affiliations*, trans. Kurt H. Wolff and Reinhard Bendix (New York: The Free Press).

——— (1968) *Conflict in Modern Culture and Other Essays*, trans. K. P. Elzkorn (New York: Teachers College).

——— (1971) *On Individuality and Social Forms*, Donald N. Levine (ed.) (University of Chicago Press).

——— (1976) *Georg Simmel Sociologist and European*, trans. Peter Laurence, (Sunbury: Nelson).

Sohn-Rethel, Alfred (1970) *Geistige und Körperliche Arbeit* (FaM: Suhrkamp) (tr. forthcoming).

Tönnies, Ferdinand (1955) *Community and Association (Gemeinschaft und Gesellschaft)*, trans. Charles P. Loomis (London: Routledge & Kegan Paul).

Weber, Max (1921) *Die Rationalen und Soziologischen Grundlagen der Musik* (Tübingen: J. C. B. Mohr, 1972) trans. Don Martindale *et al*, *The Rational and Social Foundations of Music* (Carbondale: Southern Illinois University Press, 1958).

——— (1973) *Gesammelte Aufsätze zur Wissenschaftslehre* (Tübingen: J. C. B. Mohr) trans. Edward A. Shils and Henry A. Finch, *Methodology of the Social Sciences* (New York: The Free Press, 1949).

Secondary and Other Works

The following list is restricted to works cited in the text and notes and to some of the other related works which I have found important in the course of my work.

Aliotta, Antonio (1914) *The Idealist Reaction Against Science*, trans. Agnes McCaskill (London: Macmillan).

Allen, V. L. (1975) *Social Analysis A Marxist Critique and Alternative* (London: Longman).

Althusser, Louis, and Balibar, Étienne (1970) *Reading Capital*, trans. Ben Brewster (London: New Left Books).

Althusser, Louis (1971) *Lenin and Philosophy and Other Essays*, trans. Ben Brewster (London: New Left Books).

Anderson, Perry (1976) *Considerations on Western Marxism* (London: New Left Books).

Arato, Andrew (1972) 'Lukács' Theory of Reification', *Telos*, 2.

Arendt, Hannah (1958) *The Human Condition* (London: University of Chicago Press).

Aron, Raymond (1957) *German Sociology*, trans. Mary and Tom Bottomore (London: Heinemann).

—— (1965) *Main Currents in Sociological Thought*, vols 1, 2 (Harmondsworth: Penguin, 1968).

Arvon, Henri (1968) *Lukács* (Paris: Seghers).

Bahr, Hans-Dieter (1970) *Kritik der 'Politischen Technologie'* (Frankfurt: Europäische Verlaganstalt).

Bauman, Zygmunt (1976) *Towards a Critical Sociology* (London: Routledge & Kegan Paul).

Benseler, Frank (1973) *Text + Kritik Georg Lukács* (München: Richard Boorberg).

Berger, Peter, and Pullberg, Stanley (1965) 'Reification and the Sociological Critique of Consciousness', *History and Theory*, IV. —

Berger, Peter (1966) 'Response (to Ben Brewster "Critique")', *New Left Review*, 35.

Berger, Peter L. and Luckmann, Thomas (1966) *The Social Construction of Reality* (Harmondsworth: Penguin).

Bergsten, Gunilla (1963) *Thomas Mann's Doctor Faustus: The Sources and Structure of the Novel*, trans. Clara Winston (Chicago University Press, 1969).

Bernstein, Richard J. (1976) *The Restructuring of Social and Political Theory* (New York: Harcourt, Brace, Jovanovich).

Birnbaum, Norman (1971) *Towards a Critical Sociology* (New York: Oxford University Press).

Bloomster, W. V. (1976) 'Sociology of Music: Adorno and Beyond', *Telos*, 28 (1976).

Blum, Alan F. (1971) *Theorizing* (London: Heinemann).

Breines, Paul (ed.) (1970) *Critical Interruptions New Left Perspectives on Herbert Marcuse* (New York: Herder and Herder).

Brentano, Margherita von (1970) 'Die unbescheidene Philosophie. Der Streit um die Theorie, der Sozialwissenschaften', *Das Argument*, 9.

Buck-Morss, Susan (1972) 'The Dialectic of T. W. Adorno', *Telos*, 14.

Bulthaup, Peter (ed.) (1975) *Materialien zu Benjamins Thesen 'Über der Begriff der Geschichte'* (FaM: Suhrkamp).

Carner, Mosco (1975) *Alban Berg: the Man and the Work* (London: Duckworth).

Christie, Richard, and Jahoda, Marie (eds.) (1954) *Studies in the Scope and Method of 'The Authoritarian Personality'* (Glencoe: The Free Press).

Cohen, Morris (1931) *Reason and Nature* (Glencoe: The Free Press, 1953).

Colletti, Lucio (1969) *From Rousseau to Lenin* (London: New Left Books, 1972).

Connerton, Paul (ed.) (1976) *Critical Sociology* (Harmondsworth: Penguin).

Dahrendorf, Ralf (1957) *Class and Class Conflict in Industrial Society*, (London: Routledge & Kegan Paul, 1967).

—— (1958) 'Homo Sociologicus', in *Essays in the Theory of Society*, (London: Routledge & Kegan Paul, 1968).

Dallmayr, Fred (1975–6) 'Phenomenology and Critical Theory', *Cultural Hermeneutics*, 3.

Desan, Wilfred (1966) *The Marxism of Jean-Paul Sartre* (New York: Anchor).

Dreitzel, Hans Peter (ed.) (1970) *Recent Sociology No. 2, Patterns of Communicative Behaviour* (London: Macmillan).

Durkheim, Emile (1924) *Sociology and Philosophy*, trans. David Pocock (New York: The Free Press, 1953).

Fay, Brian (1975) *Social Theory and Political Practice* (London: Allen and Unwin).

Feenberg, Andrew (1971) 'Reification and the Antinomies of Socialist Thought', *Telos*, 10.

Filmer, Paul, Phillipson, Michael, Silverman, David, Walsh, David, (1972) *New Directions in Sociological Theory* (London: Collier-Macmillan).

Fleischmann, Eugène (1964) 'De Weber à Nietzsche', *European Journal of Sociology*, v.

—— (1973) 'Fin de la sociologie dialectique? Essai d'appréciation de l'Ecole de Francfort', *European Journal of Sociology*, xiv.

Freyer, Hans (1921) *Die Bewertung der Wirtschaft im Philosphischen Denken des Neunzehnten Jahrhundert* (Leipzig: Wilhelm Engelman).

Friedeburg, Ludwig von (1963) *Soziologie des Betriebsklimas*, Frankfurter Beiträge zur Soziologie, vol. 13 (FaM: Europäische Verlaganstalt).

Frisby, David (1972) 'The Popper-Adorno Controversy: The Methodological Dispute in German Sociology', *Philosophy of the Social Sciences*, 2.

Gabel, Joseph (1975) *An Essay on Reification*, trans. Margaret A. Thompson, Kenneth A. Thompson (Oxford: Basil Blackwell).

Gallas, Helga (1971) *Marxistische Literaturtheorie* (Neuwied und Berlin: Luchterhand).

Gay, Peter (1968) *Weimar Culture the Outsider as Insider* (New York: Harper and Row).

Goldmann, Lucien (1959) *Recherches Dialectiques* (Paris: Gallimard).

—— (1964) *Towards a Sociology of the Novel*, trans. Alan Sheridan (London: Tavistock, 1975).

—— (1973) *Lukács and Heidegger*, trans. W. Q. Boelhower (London: Routledge & Kegan Paul, 1977).

Giddens, Anthony (ed.) (1974) *Positivism and Sociology* (London: Heinemann).

—— (1977) *Studies in Social and Political Theory* (London: Hutchinson).

Gramsci, Antonio (1971) *Selections from the Prison Notebooks*, Quintin Hoare and Geoffery Nowell-Smith (eds.) (London: Lawrence and Wishart).

Grossner, Clauss (1971) *Verfall der Philosophie Politik deutscher Philosophen* (Hamburg: Wegner).

Hamilton, Peter (1974) *Knowledge and Social Structure* (London: Routledge & Kegan Paul).

Hippolite, Jean (1955) *Studies on Marx and Hegel*, trans. John O'Neill (London: Heinemann, 1969).

Howard, Dick, and Clare, Karl (eds) (1972) *The Unknown Dimension: European Marxism Since Lenin* (New York: Basic Books).

Jahoda, Marie, Lazarsfeld, Paul F., and Zeisel, Hans, (1933) *Marienthal: A sociography of an Unemployed Community* (London: Tavistock, 1974).

Jameson, Frederic (1971) *Marxism and Form, Twentieth Century Dialectical Theories of Literature* (Princeton University Press).

Jay, Martin (1972) 'The Frankfurt School's Critique of Marxist Humanism', *Social Research*, xxxix.

—— (1973) *The Dialectical Imagination A History of the Frankfurt School and the Institute of Social Research 1923–1950* (Boston: Little, Brown & Co).

—— (1974) 'The Frankfurt School's Critique of Karl Mannheim and the Sociology of Knowledge', *Telos*, 20.

——(1977) 'The Concept of Totality in Lukács and Adorno', *Telos*, 32.

Jones, Gareth Stedman, *et al.* (1977) *Western Marxism A Critical Reader* (London: New Left Books).

Keat, Russel, and Urry, John (1975) *Social Theory as Science* (London: Routledge & Kegan Paul).

Kolakowski, Leszek (1975) *Husserl and the Search for Certitude* (Newhaven and London: Yale University Press).

Kracauer, Siegfried (1920) 'Georg Simmel', *Logos*, IX.

Krahl, Hans-Jürgen (1969) 'The Political Contradiction in Adorno's Critical Theory', trans. Pat Murray and Ruth Heydebrand, *Telos*, 21, 1974.

Labedz, Leopold (ed.) (1962) *Revisionism Essays on the History of Marxist Ideas* (New York: Frederick A. Praeger).

Lefebvre, Henri (1969) *logique formelle logique dialectique* (Paris: éditions anthropos).

Leiss, Williams (1972) *The Domination of Nature* (New York: Braziller).

Ley, Hermann, and Müller, Thomas (1971) *Kritische Vernunft und Revolution zur Kontroverse zwischen Hans Albert und Jürgen Habermas* (Köln: Pahl-Rugenstein).

Lichtheim, George (1970) *Lukács* (London: Fontana).

—— (1971) *From Marx to Hegel* (London: Orbach and Chambers).

Lindner, Burkhardt (1971) *Text + Kritik Walter Benjamin* (München: Richard Boorberg).

—— (1968) *Die Linke antwortet Jürgen Habermas* (FaM: Europäische Verlaganstalt).

Lukes, Steven (1973) *Emile Durkheim his Life and Work* (London: Allen Lane).

—— (1967) 'Alienation and Anomie', P. Laslett and W. G. Runciman (eds.) *Philosophy, Politics and Society* (Oxford University Press).

Lunn, Eugene (1974) 'Marxism and Art in the Era of Stalin and Hitler: The Brecht-Lukács Debate', *New German Critique*, 3.

Macintyre, Alasdair and Emmet, Dorothy, (eds.) (1970) *Sociological Theory and Philosophical Analysis* (New York: Macmillan).

Macpherson, C. B. (1962) *The Political Theory of Possessive Individualism, Hobbes to Locke* (Oxford: Clarendon Press).

Mandel, Ernest (1972) *Late Capitalism*, trans. Joris De Bres (London: New Left Books, 1975).

Mattick, Paul, *et al.* (1970) *Lenin, Revolution und Politik* (FaM: Shurkamp).

Mayer, Hanns (1975) 'Mann and Brecht: Anatomy of an Antagonism', *New German Critique*, 6.

McHugh, Peter, and Raffel, Stanley, and Foss, Daniel, C. and Blum, Alan F. (1974) *On the Beginning of Social Enquiry* (London: Routledge & Kegan Paul).

McInnes, Neil (1972) *The Western Marxists* (London: Alcove).

Merleau-Ponty, Maurice (1955) *Adventures of the Dialectic*, trans. Joseph Bien (London: Heinemann, 1974).

Mészáros, István (1970) *Marx's Theory of Alienation* (London: Merlin).

—— (ed.) (1971) *Aspects of History and Class Consciousness* (London: Routledge & Kegan Paul).

—— (1972) *Lukács' Concept of Dialectic* (London: Merlin).

Michel, Willy (1971) *Marxistische Ästhetik – Ästhetischer Marxismus*, Bd I, II (FaM: Athenaeum).

Mitzman, Arthur (1969) *The Iron Cage: An Historical Interpretation of Max Weber* (New York: Alfred A. Knopf).

—— (1973) *Sociology and Estrangement. Three Sociologists of Imperial Germany* (New York: Alfred A. Knopf).

Offe, Claus (1972) *Strukturprobleme des Kapitalistischen Staates* (FaM: Suhrkamp).

Ollman, Bertell (1971) *Alienation, Marx's Conception of Man in Capitalist Society* (London: Cambridge University Press).

O'Neill, John (1972) *Sociology as a Skin Trade* (London: Heinemann).

—— (ed.) (1973) *Modes of Individualism and Collectivism* (London: Heinemann).

—— (ed.) (1976) *On Critical Theory* (London: Heinemann).

Paci, Enzo (1970) *The Function of the Sciences and the Meaning of Man*, trans. Paul Piccone and Hansen James (Evanston: Northwestern University Press, 1972).

Parkinson, G. H. R. (ed.) (1970) *Georg Lukács The Man, his Work and his Ideas* (New York: Vintage).

Parsons, Talcott (1951) *The Social System* (London: Routledge & Kegan Paul).

—— (1950) 'Psychoanalysis and the Social Structure', *The Psychoanalytic Quarterly*, XIX.

Pascal, Roy (1973) *From Naturalism to Expressionism, German Literature and Society 1880–1918* (London: Weidenfeld and Nicolson).

Pelz, Werner (1974) *The Scope of Understanding in Sociology* (London: Routledge & Kegan Paul).

Pollock, Friedrich (1956) *Automation*, Frankfurter Beiträge zur Soziologie, vol. 5 (FaM: Europäische Verlaganstalt).

Post, Werner (1970) *Kritische Theorie und metaphysischer Pessimismus Zum Spätwerk Max Horkheimers* (München: Kösel).

Pütz, Peter (1974) 'Nietzsche im Licht der Kritischen Theorie', *Nietzsche Studium*, 3.

Radnitzky, Gerard (1968) *Contemporary Schools of Metascience, vol.* II, *Continental Schools of Metascience* (New York: Humanities Press).

Rappatz, Fritz, J. (1972) *Lukács in Selbstzeugnissen und Bilddokumenten*, (Hambourg: Rowohlt).

Rex, John (ed.) (1974) *Approaches to Sociology* (London: Routledge & Kegan Paul).

Ringer, Fritz (1969) *The Decline of the German Mandarins. The German Academic Community 1890–1933* (Cambridge, Mass: Harvard University Press).

Ritsert, Jürgen, and Rolshausen, Claus (1971) *Der Conservatismus der Kritischen Theorie* (FaM: Europäische Verlaganstalt).

Ritter, Joachim (ed.) (1971–   ), *Historisches Wörterbuch der Philosophie*, A-K (Darmstadt: Schwabe und Co).

Rohner, Ludwig (1966) *Der Deutsche Essay. Materialien zur Geschichte und Ästhetik einer literarischen Gattung* (Neuwied und Berlin: Luchterhand).

Rovatti, Pier Aldo (1972) 'Fetishism and Economic Categories', *Telos*, 14.

Sartre, Jean-Paul (1936–7) *The Transcendence of the Ego*, trans. Forrest Williams and Robert Kirkpatrick (New York: Farrar, Strauss, and Giroux, 1957).

—— (1960) *Search for a Method*, trans. Hazel E. Barnes (New York: Vintage, 1968).

Schacht, Richard (1970) *Alienation* (New York: Doubleday and Company).

Schad, Susanne, Petra (1972) *Empirical Social Research in Weimar Germany* (Paris: Mouton).

Schäfers, Bernhard (1969) *Thesen zur Kritik der Soziologie* (FaM: Suhrkamp).

Schelsky, Helmut (1959) *Ortbestimmung der deutschen Soziologie*, (Düsseldorf: Eugen Diederichs).

Schmidt, Alfred (ed.) (1969) *Beiträge einer marxistischen Erkenntnistheorie* (FaM: Suhrkamp).

—— (1971) *The Concept of Nature in Marx*, trans. Ben Fowkes (London: New Left Books).

—— (1971) *Geschichte und Struktur Fragen einer Marxistischen Historik*, (München: Hanser).

—— (1974) *Zur Idee der Kritischen Theorie Elemente der Philosophie Max Horkheimers* (München: Hanser).

—— (1976) *Die Kritische Theorie als Geschichtsphilosophie* (München: Hanser).

Schmidt, Friedrich W. (1970) 'Hegel in der Kritischen Theorie der "Frankfurter Schule"', Oskar Negt (ed.), *Aktualität und Folgen der Philosophie Hegels* (FaM: Suhrkamp).

Schneider, Michael (1973) *Neurosis and Civilization A Marxist/Freudian Synthesis*, trans. Michael Roloff (New York: Seabury, 1975).

Schönberg, Arnold (1975) *Style and Idea* (London: Faber and Faber).

Schroyer, Trent (1973) *A Critique of Domination: The Origins and Development of Critical Theory* (New York: Braziller).

Schweppenhäuser, Hermann (1972) *Tractanda Beiträge zur Kritischen Theorie der Kultur und Gesellschaft* (FaM: Suhrkamp).

Simmel, Ernst (ed.) (1946) *Anti-Semitism. A Social Disease* (New York: International Universities Press).

Slater, Phil (1977) *Origin and Significance of the Frankfurt School,* (London: Routledge & Kegan Paul).

Spykman, Nicholas J.(1925) *The Social Theory of Georg Simmel* (University of Chicago Press).

Stammer, Otto (ed.) (1971) *Max Weber and Sociology Today* (Oxford: Basil Blackwell).

Stern, Fritz (1963) *The Politics of Cultural Despair* (University of California Press).

Stern, J. P. (1975) *Hitler. The Führer and the People* (London: Fontana).

Taylor, Ian, and Walton, Paul, and Young, Jock (ed.) (1976) *Critical Criminology* (London: Routledge & Kegan Paul).

Tenbruck, Friedrich (1958) 'Georg Simmel (1858–1918)', *Kölner Zeitschrift für Soziologie und Sozialpsychologie,* 10.

Therborn, Göran (1970) 'Frankfurt Marxism: A Critique', *New Left Review,* 63.

Theunissen, Michael (1969) *Gesellschaft und Geschichte zur Kritik der Kritischer Theorie* (Berlin: de Gruyter).

Tiedemann, Rolf (1973) *Studien zur Philosophie Walter Benjamins* (FaM: Suhrkamp).

Unseld, Siegfried (ed.) (1972) *Zur Aktualität Walter Benjamins* (FaM: Suhrkamp).

Wawrzyn, Lienhard (1973) *Walter Benjamins Kunsttheorie Kritik einer Rezeption* (Darmstadt und Neuwied: Luchterhand).

Weingartner, Rudolf H (1960) *Experience and Culture: The Philosophy of George Simmel* (Connecticut, Wesleyan University Press).

Wellmer, Albrecht (1971) *Critical Theory of Society,* trans. John Cumming (New York: Herder and Herder).

Whitehead, A. N. (1926) *Science and the Modern World* (London: Fontana, 1975).

Witte Bernd (1975) 'Benjamin and Lukács: Historical Notes on their Political and Aesthetic Theories', *New German Critique,* 5.

Wittfogel, Karl (1928) *Oriental Despotism* (New Haven: Yale University Press, 1957).

Wolff, Kurt H. (ed.) (1959) *Georg Simmel Essays on Sociology, Philosophy and Aesthetics* (New York: Harper and Row, 1965).

Wolff, Kurt H. and Moore, Barrington Jr (1967) *The Critical Spirit Essays in Honor of Herbert Marcuse* (Boston: Beacon).

Wrong, Dennis (ed.) (1970) *Max Weber, Makers of Modern Social Science* (New Jersey: Englewood Cliffs).

Subject Index

Name Index